Andrew Nicol & Ed McKnight

Wealth Plan

HOW TO INVEST IN NEW ZEALAND
PROPERTY AND RETIRE ON REAL ESTATE

'The common media and political portrayal of property investment in New Zealand is that it is dominated by people buying and selling quickly as prices boom. But the reality is very different, with the vast majority of investors holding their properties for many years, if not decades. Ed and Andrew's book recognises and supports this reality and focuses on lifelong property investment, and the changes in strategy needed along the way to build wealth for retirement and passive income. Their approach focuses on how to build wealth through one's own life-cycle – not that of the housing market.' – **Tony Alexander, economic analyst and commentator**

'The humour that Andrew and Ed bring to presenting quality wealth-creation content doesn't diminish the fact that these guys really know what they're talking about. This book has a wealth of advice and should be compulsory reading for all Kiwi battlers who want to get ahead.' – **Steve Goodey, property coach**

'The most successful plans are those that are simple to execute. Opes has reduced our fear as investors, mitigated our risks and enabled us to become educated on property investment. Working with Opes we defined our goals, determined what our wealth gap was and when our most recent new-build investment properties settle we will have closed our wealth gap. This book provides the best "how-to" guide for everyday people to plan and execute their Wealth Pan. It is a must read for anyone with an interest in investment property.' – **Kathy Faulkner, investor**

'For the uninitiated, property investment can feel overwhelming. You may be aware of the financial wellbeing that can come via property investing but have no idea where to start. There are a plethora of property investing books out there, but many don't talk you through the basics, or explore the fundamentals that can help you on your way. *Wealth Plan* is perfect for people wanting to explore the ins and outs of property investing, and make informed decisions around their financial future. It's not a "get rich quick" book – the advice you find in here is sound, solid and long-term. It acknowledges that property investment can be a hard road, but that with the right strategies in place you can use it to build wealth that will help you and your family in years to come. *The* "go-to" book for anyone interested in property investment.'
– Joanna Mathers, editor of *New Zealand Property Investor*

'Andrew and Ed and the Opes team are exceptionally passionate about property and its wealth-transformative effects. They have an enormous amount of knowledge about the vagaries and nuances of property, structures to own property, and the economics of property ownership. They are fierce advocates for those clients in their care. This book echoes all of those qualities.'
– Shane Campbell, partner at Wynn Williams

'These guys change your mindset. I know things now that will shape my future! This dynamic duo have given me the knowledge for a great retirement and generational wealth down the track. This book keeps it real and is backed up with data and experience. Brilliant! – **Manuel Dalton, investor**

As you're reading this book, just remember: it's a book. It's not a financial adviser sitting in front of you telling you what to do.

While you'll read many examples of investors who have received personalised financial advice, that does not mean that what worked for them is automatically the right fit for you.

So, while you certainly will learn a lot from this book, and we hope it will make you a better investor, this book is not specific to your situation. You need to interpret it and pick the strategies that work for your situation, your goals and your starting point.

If in doubt, get some financial advice. The good news is that in many cases this is free or is available at low cost. You can always come and see us at Opes Partners to help apply the principles to your unique situation.

This book is a taster and a tempter, which we hope will help you determine your direction and goals. Seek specific advice when you get off the starting blocks and throughout the journey.

Copyright © Opes Group Holding Company Limited, 2022

The moral right of the authors has been asserted.
All rights reserved. This book or any portion thereof may not be reproduced or used in any manner whatsoever without the express written permission of the copyright holders.

This book offers financial information and is designed for educational purposes only. You should not rely on this information as a substitute for, nor does it replace, personal advice from a registered financial services provider.

Designed by Julia Murray
Typesetting by Shaun Jury
Printed and bound in New Zealand by SCG
First published in 2022 through Point Publishing Limited

www.opespartners.co.nz

ISBN 978-0-473-65491-7

Dedication

This book is dedicated to you – the reader, the investor, the Kiwi battler who wants to build a better life for themselves and for their family. The one who is willing to take on risk and take the action required to build a property portfolio. To those who don't say 'I can't do it' or 'It's too hard', but who say 'Maybe there is a way', and who ask 'How could I get it done?'

This book is dedicated to you. Because if you put the principles, the plans and the procedures contained herein into practice, you'll be on your way to property prosperity.

About the authors

Andrew Nicol

Ed McKnight

Andrew Nicol and Ed McKnight are the faces of property investment business Opes Partners. Both the pair and the company have a commitment to educating Kiwis to become more successful with money, and in particular through property.

Andrew has been investing for almost 20 years, and has grown a sizeable investment portfolio of over 40 properties. He has personally been involved in over 100 real estate transactions, whether buying or selling. In addition, he is a financial adviser. Through his clients' transactions, he has been involved in over 1,000 real estate deals.

Ed is a trained economist, and runs the numbers for the content that Opes Group produces. A property investor himself, he has a special interest in using data-scraping and technology to create new data-sets that other economists and data sources would usually not have access to.

Andrew started Opes in 2013, and in its first nine years Opes helped over 1,600 regular Kiwis buy investment properties to grow their wealth. On top of that, Opes has provided personalised property advice to more than 6,000 New Zealanders.

Together, Ed and Andrew are the voices of

the *Property Academy Podcast,* New Zealand's top business and property podcast. At the time of writing this book, the podcast has been downloaded over 4 million times. Opes has also recorded and produced New Zealand's first reality-TV-style show about property investment, *The Deal.*

Ed and Andrew are regularly asked to speak at property investment conferences, including the New Zealand Property Investors' Federation Conference and The Property Management Conference. You'll also find them regularly speaking and taking part in local property investor associations, including those in Auckland, Canterbury, Wellington, Taranaki, Waikato, Otago and Southland.

Through Opes Partners, the pair work with property investors to provide investment advice, property management, property accounting and mortgage advice.

In recent years, Opes Partners has ventured into publishing. Opes Media, a subsidiary of the core business, is now New Zealand's largest investment media publisher. The company publishes the *Informed Investor* and *NZ Property Investor* magazines.

INTRODUCTION 11

01

It's time to rethink how we build wealth

CHAPTER 1
The financial fast-track 20

CHAPTER 2
Get ready to run your own race 28

02

In the starting blocks

CHAPTER 3
Ready to hit the starting blocks? 38

CHAPTER 4
Get the money for your first property 44

CHAPTER 5
Attack that mortgage 57

CHAPTER 6
Renovate to add value 66

CHAPTER 7
Getting out of the starting blocks 77

Contents

03

Running your race

CHAPTER 8
Calculating the length of your race 86

CHAPTER 9
The hunt for 'running your race' properties 99

CHAPTER 10
Evaluating properties 113

CHAPTER 11
Assembling your team 122

CHAPTER 12
Setting up your financials effectively 136

CHAPTER 13
Being a good landlord and getting the rent right 145

CHAPTER 14
Taxing times 154

CHAPTER 15
The emotions of property investing 166

CHAPTER 16
A year in property 174

CHAPTER 17
Expanding your portfolio 178

04

Crossing the finish line

CHAPTER 18
Strategies to retire on real estate 194

CHAPTER 19
Creating a passive income through property 204

CHAPTER 20
Selling to unlock the equity in your portfolio 210

CHAPTER 21
How to find 'crossing the finish line' properties 218

CHAPTER 22
What's the future of property? 226

CONCLUSION 230

APPENDICES
Appendix A: Everything you need to know about getting and paying off a mortgage 234
Appendix B: Seven strategies to master your mortgage 245

OTHER RESOURCES 258
GLOSSARY 259
REFERENCES 264
ACKNOWLEDGEMENTS 267
INDEX 268

Introduction

If you want to learn about investing in real estate in New Zealand, and growing your wealth by doing that, this is the guide for you.

Bold claim? There's some pretty convincing data ahead (and plenty of successful investors) to back that up. You're not just going to read theoretical advice, either; we're here to give you real-world solutions and actionable steps that actually work.

This book is about investing in property over a lifetime – or at the least the lifetime you've got left. About how you use property from now and into the future to get ahead, build wealth, and fund your lifestyle. Because we're talking about investing over several decades, and how your investment strategy will change over that time. This means we're going to cover a lot of ground, rather than solely focusing on or promoting one specific strategy.

You may have picked up this book because you have got a little voice niggling and reminding you that you need to plan for your future. Maybe you have some aspirational life goals to tick off? You see house prices increasing and think 'Will my kids ever be able to afford their own home? How can I help get them on the property ladder?' Or you might just be focused on being able to enjoy a comfortable retirement.

Here's the blunt truth. This book alone isn't going to help you do any of that – that is, unless you actually go out and do something with the knowledge you have, once you're finished reading it. If you buy this book, read it, put it down, walk away and do nothing, your wealth will continue on its current trajectory. Ultimately your financial situation will be $40 worse off after paying for the book (or $3 worse off if you bought it second-hand from the op shop). We can give you the know-how, but you've got to take action.

There are five core ways you can invest and grow your money: shares, savings, building a business, managed funds, and property. This book specifically champions residential property investment as the asset class where Kiwi investors can quickly build a decent-sized portfolio.

What makes us so sure? Property is the only form of passive investment where you can borrow the vast majority of the money to buy an asset. If this is the first time you're learning about investment property, then it may surprise you to know that most property investors even borrow the deposit when purchasing real estate. What other investment is there where you can buy a

INTRODUCTION

$1 million property with less than $5,000 cash in your bank account? Throughout this book you're going to learn the specifics of this – along with the risks and rewards, and who can and can't do this.

To be clear, there is a place for all of the five core asset classes in your portfolio. If you are comfortable with a higher level of risk, you might also wish to pursue the higher returns that shares can bring. Similarly, if you're risk-averse, you might be tempted to simply save your money with a bank. In this case you'll get a lower return, but both your income and the value of your assets will be predictable.

Having weighed up their options, many Kiwis opt for property, with its mix of capital growth, yield and income security. Often people find that the more they understand what building a property portfolio can do for them, the more they like it.

How is this book different from other property investment books?

Several other New Zealanders have written top-notch books about how to invest in property. So what's new in this one? In this book we lay out a framework for which property investment strategies to use through the three main stages of your life. You see, it's not about using only one strategy, it's about using them all but at different times.

Although a bit boring-sounding, this book also includes a financial-planning perspective. That reflects the people it's written by – one a financial adviser, the other an economist – which really means two things for you:

1 **This is a practical guide** for how to use property to achieve your specific financial goals.
   After all, most Kiwis don't want to invest in property just 'because'. Instead, the goal is to achieve a comfortable retirement, build a passive income, or achieve financial freedom. This book is written to help you identify your specific goal and use property to achieve it – in a data-driven, non-'woo woo' way.

   Importantly, we'll guide you through the **eight key steps** that will help you to build a portfolio of properties you can live off.

   - Step 1   Buy your starter property (usually your own home).
   - Step 2   Build your equity by aggressively paying down your mortgage or renovating the property to increase its value.
   - Step 3   Buy your first investment property.
   - Step 4   Manage your investment property.
   - Step 5   Expand your portfolio.
   - Step 6   Sell your properties.

Step 7 Buy crossing the finish line properties (optional).

Step 8 Live off your income.

2 **This book isn't tied to one specific property investment strategy. Instead, it recognises that the way you invest in property will change as you progress through life.** In fact, there are three different life stages when it comes to property and the way you invest in each phase is different. That's why the bulk of the book gives you the game plan for each life stage, as well as when to transition through each.

Who is this 'we' we keep talking about?

Before we get going, though, you probably want to know who is this 'we' we keep mentioning. You'll have got the basic CV stuff from the 'About the authors' section, but here we share a bit more of our personal journeys, not as an ego trip but as real examples of what this book is talking about when it comes to the property investment journey over our retrospective lives.

We're Andrew and Ed from Opes Partners. Not married to each other (although it sometimes feels that way!). We spend 80 per cent of our time together, finish each other's sentences and as much as we bicker, we're a team.

In fact, it was our own personal experience of what property investment really involves that informed the form and make-up of the Opes Group, which employs in-house property managers, mortgage advisers, property accountants, real estate agents, renovation consultants and data-crunchers. This end-to-end service gives us the insights, the stories and the understanding of what works for the average Kiwi. So the ideas you'll read within the book haven't appeared out of thin air: they've been tested and refined through our own experience and the experience of the investors who have gone before you.

Between the two of us, Andrew's got the most experience. He bought his first property at 19, and built a successful portfolio through hard work, perseverance, taking risks and just getting it done. With over 100 property transactions under his belt, Andrew has given almost every way to make money in real estate a go.

INTRODUCTION

ANDREW'S STORY

My parents were very much blue-collar workers. Growing up in Waltham, a pretty poor area of Christchurch, we didn't have much money. I cottoned on pretty early to the fact that my parents hadn't been taught a lot about finances; I could hear them worrying about money at night.

I knew my parents got paid monthly, and for the first two weeks of every month we lived like kings. We were 'rich' . . . at least for a short time. And then invariably for the last two weeks of the month Mum would pull out the Tegel chicken 'off-cuts' from the deep-freeze. (In case you're wondering, those are the parts of the chicken that didn't make it to the stores. Enough said.)

One of my big incentives for getting into property investment was that I didn't want to live the same way as my parents and carry the same burden of worry. Seeing my parents' struggle motivated me to take a very different path.

So as a kid, I would dream up money-making schemes. One summer, my little brother caught a bunch of tadpoles in the creek near our house. He wandered down to the pet shop and sold them for 10 cents each. At last, I'd found the way I'd make millions. Believing we were on the brink of becoming the next Rockefellers, I got my dad to drop me and a friend off in the same spot. We scrambled down the bank, parting the weeds as we went, ending up to our knees in mud. After six miserable hours in the bush frog-hunting, we were filthy and lost. And frogless. We battled our way back out, with a grand total of zero tadpoles in hand. My first capitalist venture was far from a resounding success.

My next get-rich scheme was selling coconut ice. I'd whip up a batch of this Kiwi classic, messing up the kitchen in the process. I'd then go door-to-door convincing neighbours to give me 50 cents for a product that should have been called 'inedible ice'. This was back when I could trade on my cute looks. The charm didn't work with Mum, though: she promptly put a stop to my sweet-making efforts – no doubt in no small part because I was using all of her ingredients for free, never mind the mess. But while it lasted it was a very profitable business for one of us.

When I left school I got a job working at a bank. It was there that I realised that you don't necessarily get rich by starting with lots of money, but by using what money you do have the right way. Working with Tony Mounce, a mobile mortgage manager and local Christchurch legend, I began to understand finance. He changed my life.

I'll never forget the day Tony and I were driving along between appointments and I told him I was thinking of buying a property. I'd saved up a $10,000 deposit and had been hitting the open homes. He said, 'That's enough, just buy something.' So I did.

My biggest problem up until then had been making a decision. I'd been to a whole lot of viewings and hadn't actually moved forward with anything. Tony's blunt encouragement pushed me across the line. For many Kiwis, this is how your property investment journey will also begin. You're thinking about investing in property, you talk to a friend and, following their encouragement, you take the plunge.

We talk a lot in this book about building equity and leveraging off that equity to buy more properties. But at the start of my journey I was reliant solely on my savings to buy a house. Nearly everyone is going to be in this position to start with.

It's not easy to pull that first deposit together. But the stats show that in New Zealand first-home buyers are finding a way to make it happen despite higher house prices. **Since 2017 the average age of a first-home buyer has dropped from 35 to 34, even though house prices have increased 35.3 per cent over the same period.**[1]

Looking back, I did all the things people say you should do to save a deposit. I hardly went out. I limited the amount I spent on alcohol. I lived with my parents. When I did finally move out of the main house, I lived in a granny flat in my parents' back yard. Nothing fancy.

And I saved hard. I was prepared to make the sacrifices then so I didn't have to make as many sacrifices later in life. That's the truth that everyone knows, but nobody likes to admit. You're going to have to sacrifice something one day.

Once I had my $10,000 deposit – and that prod from Tony – I was a fresh-faced 19-year-old sealing the deal on my first rental. It would be fair to say that those negotiations were initially tumultuous. Looking back, I reckon the real estate agent saw how green I was and wanted to take advantage. It was a run-down old four-bedroom house, and he did a good job trying to get the price up for the vendor. I got cold feet and pulled out of the deal.

. But after a couple of months I saw it was still for sale, so I ended up buying it. You'll read all about that one in Chapter 3, but the key message is that this was a property where I got a lot wrong. I did a very poor job on the renovations, didn't use a property manager, and didn't do a background check on the tenants. Thankfully I've learned from my mistakes, and in this book I will share those and many other lessons so you can avoid making the same ones.

We like to play board games in the Nicol household, and one Christmas we pulled out *Family Feud*, the game that pits your family's answers to a range of questions against the results of a survey of 100 Kiwis. The most popular answer is #1 on the list, and the top six answers are listed on a card.

The very first question asked was 'How do you get rich?' I immediately pressed the buzzer and thought: 'I know this – property.' Turns out, that was number five on the list. Next my dad got a turn. 'Work hard,' he said, at which point I laughed obnoxiously. Although my dad had worked hard his entire life, it hadn't made him rich. But his guess was number two on the list. The top spot went to 'saving'.

What this game told me is that the average New Zealander thinks the way to get rich is by working hard and saving – rather than understanding how to make their money work hard

> for them. I've still got the card from that game somewhere in my office, to remind me that most people have got it wrong. Because I know that property investment done well will create lasting wealth. That motivates me. I hope that motivates you, too.

Complementing Andrew's experience, Ed brings a razor-sharp focus on facts. He's an economist and spreadsheet savant, helping New Zealanders understand the mechanics of how and why property works.

He started his property journey over a decade later than Andrew, so his portfolio is smaller, and the properties are more expensive than when Andrew was starting out. That adds another perspective to the book from someone earlier in their investment race.

Nothing greases Ed's gears more than devouring an economic report from the Reserve Bank or a 143-page document about tax changes from the IRD. And sadly, that's not even a joke.

ED'S STORY

I haven't owned as many properties as Andrew, yet . . . Whenever people ask me how many I own, I tend to reply 'Not enough'. I've always been preoccupied with numbers, money, spreadsheets, formulae, and the potential to build wealth.

That's only half true, though. Like Andrew, I come from pretty humble beginnings – growing up in Hāwera, a small town in South Taranaki. From an early age, I was wondering how to turn one dollar into more. I remember mowing lawns and thinking: 'If I want a million dollars in 10 years' time, and I double my earnings each year, how much do I need to earn in the next 12 months?' ($977.52 post-tax by the way. Sorry. Numbers; can't resist.)

While pushing a lawn-mower one day, I started thinking about the rental listings I'd seen in the local newspaper. I figured if a property was worth $200,000 it would rent for $200. At the time, I reasoned that someone could buy a property and pay off the mortgage in less than 20 years just using the rent. I wondered why everyone wasn't going out to buy property.

Of course, these days I know more about interest costs, rates and insurance, and I understand that it's definitely not that simple. But my conclusion remains the same: why aren't more people doing this?

My aspirations ramped up at Turuturu School, where I became the self-appointed chief canteen monitor every Tuesday, counting the tuck-shop takings. My best friend's dad chewed me out one day, and told me in no uncertain terms that I needed to work more collaboratively. Andrew's been telling me the same ever since.

I never wanted to be an economist. It happened by accident when I couldn't take accounting because of a timetable clash. So I was stuck in economics class instead. I've got to pay tribute to Vinder Taylor, whose descriptions of maximum and minimum prices as maxi and mini skirts unsurprisingly brought the subject to life effectively at Dilworth, an all-boys' boarding school.

What they don't tell you about economics is that it's not about the spreadsheets, it's about trying to sort facts from fiction. Facts can be confronting. For instance, in 2019, according to the Commission for Financial Capability, 69 per cent of Kiwis worried about money.

And that number is not going to change unless New Zealanders make a change in the way they view money. Like Andrew, I want people to know that to invest in property you don't necessarily need cash. You need access to capital.

When I bought my first property, a two-bedroom apartment, the mortgage was topped up with a small loan secured against my mother's house, which enabled me to get over the start line. Banking rules had tightened, so I needed a bigger deposit than Andrew did back in the day. Getting access to capital from a family member when you don't have enough, like I did with my mother's house, can help first-home buyers and investors who are just starting out.

I also believe that investors need to let go of the traditional idea of a property ladder. You don't have to start by owning your own home. At least not the way it's traditionally thought of (see Chapter 3 for more details). I'm currently still renting. But I also own a couple of properties. I'm what you call a 'renter landlord' or a 'rent-vestor'.

It's just me, no kids, so I don't need a lot of space. There is no point in me purchasing a massive home to live in. A much more efficient use of my deposit and equity is to buy rental properties for others to live in, while I live in a small, one-bedroom rental. That's not just a better outcome for me; I'm able to provide warm, dry rental accommodation for multiple families rather than consuming those resources myself. In this way, investors can be part of the solution to the housing problem.

Whether you're just starting out and are earlier in your investing journey, like Ed, or further along, like Andrew, this book has something for you. It's designed to take you the whole way from your first steps in property through to reaching your end goals as an investor. We'll cover everything you need to help you gain the freedom that comes from a property portfolio that can increase your wealth. So, no matter what stage you're at – whether at the start, or buying your third, fourth or tenth investment – this book will give you the tools, strategies and guidance you need to get from the starting blocks to the finish line. Ready? We'll show you how.

01

It's time to rethink how we build wealth

Chapter 1

The financial fast-track

If you're like us, no one ever sat you down and explained how to apply for a mortgage, buy a property, or strategically use debt. That's not to blame your parents, but it could mean that nobody's ever told you about the fundamental principle of 'leverage', which can help you achieve out-sized returns.

It could also mean that you're not used to, or comfortable, talking about money. It's not uncommon for married couples we're working with at Opes Partners to ask for retirement planning advice, when they have not yet talked with each other about what they want their retirement to look like financially.

If that sounds familiar to you, then there are five principles you need to be across. We call these the *financial fast-track*, because once you've got these principles down, you won't have to stumble about trying to figure them out yourself. Instead, these five mindset shifts will give you the inside track so you can be a successful investor.

Principle 1: It doesn't matter where you start. What matters is where you're going

From our experience working with thousands of New Zealanders, many have an 'ostrich with its head in the sand' mentality when it comes to money. Although it turns out that ostriches don't really stick their heads in the sand to hide from predators . . . But, anyhoo, the general idea is still applicable, so let's be sticking with the ostriches.

There are two different species of ostrich we meet at Opes. The first are those who have never thought about their financial future with any rigour. These are the people who haven't planned, so don't reach their financial potential. The others are those who are so far behind that they don't look at their finances at all. Perhaps they're embarrassed about their current financial position. It's not that they think if they ignore their finances their challenges will go away; usually these people are intelligent and hard-working. Rather, their problems seem so unmanageable that they'd rather not go through the mental anguish of acknowledging their starting point. The sand offers a more comforting view.

We know. Because we've been part of that second group, too. We might be writing the book on property investment, but it's one grounded in experience – not all of it good. For example, at his worst, Ed had $16,500 of overdraft and credit card debts. That's a lot when his base salary was only $45,000 at the time. It was terrifying. He'd done all the classic things you see on the TV sitcoms when people are deep in debt. He'd avoided logging into his banking apps, terrified of what he'd see. No sooner had his credit card bills arrived in the post than they were filed . . . in the bin. He just didn't want to see the number at the bottom of the statement.

'I felt such a failure, a loser. I mean, I'm meant to be smart. I'm an economist for goodness' sake – I'm meant to be *good* with money!' Fair point. But while it's natural to be hard on yourself in such situations – it's not your starting point that will define your success: it's *what you do next*. It's where you're *going*.

Eventually Ed did dig himself out. The first step was to face the reality of the situation, and the second was to do something about it. And you'll read the strategies he used later in the book (a combination of the Debt Destroyer and the Earn, Baby, Earn strategy for those who can't handle the suspense).

And in making a plan, and taking positive steps to improve matters, chances are there will be positive flow-on effects in other areas of your lives, too. Financial matters have an uncomfortable habit of seeping into all aspects of our lives: for example, in 2020 the Commission for Financial Capability found that one in five adult New Zealanders have had relationship problems caused by money.[2] On top of that, 69 per cent of New Zealanders are concerned about money[3] – meaning, statistically speaking, that 7 out of the 10 people reading this book may have some lingering financial concerns.

And if you're one of them, you need to get started. The sooner you start to put a plan in place, the sooner you can start to change. It doesn't matter whether you are currently deep in debt, or are a doctor earning well into the six-figures per year. Remember: your starting point – where you are today – doesn't matter as much as where you are going, and where you could be on track to be. The key is to get started.

Principle 2: You need more assets

When you crawl into bed and start thinking about your future, or someone asks where you want to be in 20 years, what do you think about?

We've asked a lot of investors this question over the years. Their answer isn't what you might think. Most investors we've worked with don't want the biggest house on the street. They don't want to drive around in a Ferrari, and flying around in a private jet isn't on their priority list. That's not to say that wanting these things is bad or undesirable. If that sort of lifestyle motivates you, go for it. We love the ambition.

But for most regular New Zealanders who are starting their property investment journey, they're motivated by something else. They want a comfortable retirement. They want to buy a new car every few years. They want to travel more than they currently do, provide for their families and live mortgage-free.

We'll get into goal-setting in much more depth later. The point here is that, as we have learned from dealing with thousands of investors, most have a picture in their mind about how they want life to go. They have a picture in their mind about how their future will look. But experience also tells us that most investors have a *wealth gap*. There is a difference between the cost of the lifestyle they want to live and where their current investing behaviour will take them. They're not on track to build the level of assets needed to make their ideal lifestyle a reality.

Running these numbers – as you'll get the chance to do – is scary. It's scary seeing that you have a wealth gap and aren't on track to hit your goals. But this is just the maths of it. And it's normal. Most people have a wealth gap.

What's the solution? Yes, you've guessed it: creating a Wealth Plan is part of it. But the real solution is to build your assets. You need to own more. You need to invest more. You need to have something to your name and take calculated risks to get the returns needed.

And although property could be an option for you, you don't have to invest in property. There are other options. But you do need to choose an investment option. You do need to *do* something.

Principle 3: Saving is not enough to achieve financial freedom

Many of us are worried about our financial situation, with 60 per cent thinking about it while at work.[4]

Yet think back to the game *Family Feud* discussed in Andrew's backstory. That (albeit unscientific) poll shows that most Kiwis think saving will help them achieve financial freedom. And therein lies the mismatch. While we think savings are the main driver to improve our finances, the bulk of us are still worried about money. One response is to say maybe we're just not saving enough. But from our experience it's simply that 'saving' alone is not enough to build wealth.

According to Massey University's research, if a Kiwi couple, both aged 45, wants to retire in 20 years and live a comfortable retirement, they'll need to hit 65 with a nest egg of $1.2 million. That assumes they'll own their own home without a mortgage and will receive New Zealand Superannuation from the age of 65.[5] So how could you build up that $1.2 million over the next 20 years?

Imagine you put $100 a week under the mattress. At the end of those 20 years you would have $104,000 in cash. While that might sound like a lot, it's just 8.6 per cent of what you need in this scenario. And that's after 20 years of saving! It's certainly not going to see you and your family retire comfortably. Saving alone is simply not enough for most of us. So instead of putting your money to bed, how about putting your money to work for you?

Let's say you bought a $600,000 investment property at the beginning of that period and borrowed all of the money to purchase it (we'll go through the exact mechanics of this in Chapter 7). The rent you receive may not cover all of the costs of the property, so your $100 a week goes towards topping up the mortgage after the rent, rather than into a savings account. In 20 years, with the property going up in value by 5 per cent a year, it is estimated to be worth just under $1.6 million. After paying off your mortgage and paying for the real estate agent, you're estimated to have $912,000 worth of equity, and so have made 8.77 times more money through property than just squirrelling your savings away under your mattress.

By investing in this single property, you would have made 76 per cent of the money needed for your comfortable retirement. That leaves just under a quarter that can be built through KiwiSaver, shares, another investment property, or some other investment plan.

The reason property gives a good return isn't because it increases by, for instance, 5 per cent a year. It's because of 'leverage'. When you buy property you use the bank's money – through a mortgage – to purchase a more expensive asset than you could otherwise afford. Then when that asset increases in value you keep the extra wealth generated. You don't have to share it with the bank – or the tax man (conditions apply, see Chapter 14).

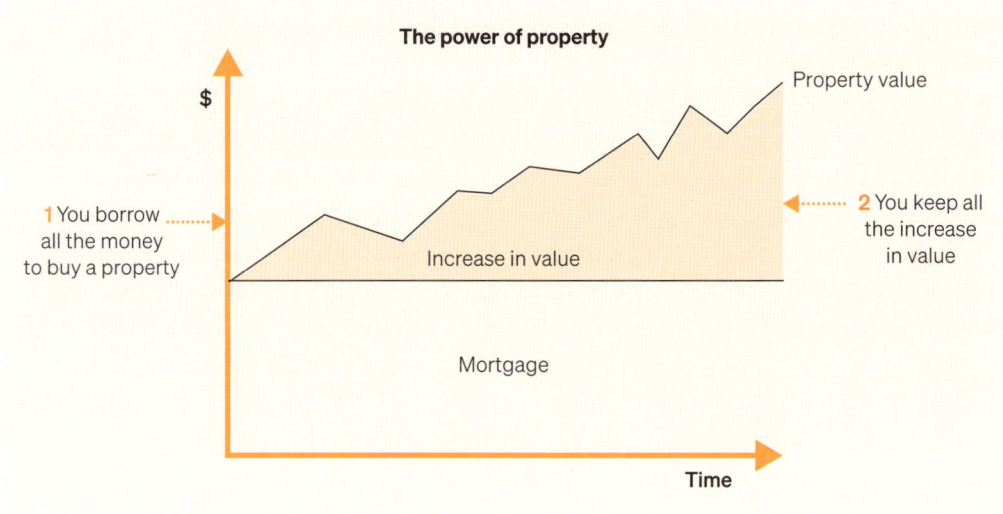

Let's say that you have $200,000 that you can use to buy a $1 million rental property. If that house increases in value by 5 per cent in the course of a year, it's worth $50,000 more. You might say 'that's not bad, a 5 per cent return on $1 million'. But in fact you only put in $200,000 to make the additional $50,000. That's a 25 per cent return on the money you invested, not 5 per cent.

It's obviously not as simple as that, otherwise there wouldn't be a whole book to read. With all investments, problems will crop up. You might get a bad tenant or the property market might be flat for a while. And of course, while asset values tend to increase over the long term, they do go up and down in the short term.

What does that all mean? Although we are 'property guys' and this is a book about investing in property – property itself isn't the 'secret sauce'. It's leverage. The fact you can borrow against it, and it tends to go up in value over the long term (15 years+). That combination. That's the special stuff.

If the bank would lend you money to buy watermelons and watermelons increased in value (held their value and earned an income), we might be writing a book about investing in tropical fruit instead.

What's the key message? If you're saving for your retirement, saving will not be enough on its own. You need to buy assets that you can leverage, and you need assets that tend to increase in value.

Principle 4: You need to take some risk

If saving isn't enough to help you live a comfortable retirement or set you up for your financial future, then it's obvious that you've got to do something else. Yes, that means investing, which will bring a higher return. But that will also come with some risks. In other words, you need to be aware that sometimes there will be problems. Things can go wrong. That's okay, you'll get through it, as long as you are prepared, take a long-term approach, and put plans in place to handle those problems.

Throughout the book you will read story after story of where things have gone wrong in property for real investors. Tenants not paying rent on time, tenants up and leaving without notice, property managers skipping town with the rent you're meant to get, property prices going up and going down, people losing their jobs, and the constant changing of the laws you need to follow . . .

Of course you can and will put plans in place to protect yourself. But you need to accept that as a long-term property investor – that is, holding properties for 10 or more years – at some point your properties will hack you off. Something is not going to go your way. That is a natural part of investing. You need to accept it and you need to prepare for it. And the reason you need to accept it is that the risk-free option – savings – will not get 99.9 per cent of people reading this book where they want to be financially. So you have to take some risk.

Principle 5: Others don't need to fall behind for you to get ahead

You might wonder whether investing in multiple properties takes away from someone else's ability to buy their first home. Some property investors we've worked with do not tell their family or friends that they invest because they're worried about negative stereotypes. But we want to flip your thinking on all of this.

According to Statistics New Zealand, 35.5 per cent of properties are currently rented.[6] Some commentators might have you believe this number is the highest it has ever been and that home ownership is perpetually in decline. But take a look at the graph overleaf. It shows that today a smaller proportion of households rent than in the 1930s, 1940s or 1950s.[7] While the number of Kiwis renting rather than owning their homes is now higher than in the 1990s, historically it has been much higher.

But let's assume we could get home ownership back to the levels seen in 1991, when renters were at their rarest. At that point just over 26 per cent of our population rented. Let's use that as the 'theoretical floor' for the number of Kiwis who will always rent. Based on our population of 5.1 million,[8] that means we need rentals for at least 1.28 million people, because there is an average of 2.7 people per household.[9] Right now we'd need over 472,000 rental properties to house them all.

However, currently the government through Kāinga Ora has just 60,000 state rentals,[10] under 13 per cent of what's needed to house the theoretical minimum of people who rent. That tells us that the government (and it doesn't matter which political party they represent) can't provide rental accommodation for everyone who needs it. *We need private landlords to supply that housing.*

It is sometimes argued that without property investors house prices would be lower and renters would be able to afford to buy their own home. But, as the graph below shows, there have always been some people unable to afford their own home no matter what the house price. Back in 1991 property prices were 7.05 times cheaper than now,[11] and yet over a quarter of the population still rented.

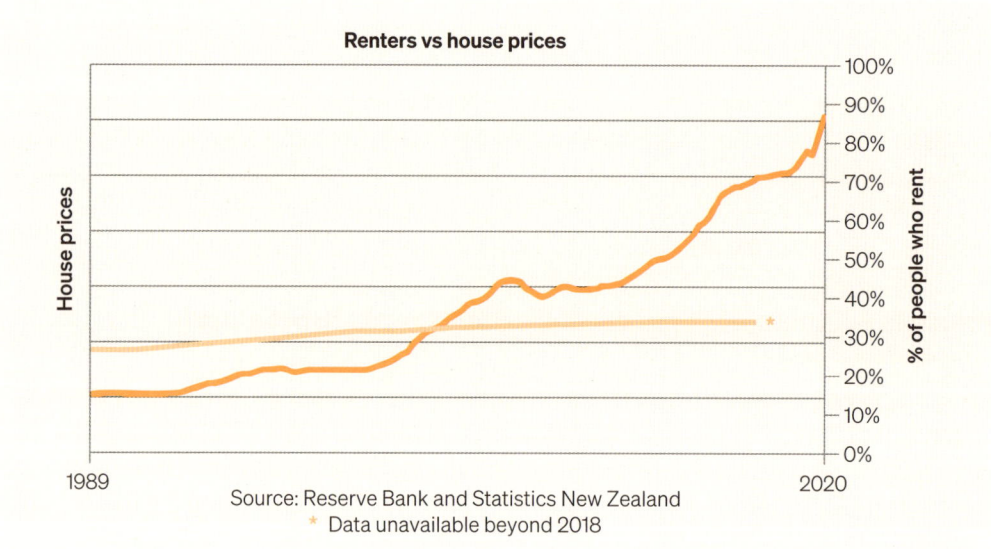

In reality there are also pockets of society for whom renting is simply more appropriate than owning their own home. What about the students who move to Hamilton to go to university and don't have family to live with? They can't afford to buy their own place to live, and the university's resources are better spent on teaching than building mass student housing. What about workers who need to move between cities for a few months or a year? Hotel rooms aren't always an affordable or desirable option. What about young people who are just entering the workforce and starting to save for their deposit? In the first few years, they couldn't afford to buy even if house prices were at 1980 levels.

Private investors have a part to play in all these scenarios.

The truth is, every country and community needs private landlords to invest in housing, because not everyone is going to be able to, or find it practical to, buy their own home. It doesn't make sense for the government to tie up resources providing housing for those who can access it from the private market, when that money can be better spent on healthcare, education and directing their housing support to those whose needs can't be met by the private rental market.

Summary

To invest in property you need to look towards the financial fast-track, which is made up of five principles:

1. **Don't feel down about the state of your financial situation today. You are where you are.** You need to focus on where you are going and what you'll do to get there.
2. **Most investors have a wealth gap.** There is a difference between the lifestyle they want and what they're currently on track for. To close that gap you need to build your assets.
3. Saving alone is unlikely to be the best way to build wealth and assets, especially if you want a comfortable retirement. Leverageable assets, like property, can produce out-sized returns.
4. **You need to take some risks.** That's the only way to get a better return than putting money under a mattress.
5. Growing your wealth through property doesn't mean others have to fall behind. You can help rather than hinder other Kiwis by providing good-quality housing.

In the next chapter, we'll introduce the three phases of purchasing and investing in property. You'll be able to use this framework to identify where you are right now and what you need to do to transition into the next stage of investing. Property investment is a marathon, not a sprint, so let's dig into what you need to do to start the race.

Chapter 2

Get ready to run your own race

Are you ready to get rich slowly? We need to warn you upfront that our approach to property investment is one that pans out over 15, 20 or more years. That's why we liken going on the property journey to being a long-distance athlete on the track. The old sprint versus marathon comparison. That journey can be broken up into three further stages of property investment; when you're:

→ **in the starting blocks**
→ **running the race, and**
→ **crossing the finish line.**

The rest of the book is broken up into these three phases, so in this chapter we'll give you an overview of what you'll learn in each section, as well as a case study of what it looks like to move through each of them.

Stage 1: In the starting blocks

The first stage of any property race begins at the starting blocks. The goal is to get your first property, build some equity and get yourself in the position to buy your second. So in this section we're going back to basics. We cover what a starter-block investor looks like, how to get the lending for your first property, the two strategies you can use to build equity, and what properties to buy and which ones you should avoid. You'll also learn how to figure out when you're ready to buy your second property, and how to build equity fast. At the back of the book, there's a whole appendix on mortgages, which provides additional strategies and detail on the process banks use to assess your mortgage application.

Before we move on, though, we need to talk about the E-word. Equity. Because you're going to hear it a lot.

What is equity?

Most investors we work with don't have $150,000 in cash to use as the deposit for an investment property. In some instances, they may only have $5,000 saved in their bank account. So how do they get the deposit to purchase a rental? They borrow it. And they use their own home to secure[*] that borrowing.

This concept can take a bit to get your head around, but once it clicks, property investment is going to feel more accessible and achievable. It starts with understanding the difference between 'equity' and 'useable equity'.

Equity is the wealth you have within your home. It's the difference between what your property is currently worth and what you owe on your mortgage. So if your home is valued at $1 million and you owe $600,000 to the bank as a home loan, you have $400,000 worth of equity. This means if

---

[*] To 'secure' means giving the lender (usually a bank) something to sell if you stop paying your mortgage. So if a bank is going to lend you money for the deposit for a property, they will need to secure it against something, which, more often than not, is a house.

you sold the property and paid back the bank what you owed on the mortgage, you'd be left with $400,000 before paying your real estate agent and lawyer.

You can borrow against some of this equity in your home to get the deposit for your investment property. However, you can't go to a bank and borrow all $400,000. That's where the concept of 'useable equity' comes in. *Useable equity* is the money you can actually borrow against a property to get the deposit to purchase another one.

In the above example, while the homeowner has $400,000 of equity, they have only $200,000 of useable equity. (We'll teach you how to calculate all of this in Chapter 7.) That means the prospective investor could fund a deposit for properties worth between $500,000 and $1 million, depending on what they buy.

In our minds, equity, and in particular useable equity, is the building block of wealth. So we'll talk about it often. We give it three whole chapters, in fact – Chapters 5, 6 and 7. Once you have enough useable equity to purchase your second property, you'll spring out of the starting blocks and into your next stage: running the race. It's entirely do-able, even for the 'average' New Zealander, so quell your nerves, cast doubt aside and stick with us. We'll show you the way.

Stage 2: Running the race

Once you're out of the starting blocks, having built enough useable equity to purchase your second property, the challenge becomes pacing yourself. At this second stage of the race, it's about laying down the groundwork to buy multiple investment properties for the long term. This phase is the longest part of the property journey, so there's a lot to learn. And because you're in for the long haul, we'll spend the most time here. The goal is to *build your wealth*, which will then provide a passive income in the third phase – crossing the finish line. The bigger the passive income you want, the longer you'll stay in this stage and the more active you'll be.

While you're running the race, you need to learn what properties you should buy, how to choose a city or suburb to invest in, and how to analyse the data to make an informed investment decision. All of this is covered in Section 3 of the book (see page 85).

You'll also learn how to be a landlord, from understanding and complying with tenancy law through to managing your properties' cashflow and bank accounts. You'll be given strategies for identifying which debt to pay off first, and determining how to set up and track your financial position, including managing cashflow. You'll also meet the people you can't and shouldn't live without at this part of the journey – a team of property experts who'll help your property investment business succeed through every step.

To make this practical and real-world focused, throughout the book you'll hear the ups and downs other investors have faced. You'll read a few horror stories, and some feel-good ones, too.

Together, we'll look at the government rules and regulations around owning property in New Zealand, before we lead you towards the finish line . . . where you'll reap the rewards of a race well run.

Stage 3: Crossing the finish line

When the finish line is in sight, your investment goals tend to change to suit this period of your life. Often this is the stage where you are older and want to transition from working hard for your money to where it starts working hard for you. You get to decide where the finish line is, because you can make this transition when you're 45 if you have enough equity, or you can do it at 75 if you start later or need to take your time. The primary focus of this third stage is *passive income*.

It's useful to define what we mean by passive income here, because people use the term to mean different things. We're not talking about joining Arbonne or some pyramid scheme here. Instead, this is about building up assets that continue to pay you a sustainable flow of money when you decide to stop working. In simple terms we're talking about buying high-income properties, and setting them up so that, after the rent comes in and the expenses are paid, you receive regular income when you decide to work less.

We'll share what we see as the best types of properties to hold at this stage, and we'll go over how, what and when to sell for a profit, with some great insider tips and tricks.

Which stage am I in?

Your investing stage determines the strategies you'll use to grow your wealth, but before you can put any of those strategies into action, you need to determine where you're at. Our quick quiz below can help you figure out where you are starting from now:

THE LIFE STAGE QUIZ

1. Do you own your first property yet? No – *You're at the starting blocks.*
2. Do you already own two or more properties, or do have enough useable equity to buy your second? Yes – *You're running the race.*
3. Do you own multiple investment properties that you've held for 10+ years (or have a lot of cash in the bank?) Yes – *You could be crossing the finish line.*

IT'S TIME TO RETHINK HOW WE BUILD WEALTH

For more detail, the table below gives an indication of what tends to happen in each of the three stages.

When you're at the starting blocks, you're saving up to buy your first property, whether your own home or an investment. Once you have your first property, your goal becomes to build enough useable equity to buy your second property. You're typically younger in life and have high debt levels.

When you're running the race, you are purchasing your second property (often your first investment) and building a portfolio of assets to grow your wealth. Your debt level compared with your assets will start out very high as you borrow to invest. It will gradually reduce as your properties increase in value and you pay off some of your debt. Typically, at this stage you are younger to middle-aged.

Once you're near to crossing the finish line, you'll be looking forward to the end of your working life and wanting to slow down. You'll sell your properties to reduce your debt, and purchase high-income properties and start living off the rent you're receiving.

WHERE AM I?	STARTING BLOCKS	RUNNING THE RACE	CROSSING THE FINISH LINE
Properties owned	Don't own a property yet. **Or** Own your own home / first rental, but don't have enough useable equity to buy your second property.	Own two properties or more (e.g. own home + investment). **Or** Have enough equity to purchase a second property (e.g. first investment property if you already own your own home).	Own three or more investment properties and have owned them for 10 years or more.
Debt levels	High	High moving to medium over time.	Low
Indicative age range	20–35 years	30–65 years	60+ years
Goal of stage	Buy first property and build equity.	Build a property portfolio over many years.	Buy high-yield properties. Live off rental income of properties.

Just before you think 'I've left it too late' or 'I'm too old', the age ranges in the previous table are indications only. Your race may follow a very different path. For instance, you might purchase your first home at 45, and you might not transition into running the race until you're 50. That's okay, and still totally do-able. Be aware only that the earlier you start, the more properties you typically have time to buy, which means a higher passive income when crossing the finish line.

Before you read the whole book, we want to cut to the chase: what can the strategies in this book do for you? As this book is based on the real world, rather than abstract theory, we can best illustrate this by way of a real example: the story of a typical investor who we've worked with for the better part of a decade. She was, and is, a single mum, living in Auckland, on an average income, who's used investment property to build a better life. This is the classic story of someone who has followed the principles in this book to transition out of running her race and eventually cross the finish line. This is the sort of strategy you might decide to use in your own property investment race by the time you've finished the book.

> **CASE STUDY**
> ### Building your life through property
>
> Andrew first met Tanya when setting up Opes Partners back in 2013. At the time she already had two investment properties, which she'd owned for a decade each.
>
> She was 57 at the time, and like most parents had one eye on her two teenage sons. They were both almost ready to graduate high school, and she wanted to help them get into their first homes when the time came. But she also had the other eye on herself. She wanted to use property to build a passive income. In other words, she wanted to grow a property portfolio so she could then live off the rental income the properties produced. That would mean she could look after herself in retirement, without needing to rely on her kids or the government superannuation.
>
> Here's what her portfolio looked like when we first met. As well as her own home, she'd purchased an Auckland-based property for $300,000. That was in 2002. The year after, she'd purchased another in Hamilton for $180,000. (Yes, those were the days!)
>
> So Tanya had already done some of the heavy lifting, since she'd been investing for over a decade. She was already partway through running her race. But if she'd tried to cross the finish line and build a passive income at that point, she would have made only $23,750 a year from her properties. Not bad, but not enough for her to retire on either.
>
> What was the issue? She didn't have enough assets. Yet. Her race wasn't over. She needed to grow her wealth so that by the time she hit retirement, she could have a half-decent passive income.

She set a goal to retire by the time she was 65, in 2021, which gave her eight years to increase her assets. To do this, we organised for her to buy a standalone house in Christchurch for $400,000. That was in 2013. Then, four years later (in 2017), she bought an apartment in Wellington for $525,000. At the same time she held on to her previous two investments. So over 15 years Tanya had bought four investment properties – about one every four years. And she spent a touch over $1.4 million in total.

By the time she hit retirement, her portfolio was valued at a whopping $3.5 million. Over those 19 years, Tanya made $2.1 million by her properties increasing in value. (Though bear in mind that she had a significant amount of debt held against these properties.)

What did she then do? She set a plan to sell her three standalone houses and use the money to pay off the debt on her apartment. She then bought another apartment, which had a high rental income. She didn't need a mortgage for this, since she still had money left over from the sale of her other properties.

Today, she's crossed the finish line. She owns two apartments, which she keeps as rental properties. She doesn't have a mortgage on them, nor does she have a mortgage on her own home.

Together, these rental properties earn her $79,000 a year. That's after paying all her costs, like rates, maintenance and insurance. This $79,000 is her passive income. Without getting out of bed in the morning, Tanya can live off $1,500 a week (pre-tax), before even factoring in her New Zealand Superannuation. If you add that in, too, Tanya earns just shy of $106,000 a year. This will continue for the rest of her life, whether she lives to 82, 92 or 102.

But that's not all. During this time, she's used the equity in her properties as part of the deposit for her sons' first homes. One now lives in Foxton, and the other lives in North Auckland.

What does she do now? She lives life to the full. There's no mortgage to pay. She spends the income from her rental properties without worry, knowing that there will be more next week. She doesn't have to worry about whether the money will run out, or whether her electricity bill will be too high during winter. She's got choices. And while she's not a gazillionaire, she lives comfortably.

She travels with her friends when she wants to. But she's planning to stay in Auckland more, since she's now got a grandchild on the way.

Tanya's story demonstrates many of the principles you will read over and over again in this book. She wasn't on a massive income, and she didn't aspire to go shopping at designer stores every week. She wanted to sort herself out in retirement, build a passive income and help her kids. And to do that she didn't need 10 properties or a fancy new strategy. She just needed to pick the right properties, invest for the long term, and keep her eye on her ultimate goal.

That's what this book is about.

Summary

There are three stages of how you will use property throughout your lifetime:

→ **STARTING BLOCKS: where you purchase your first property and get in the position to buy your second. To do this you will focus on building your useable equity, which allows you to begin acquiring a portfolio of investment properties.**
→ **RUNNING THE RACE: where you grow a portfolio comprised of multiple properties that build your wealth further.**
→ **CROSSING THE FINISH LINE: where you use your wealth to purchase high-yield properties with low debt and live on the rental income.**

To move through these phases you'll need to identify how much wealth you will need when you transition into crossing the finish line. This becomes your goal and helps to identify how many properties you need to buy. In the next chapter we'll dive deeper into the starting blocks, looking at the initial game plan for how to start, and then move through this stage.

02

In the starting blocks

Chapter 3

Ready to hit the starting blocks?

If you're in the starting-blocks stage, you either don't own your home yet, or you have your own home but aren't ready to purchase your first investment. Chances are you're earlier on in life, and are figuring out how to climb the property ladder. Your main issue is usually equity. You don't have enough of a deposit to go out and build a portfolio of properties straight away. So you need to build enough deposit to get into your first property, and then build enough equity to purchase your second. There are two steps you need to take at this point.

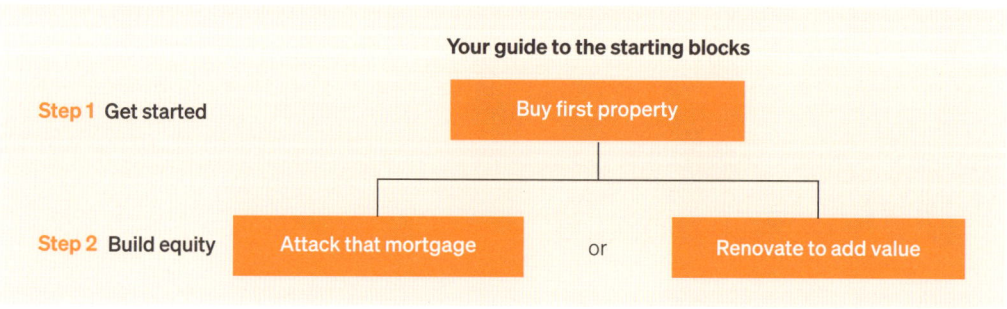

Step 1: Buy your starter property

Your first big strides are all about securing your starter property and being able to pay a mortgage. This could be your first home that you'll live in for the next few years, or it could be an investment. Everything you're doing at the starting-blocks stage is with the aim of creating equity – that is, wealth which you can use to purchase more rental properties.

Most Kiwis do eventually meander out of the starting blocks. They purchase their first home, slowly pay down their 30-year mortgage, and eventually the property market appreciating puts them in the position to purchase an investment property. But if you're not ready for that first investment property yet, and want to sprint out of the starting blocks, there are two strategies you can use after purchasing your first property.

Step 2: The strategics

Option A: **Attack that mortgage**

Really gung-ho investors with their eye on the prize aim to pay off their home loan as quickly as possible. Because you're typically younger, you are more likely to earn a decent income and have relatively low living expenses. This allows some investors at the starting blocks to increase their mortgage payments beyond the minimums required. The combination of paying down debt and their property increasing in value allows those at the starting blocks to move on to the next stage more quickly – purchasing their next property and starting to run the race.

Option B: **Renovate to add value**

An alternative path is to take an active investment approach, which involves renovating your property and sometimes shifting it on, to *manufacture wealth*. To take this path the properties you're attracted to will be older, cheaper (relative to the rest of the market), potentially run-down, and have definite value-add potential. This doesn't have to be your approach. But if you are lean, keen and green, and you want to get your hands dirty, this could be the right fit for you. This strategy has both advantages and pitfalls compared with the more passive approach.

Both are legitimate. Ed chose the first strategy, while Andrew chose the hammer-wielding active approach. If you choose to renovate, your approach will be dictated by how much money you have and whether you have the time, skills and inclination to renovate.

Property investment strategies

The two options mentioned are specific applications of the two most common property investment strategies. Option A is a passive buy-and-hold strategy, while option B is the renovations-focused active buy-and-hold strategy.

While these are the most popular property investment approaches, they are not the only ones. Following is a quick introduction to the three most common approaches.

PASSIVE BUY-AND-HOLD

This involves investing in a well-maintained or new-build property, renting it out, and then owning it for the long term. You primarily make money through capital gains as the property increases in value over time. You'll also make money and increase your wealth through the rental return and paying down debt, if appropriate.

BRRRR / ACTIVE BUY-AND-HOLD

The active buy-and-hold strategy is also commonly called 'BRRRR', which stands for 'buy, renovate, rent, refinance and repeat'. This involves investing in properties that could use some love, renovating them to add value (e.g. adding bedrooms), and then continuing to hold them over the long term. Here, you make money through the rental cashflow, the uplift in value from the renovation, the property going up in value over time and any debt repayments. Refinancing means you can then use the equity to purchase another investment property.

BUY AND FLIP / FLIPPING

Similar to the BRRRR strategy, flipping involves buying a property that needs work and undertaking renovations. The difference is that you sell the property soon after you've increased its value. The benefit of this strategy is you get access to the uplift in value created from the renovations once you sell the property. The drawback is that you need to pay tax on the uplift in value (more on this in Chapter 14).

Although there are these three core property investment techniques, typically investors at the starting blocks avoid flips because:

→ **you pay a significant amount of your gains to the IRD through taxation**
→ **you tend to make the most money by holding your properties over the long term, and receiving capital growth, rather than by selling quickly.**

Because of this, we've not provided detail about flipping in the book. Nonetheless, some investors at the starting blocks *need* to flip properties because they can't afford a quality long-term hold property. So they might do a flip, then transition across to more of a holding strategy.

To get a sense of how a starting-blocks investor gets going, let's look at how Andrew did with his first property.

CASE STUDY
Andrew's first investment property

Like most first-time investors, I didn't have a lot of money, so I had to buy a cheap property in a less-desirable area, with a small deposit. This is everything I would steer an investor with more money away from now. But this is still the pathway for many investors in the starting blocks today.

In 2003 I was 19, and working at a bank. I had saved a small, hard-won nest egg. With my $10,000 deposit burning a hole in my pocket, I convinced my girlfriend at the time to chip in an extra $5,000. I found a four-bedroom property in Christchurch advertised at $179,000. Now remember, this was back in 2003. Christchurch property prices have increased 240 per cent since then, and the same property might be worth $700,000 at the time of writing.[12]

My plan after purchase was to use the second option that investors at the starting blocks have: renovating the property to increase its value (i.e. the BRRRR strategy). Then, after renovating the property, I intended to rent the rooms out individually, since that usually means more cash coming in.

I went around to the property to have a look at it, only to discover that the real estate agent had advertised it at a lower price than it was actually selling for to get more people through the door. The owners actually wanted $279,000 – way beyond my budget. I walked away and went on to lose a few more properties at auction.

Several months later, a few real estate agents were starting to recognise me. One came to me with a prospect: a four-bedroom house 'with potential'. It was the very same one I had walked away from, but this time the vendor had dropped their expectations and had a much more realistic price in mind.

After some back and forth, I bought it for $200,000. Importantly for you starting-blocks investors, I negotiated two things:

→ **A deferred settlement. That meant that I had the ability to purchase the property but I didn't have to pay the money for a few months.**

→ **Early access to the property.** That meant my long-suffering girlfriend and I could go around there in the interim to do some cosmetic 'sprucing up', even though we didn't technically own the property yet.

This was important for me starting out, because I didn't have the money to pay the mortgage and renovate the property at the same time. I needed tenants as soon as the mortgage payments were due.

I'd leave my bank job at 6pm, stop by the local Thai takeaway to get dinner, and then we'd spend the evening cleaning and painting the place. We'd finish up at midnight, go home and do it all again the next day. Looking back, the deal was a bit unusual. Some of that was to my benefit, some of it was just a bit strange.

On the positive side, the deferred settlement and early access worked in our favour. We were renovating the property without having to pay the mortgage. This was important, as we didn't have the money to pay the mortgage without tenants. But it did mean that we were painting the property while the previous owners were still living there. Awkward. The owners were getting divorced and, because they were starting new separate lives, they were more concerned about getting the right price for the property than moving on quickly (hence their high starting price). So, although awkward, this part worked in our favour.

On the negative side, I now reel in horror at my idea of 'modernising' the property. The only renovations work we really did was cleaning, wallpapering and repainting. We used horrible wallpaper and gave each room a different-coloured feature wall. One room was brown, another was blue – clearly, 19-year-old me had great taste!

Finally, the property was ours and ready to rent. But as a cocky (and naïve) investor, I shunned using a property manager – after all, 'they cost money' – and got my own tenants in. As in: without the proper credit and reference checks that a reputable property management company would do. In fact, a guy in the industry who I now respect warned me that I should sell immediately. 'The house is the best it will ever be,' he said. 'Hold on to it and it'll break your heart.'

And it did. I ignored that advice and went on to have a dreadful experience with terrible tenants. That forced me to change the property from a 'hold' to a 'flip'. I sold after six months for $230,000, and walked away with an extra $27,000, having spent only $3,000 on renovations. I know that doesn't sound like a lot, but wallpaper, a couple of tins of paint, brushes and rollers didn't (and still don't) cost much. Ultimately this allowed me to buy my next property, which would help me get out of the starting blocks, and was a better-quality hold property overall.

Summary

At the starting blocks, your goal is to purchase your first property and get in the position to buy your second. The game plan is to buy your first property and then do one of two things:

→ use the **passive buy-and-hold strategy**, while paying down your mortgage aggressively, or
→ use the BRRRR strategy, renovating properties to increase their value – this is sometimes called the **active buy-and-hold strategy**.

How do you pick the right strategy for you? It starts with understanding what's involved with each of them, and then selecting the one you can commit to, and make work for you and your lifestyle.

To help you do this, the next three chapters are dedicated to the stages of investors in the starting blocks. In the first you'll learn how to get the money together to purchase your first property, including the basics of how to work with the banks to get your mortgage approved. The following two chapters then show you what's involved in the strategies to build equity. The first deep-dives into the passive approach, the second focuses on the active strategy.

Now you are ready for **Step 1: Buy your first property.**

Chapter 4

Getting the money for your first property

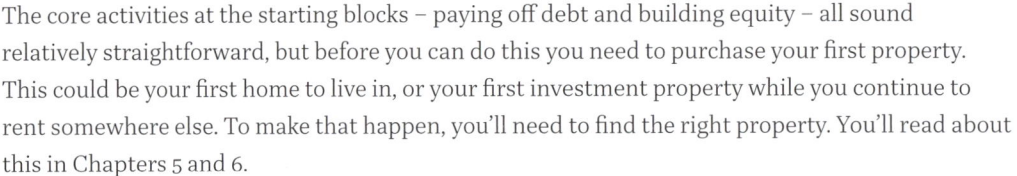

The core activities at the starting blocks – paying off debt and building equity – all sound relatively straightforward, but before you can do this you need to purchase your first property. This could be your first home to live in, or your first investment property while you continue to rent somewhere else. To make that happen, you'll need to find the right property. You'll read about this in Chapters 5 and 6.

But before you can go shopping for properties, you've got to deal with the bank and get a mortgage. In this chapter we're going to start by talking about the amount of deposit you need for your first property, given that this is what usually holds most first-home buyers back.

We'll then talk about ways to pull your deposit together using 'The Fast Five'. These are the top five sources that first-home buyers can use to secure their deposit. The chapter then concludes with a discussion of the three misconceptions a lot of starting-blocks investors have about purchasing their first property.

Chapter 4 Getting the money for your first property

Do I have enough money to get into and out of the starting blocks?

The confusing thing about mortgages is that while the rules are often clear, there are always exceptions to the rules. The amount of deposit required to buy your first home to live in is a good example. Generally, many first-home buyers purchase with only a 10 per cent deposit. That may sound surprising, since you may have heard that owner-occupied properties require a 20 per cent deposit. Here's the situation:

→ For owner-occupiers, anyone with **less than a 20 per cent deposit** is considered a 'low-deposit borrower'.
→ In 2014 the Reserve Bank introduced **loan-to-value ratio (LVR) restrictions**. This limits how much each bank can lend to people with low deposits. The vast bulk of home buyers therefore need a 20 per cent deposit or more.
→ However, there is an exception: up to 10 per cent of each bank's lending can currently go to **low-deposit borrowers who are purchasing their own home to live in**, as opposed to an investment.
→ While these low-deposit loans can go to anyone, they are most heavily used by **first-home buyers**. So although only 10 per cent of borrowers can access these loans, in practice 37 per cent of first-home buyers purchase with low deposits.[13]
→ Who gets to borrow using a lower deposit is up to the bank. Since these low-deposit loans carry risk for the lenders, they tend to approve them only for **borrowers who appear to be lower-risk** and have good incomes.
→ So while one first-home buyer might get approved with a 10 per cent deposit, another might require a 20 per cent deposit if the bank decides they are riskier. This type of complexity is one of the main reasons **it's best to work with a mortgage adviser** to help you navigate the bank's requirements. (See page 126 for how to find a good mortgage adviser.)

As a quick guide, here's how much deposit you need, based on the property you are buying and whether you are a first-home buyer, second- (or more) home buyer, or an investor.

	BORROWER TYPE	DEPOSIT REQUIRED	DEPOSIT MULTIPLE**
Own home	First-home buyer	10 per cent* or 20 per cent	10×, or 5×
	Second+-home buyer	20 per cent	5×

IN THE STARTING BLOCKS

	BORROWER TYPE	DEPOSIT REQUIRED	DEPOSIT MULTIPLE**
Investment	Existing property	40 per cent	2.5×
	New-build property	20 per cent	5×

* Subject to bank approval and buying outside of the loan-to-value ratio (LVR) restrictions.
** Multiply your deposit by the factor given, to see what you can potentially afford.

The Fast Five: how to get your deposit together quickly

As a first-time property buyer, the price of the property you can buy is usually dictated by the size of your deposit rather than by your income. So you have a good incentive to scrape together every last dollar for your deposit.

So long as the bank is willing to lend you the money based on your income and expenses, with a 10 per cent deposit, then every $1 you can get together represents $10 you can spend on a house: $1 from you, $9 from the bank. If you can scrape together an extra $1,000 for your deposit, that's an extra $10,000 to spend. There are five main ways first-home buyers can build their deposit, which together we call *The Fast Five*. You may not be in a position to use all five of these. But if you can use four or five of them you will build your deposit faster than if you rely on only one.

1. KiwiSaver

KiwiSaver is the government-initiated programme where New Zealanders are encouraged to save for their first home or for retirement. There are significant incentives to investing in KiwiSaver if you are an employee. Chief among them is that for the first 3 per cent you save you will effectively more than double your money, since your employer will match your contribution and the government will chip in, too. We won't go into too many details here, since KiwiSaver is widely understood.

However, what is typically not as well known is that when using KiwiSaver for your first home you can't take all of your money out. When purchasing your first home you need to leave $1,000 in your KiwiSaver. If you have $26,000 in your account, you can access up to $25,000 for your first-home deposit. If purchasing as a couple, the KiwiSaver accounts together will typically make the foundation of a deposit.

2. Government support

The next building block is the First Home Grant and other government support.

The First Home Grant is a programme whereby the government will give you money towards your deposit that doesn't need to be repaid. You can access up to $10,000 per person. But whether you are able to get the grant and how much you get depends on three things: how long you've been contributing to KiwiSaver; your income; and the price and type of property you're buying.

At the time of writing, here are the rules. You can get access to the programme if you've been contributing to KiwiSaver for three years or more. You receive $1,000 for each year that you've contributed, up to a maximum of five years (this doubles if you are buying a new-build). If you've been paying into KiwiSaver for four years, you're eligible for $4,000 if purchasing an existing property, or $8,000 if purchasing a new-build. If you've been contributing for six, you're eligible for $5,000 for an existing property or $10,000 for a new-build. This means there is twice as much government support if purchasing a newly-built or soon-to-be-built property.

But to access the programme you need to meet the income requirements. To be eligible, you need to have earned $95,000 or less in the preceding year if purchasing by yourself, or $150,000 collectively if purchasing as a couple or group.

Finally, there are price caps that your property has to meet or fall under. These price caps will change regularly, so it's best to look online for what they currently are at the time you are making the application (visit opespartners.co.nz/book). At the time of writing, in Auckland the maximum purchase price for an existing property or a new-build is $875,000. For most of the Wellington region it is $750,000 for an existing property and $925,000 for a new-build. For Christchurch and the surrounding districts it's $550,000 for an existing property and $750,000 for a new-build.

But the First Home Grant isn't the only government programme you can access. Another recent addition is the First Home Partner. This is a scheme whereby the government will give you up to $200,000 for the deposit on your property, and take an equity stake in your property. You still need a 5 per cent deposit, but this can be a big, big help for those struggling to pull a 10 or 20 per cent deposit together.

Let's say you want to buy a $750,000 new-build property. You have $32,500 available in your KiwiSaver as a deposit. The government could give you another $112,500 (15 per cent) as your deposit, and then they will own 15 per cent of your property. You then have up to 15 years to buy them out of their share. You can do this either by paying them back, or by borrowing more against your property as it increases in value to pay them out.

The good thing about this scheme is that there are no house-price caps. You could theoretically buy a $2 million house, as long as you are underneath the income cap ($95,000 for a single person, or $150,000 for a couple or group).

It's worth noting, though, that you have to buy a new-build and the government picks and chooses who it wants to support. If you're buying a luxury home, there is a very good chance they could turn you down.

Over time these government schemes will change. The income caps will change, the house-price caps will change. But while the specifics will change, for decades this type of government support has been a major help for first-home buyers.

3. Sale of assets

In building your deposit, you might also consider selling some of your assets. Cars are an obvious one. If you have a car that's worth $10,000, you might decide to sell it to buy a car worth $5,000. This would give you $5,000 in cash for your deposit, which translates into an extra $50,000 to spend on a property if using a 10 per cent deposit. If buying with your partner and you both have cars, one option may be to sell one and share the other for a short time until you can buy another. This might be a sacrifice you're willing to undertake to get you over the line to buy your first home.

4. The Bank of Mum and Dad

Just as you can use the equity in your own home as the deposit for an investment property, you can use the equity in other people's homes, too. This generally involves a hand-up from a close family member to kick-start your property journey. This is also why this tactic is commonly referred to as 'the Bank of Mum and Dad'.

Some people don't like talking about this option. Parents might dismiss it because their own parents never helped them into their first home. Or you might be thinking that you wouldn't want a house your parents helped to pay for. That's totally fine if that's your point of view. Like all the strategies on this list, not every one of the 'Fast Five' building blocks will be used by everyone. Having said this, it is important to tackle some of the misconceptions people have about the Bank of Mum and Dad.

People often think using the Bank of Mum and Dad means you've got rich parents who will hand you wads of cash. It doesn't. Rather, they might guarantee part of your deposit using their own property as security with the bank. Usually this means borrowing money from the bank using a product like a revolving credit, and then transferring the money to the first-home buyer's solicitor once ready.

This works in one of three ways:

→ Your parents give you the money and you don't have to pay it back. That's called **a 'gift'**.
→ Your parents lend you the money, but, you don't need to pay them back until you sell the house. That's called an **'interest-free loan without time commitments'**.

→ **Your parents lend you the money (either from their own funds or from the bank) and you make normal repayments.**

In New Zealand, mortgage advisers report that about half of all first-home buyers purchase properties with the help of their parents.[14] While it's human nature for parents to want to help their children, this pathway is not without its pitfalls.

For example, let's say you give your child money towards their first property, which they're buying with a partner. If the couple then breaks up, you probably don't want the now-former partner taking part of the deposit you gave them. That's why it is wise to cover off such contingencies from a legal perspective with any loan, so you are not caught off-guard by changing circumstances.

5. Saving and increasing your income

If you've stuck with us through the first four strategies and don't quite have enough deposit yet, this is where you might set up a savings scheme.

A lot has been written along the lines of 'if you want to save for a house, stop paying $22 for avocado on toast'. Cut us a break. Avo on toast at your local café – alone – isn't what's stopping you from purchasing your first property: after all, $22 a week will only save $1,144 in a year.

And while it's true that every dollar saved starts to add up – and budgetary sacrifices may be necessary – increasing your actual income is a strategy most people forget about. Let's get back to that avocado on toast again. Do you really have to give up the avo? Or is there another way you could save that $1,144 a year and still be eating the green stuff? One way is to upskill in your job, learn new skills and then ask for a pay rise. If you're currently earning $70,000 a year, you need just under a 2.5 per cent pay rise to earn enough extra income (after tax) to save the same amount as giving up the avo. So you could either give up the café visit every week, or you could have one awkward conversation with your boss. Or you could do both and get into your first home even faster.

Let's say your boss says 'no'. No trouble, you can also increase your income through a side hustle. If you want to see what's truly possible, the case study coming up at the end of this chapter will blow you away.

Let's presume you need an extra $10,000 deposit to get started. That's where you could set aside enough money each week to save that extra bit. Say you identify ways to earn more (or spend less) and find a way to put aside $200 a week. After a year at 2 per cent interest you'd have $10,500 to use for your deposit. It's simple. It's obvious. But it works once you set it up right.

Once you go through The Fast Five, add up all the ways you could potentially get your deposit together, and then multiply it by 10 if you are using a 10 per cent deposit, or multiply it by 5 if using a 20 per cent deposit. This will give a rough guide for what you'll be able to afford from an equity perspective. Of course, you'll still need to get approval for a mortgage based on your income, too, so don't go signing an unconditional offer on a property (just yet).

Three misconceptions about buying your first home

As part of Opes Partners, we run a service called Opes First Home. This is where first-home buyers get help from a first-home coach to pull their deposit together, and then find the right first home. Through working with first-home buyers we've found there are three misconceptions that they often need to overcome.

1. 'The average price of a property is $890,000, so I need to spend $890,000'

With the median sale price for New Zealand sitting at $890,000[15] at the time of writing, you might well be wondering how you are ever going to be able to afford a property. While the median house price is widely reported, the truth is you don't have to buy the median property as a first-home buyer. There is a wider range of properties available than most first-home buyers think.

Something that will likely surprise you is that while the median house price for New Zealand is $890,000, that doesn't mean that most properties sell for between $800,000 and $900,000. In fact, the most popular price bands are significantly more affordable. In the year to March 2022,

the most popular price band for properties in New Zealand was $600,000–$699,000. In simple terms that means that more properties sold for prices starting with a 6, rather than starting with an 8.[16] The median house price is just an average; it doesn't mean that you have to purchase at the average.

In addition, first-home buyers tend to buy cheaper properties than the market average. According to CoreLogic's *First Home Buyer Report*, between July and September 2021 the average Auckland first-home buyer spent $900,500 on their first property. That compares to $1,050,000 for the average Auckland property sold over the same period.[17] So first-home buyers in our most populous city spent just over 14 per cent less than the average for all property buyers. This trend is consistent across all major centres, where the average first-home buyer purchases property at a cheaper price than the average property.

To be clear, this does not mean that property is inexpensive. Of course it's expensive, it's a house. But you don't need to look at the average price of properties across the country and think that you need to buy the average property.

2. 'I can't get a property for underneath the First Home Grant house-price caps'

With the First Home Grant house-price cap set at $875,000 for a new-build in Auckland, you might wonder how you are going to find a property for $875,000 when the average first-home buyer spends more than this. One tactic is to get the property under contract for a lower purchase price.

For instance, we were dealing with a first-home buyer through Opes First Home who was interested in a soon-to-be-built two-bedroom townhouse in Auckland that had a car park. At the time the First Home Grant house-price cap was $700,000 and the property was advertised for $730,000. This buyer needed the First Home Grant to afford the property. However, they wouldn't be able to get the grant for this property since it was priced over the cap for Auckland. But since the property wasn't built there was still a lot up for negotiation, even if at first it didn't seem that way. In this case, the developer agreed to our suggestion to reduce the price to $700,000 and reallocate the car park to another property in the project. That meant that our first-home buyer could purchase with the First Home Grant, and the developer could increase the price of the other property he was building as it now had two car parks.

Of course this has required some obvious trade-offs. The first-home buyer now doesn't have a car park as part of her property. She'll need to either find on-street car parking or hire one of the car parks from her new neighbours. And while we don't have data to back this up, there is a chance that the long-term value of the property may not increase as quickly. But in doing this she gets $10,000 in government money she wouldn't have otherwise got, which enables her to purchase her first property.

Some of you reading this may baulk at the idea of buying a property without a car park. But at some point you need to make sacrifices. For this first-home buyer, there were two choices. Buy a house now, meaning making a sacrifice today because she wouldn't have a car park. Or wait, save more and eventually pay more for a house, and not have access to the First Home Grant. That would mean saving a larger deposit and paying more for the house, but getting one with a car park.

While it's not always obvious, there can be considerable room to negotiate with developers when purchasing a new-build as a first-home buyer. For example, because new-builds typically come with curtains, landscaping and some appliances, you can negotiate to remove any of these to reduce the price. You can then add these finishing touches yourself. If you don't have the money to buy the complete package, these are some of the trade-offs you might be willing to accept. In some instances this will help you get properties into a range you can afford, and potentially underneath the First Home Grant house-price cap. Everything is up for negotiation.

3. 'I need to live in my first home for a while, so it needs to be close to where I want to live'

When you're in the starting blocks you have a choice: you can decide either to live in your first property as an owner-occupier or buy it as an investment property. The benefit of purchasing as a rental often means that you can buy a property more cheaply because you can sacrifice on location. For instance, if buying on the fringes of a city, the price will likely be significantly cheaper than in the centre, even if you would prefer to live in a more central location. By being hung up on where *they* want to live, and assuming that they will have to live in whatever property they buy, many first-time buyers miss the opportunity to purchase a first property with the intention of turning it into a rental, and purchasing at a cheaper price than would otherwise be the case.

Generally, though, even if a first-home buyer intends to have the property as a rental, they'll still start off treating it as an owner-occupier, and then turn it into a rental property later. This is because doing so means that a lower deposit is required. For instance, if purchasing an existing property as a first home you'll need a minimum 10 per cent deposit, whereas if you purchase the same property as an investment you'll need a 40 per cent deposit.

In addition to this, if you purchase a property as a first-home buyer initially to live in yourself, then you also are able to access your KiwiSaver and – depending on your financial position – the government's First Home Grant. If you initially buy it as an investment, you won't have access to either. Even if you go on to purchase an owner-occupier property later, you won't be able to access your KiwiSaver for that purchase because you are no longer a first-home buyer. A bit tricky, right?

So if you are purchasing a property with the intention of turning it into a rental, there is an obvious catch: you have to live in it, at least for a short while. For this set-up to be considered legitimate, you'll need to live in the property for at least six months under the current rules. This is a common set-up for those living in Auckland who can't afford to buy in our largest city.

One Auckland-based first-home buyer we worked with was in this exact position. He and his partner were both freelancers, and so had the ability to move easily without needing to find new jobs. They decided to purchase a property in Dunedin, at a time when the average value of a property in Dunedin was 63 per cent cheaper than Auckland.[18] They moved south for six months to meet the requirements to withdraw their KiwiSaver, then flew back to Auckland, turning their Dunedin property into a rental. After three years the Dunedin property had increased in value substantially, and they were able to use the equity in the investment property to buy their own home in Auckland.

To sum up, if you don't own any property yet and you want to purchase a house to use as a rental, *there is a good incentive for you to initially treat it as an owner-occupier*. This means you're probably not going to buy your first property where you want to live long term. But you may be able to buy a property in a small town, or somewhere that's a bit more rural, or perhaps with a longer commute to work. Purchasing initially as an owner-occupier and turning it into a rental is nevertheless a worthwhile strategy.

Our next case study is a perfect example of the principles contained within this chapter being used in practice. We're actually in awe of this investor, and how she saved $57,000 in one year (on a single income, no less) to buy her first home. It's an example of just what can be done with grit, determination, some smarts – and knuckling down to some hard saving.

> **CASE STUDY**
> ### How a first-home buyer saved a $57,000 deposit in 12 months
>
> Simran Kaur – founder of Girls That Invest – saved $57,000 to purchase her first property. One of the most remarkable things is that she was 24 years old when she opened the front door to her first home, having put down a 10 per cent deposit.
>
> Pulling together a $57,000 deposit in a single year takes one hell of a commitment. No, she wasn't earning $200,000 a year either, although she admitted that she does have a reasonably good graduate salary as an optometrist. Pay on average for someone starting out in that profession is $65,000–80,000 annually.
>
> Simran set a goal to buy a house within two years. Her first step was to calculate how much she wanted to spend on a house, how much deposit would be required, and how much she would have to save. She thought she'd need a $55,000 deposit, meaning that with a 90 per cent loan she'd be able to buy a house for $550,000.

The next step was to run through The Fast Five. Starting with her KiwiSaver, she estimated that over that time her KiwiSaver would add up to about $10,000. But she couldn't access three of the other steps in The Fast Five – the First Home Grant, sale of assets, or the Bank of Mum and Dad – so she had to use the only other deposit builder available: savings. That's right: she would need to save an extra $45,000.

To save $45,000 in a single year she did four crucial things. First, she set a savings goal of $500 per week. No, she wasn't living at home with Mum and Dad for free. She was paying rent in a four-person flat, splitting the bills, etc. She still enjoyed herself and went out with friends, but she stuck to a budget (and made her own coffee!).

Next she had to find a way to increase her income. She ran two side hustles: selling clothes and accessories online to bring in money above and beyond her salary. Both of these businesses got a boost during Covid when everyone was locked up at home and spending online. Simran admits she probably couldn't have achieved her savings goal so quickly on her optometrist income alone.

Thirdly, she limited her expenses. One way she kept track of this was to input her spending into the free version of Spendee, a budgeting app. This kept her accountable, and revealed she was spending a lot on food. In her own words: 'That showed me where my priorities were. If I'm spending a lot on food then that's my priority, rather than saving for my first home.' To limit this, she set a weekly budget of $100 for food, and challenged herself to trim it to $80 to see if she could get by. It became a bit of a game to shave off bits of spending to see if she could do it. Knowing that her first home wasn't far off made the sacrifices easier to accept. As did knowing they were temporary and that she'd be better off for the rest of her life.

The fourth and final tactic was to put her savings to use while she was accruing them. Simran was confident enough to put her savings into shares, using the Hatch app. As she got closer to her savings goals, she withdrew them and transferred them into cash to guard against the shares decreasing in value.

Ultimately she purchased a two-bedroom standalone brick home in Hamilton for $565,000 at the end of 2020, in a sharply rising market. She put down a $57,000 deposit – just above 10 per cent. Here's how the numbers worked:

Personal savings – $29,000
KiwiSaver – $9,000
Shares – $19,000 ($14,500 savings, $4,500 uplift in value of shares)
Total deposit amount: $57,000

> She'll also use this property to blast out of the starting blocks. It needs a little bit of work done, so she can renovate the property to increase its value. She also intends to turn it into a rental property one day in the future, since it's near the hospital, and close to amenities.
>
> So what principles from the chapter did Simran use?
>
> 1. She bought with a 10 per cent deposit.
> 2. She wasn't able to use three of The Fast Five deposit builders – the First Home Grant, the Bank of Mum and Dad, or sale of assets. So she focused on the other two: KiwiSaver and savings.
> 3. She bought a property for $565,000, which was 22.5 per cent below the average value of a property in Hamilton at the time.[19]
> 4. She treated the property as an owner-occupier, and at some point in the future intends to turn it into a rental when she decides to move back to Auckland.
>
> Yes, this story has a happy ending. Simran ended up buying (and living in) her first property in Hamilton, after a solid year of saving. Even though she is from Auckland, she took a graduate job in Hamilton as she knew her expenses and rent would be lower, making her salary go further.

You have to do something

From our experience, there is a lot of negativity surrounding first-home buying today. Whenever we take to social media to promote a tactic for first-home buyers to get ahead, we always get slated in the comments section.

Here's the thing. Not every tactic will be available and applicable for everyone. But you don't need to use every single tactic to buy your first home. You don't need to be a rent-vestor, *and* buy in the cheapest area in New Zealand, *and* use your KiwiSaver, *and* get the First Home Grant, *and* start a side hustle, *and* use the Bank of Mum and Dad, *and* sell your car, your computer and your soul. But you do have to do *something*. If you dismiss every tactic, and worry that none of them will work for you, your first property will stay out of reach. Find a combination that will work for you.

We can understand that some people feel that 'all hope is lost'. That they'll never be able to purchase a property. However, we don't see that sort of despair in the numbers. Rather, they tell quite a different story. Right now, as we write this, the share of properties being bought by first-home buyers is at a record high. Of all houses bought in July–September 2021, 26.4 per cent were purchased by first-home buyers.[20] That's well above the long-term average of 21.8 per cent. In fact, this is the highest proportion of properties purchased by first-home buyers since the records began in 2006.

IN THE STARTING BLOCKS

Our message for prospective first-home buyers feeling despondent at the sight of high house prices: don't let negativity get in the way of you buying your first property. Find the tactics that work for you, and make it happen.

Summary

To calculate how much you can afford, you need to:

→ Decide what **percentage deposit** you will aim to use. Many first-home buyers use 10 per cent. Talk to a mortgage adviser to see what's possible for you.
→ Use **The Fast Five** to add up the various ways you could pull together your deposit from KiwiSaver, the First Home Grant and government support, sale of assets, the Bank of Mum and Dad, and savings.
→ Multiply your deposit by the **deposit multiple** taken from the table on pages 45–46; this will give a sense of what you may be able to afford.
→ When looking for properties, most first-home buyers purchase properties **well underneath the average price**. In the case study on page 53, Simran bought 22.5 per cent below the average value of a property in Hamilton.[21]
→ If you can't afford to purchase in the city you live in, **consider buying in a more affordable town**, living there for a short time, then turning the property into a rental and moving back to where you'd prefer to live.

When you have your bank finance sorted, it's time to go shopping for property, and get into the position for running the race. The next two chapters present different ways to do this. The first delves into the passive buy-and-hold strategy, where you'll pay down your mortgage aggressively. The second delves into the renovations-focused BRRRR strategy.

Now you are ready for **Step 2: Build equity**.

Chapter 5

Attack that mortgage

Once you own your own home, the next step is to build the equity that will help you purchase your next property. This chapter explores the *passive buy-and-hold* strategy, where you'll purchase a low-maintenance property and aggressively pay down the mortgage. In this chapter we'll cover this strategy in depth, answering three critical questions:

1. What sort of properties am I going to buy under the passive buy-and-hold strategy, and what should I look for?
2. Where do I find these properties?
3. What are the precise steps I can take to build equity when using this strategy?

What sort of properties am I going to buy, and what should I look for?

In today's environment, passive buy-and-hold purchasers tend to favour new-builds when buying their first home. These are properties that are bought either off the plans or have recently been built. Purchasing (or building) a brand-new property hasn't always been the typical path a first-home buyer would go down. However, there are three factors that are different today compared with even 10 years ago.

It's easier to buy new-builds with a low deposit

In the last chapter we talked about how the Reserve Bank requires the bulk of loans to owner-occupiers to have a 20 per cent deposit. But there is a small 10 per cent of people who can borrow with lower deposits, and the banks need to select who they give those loans to. One thing we didn't mention is that there are no restrictions for new-builds under the loan-to-value ratio restrictions. That means that as long as the bank is willing to lend to you with a lower deposit, they don't have to decide whether you fit into the 10 per cent of loans that can have a smaller deposit. In effect, first-home buyers can more easily access a low-deposit loan for a new-build compared with an existing property.

Double the First Home Grant support

If you purchase a new-build, and can meet the First Home Grant criteria (see page 47), then you are able to get twice the amount of 'free' money from the government compared with if you are buying an existing property. There are also often higher house-price caps, which mean that these grants are more accessible if purchasing new.

Tax advantages for a rental property

If you are purchasing your first home with the intention of turning it into a rental property, a new-build is often more attractive for passive buy-and-hold investors. As you'll see in Chapter 10, new-builds have significant tax advantages when turned into rental properties. That's because new-builds pay less tax compared with the equivalent existing property, since the mortgage interest costs are deductible (see page 158).

Where do I find these properties?

Because you are relying on two factors to increase your equity – your property increasing in value and paying off your mortgage – it makes sense to purchase the sort of property that is more likely to benefit from the natural capital growth occurring in the property market. We'll discuss the thinking of what to look for extensively in Chapter 9, but there are eight principles for capital growth:

1. **Properties in areas that are currently undervalued** tend to receive higher near-term growth than those where prices are currently overvalued. See the data for which regions are currently over or undervalued at opespartners.co.nz/book.
2. **Properties in areas with high population growth** tend to increase in value more quickly than those in areas with lower population growth.
3. **Properties in areas with larger populations** tend to have more consistent capital growth than those in areas with smaller populations. (Note: this is the total number of people, as opposed to how quickly that population is growing.)
4. **Properties closer to the centre of the city** tend to increase in value faster than those on the outer edges of the city.
5. **Properties in higher-end suburbs** tend to increase in value faster than those in less valuable areas.
6. **Standalone houses and townhouses** tend to increase in value faster than apartments.
7. **Two- to four-bedroom properties** tend to increase in value faster than one-bedroom properties.
8. **Properties that are bought at or under valuation** have more room to increase in value compared with those that are bought above valuation (i.e. if you've overpaid there's less room for capital growth).

You'll never find a property with all eight principles and factors. But you can (and should) weigh up your purchasing decisions based on these factors. It's better to take a 'good deal' when you can, rather than delaying and waiting for a deal that is observably perfect. These latter types of deals are often like unicorns; they don't exist.

In terms of where to find these properties, there are three main paths you can take to find the right deal: look for these properties yourself, using websites like TradeMe or Realestate.co.nz; approach developers directly; or work with a buyer's agent (also called a first-home coach), like Opes First Home, who approaches developers and negotiates the deals on your behalf.

How to build equity

Once you've got your first property and it's potentially increasing in value, it's time to kick it up a notch. The good news is you'll already be creating more equity by paying off your mortgage and being in the property market. But you can get out of the starting blocks and purchase your second property faster by attacking your mortgage and paying it off more aggressively. Every extra dollar you pay off your mortgage is worth up to another $5 you can borrow for a new-build investment property, or $2.50 for an existing property. Of course this is assuming you have 20 per cent equity, and you meet the bank's income requirements.

It's important to realise that you don't have to pay your mortgage off at the minimum rate the bank sets for you. In fact, your mortgage will be much, much cheaper overall if you make higher repayments. This has a compounding effect. The faster you pay off your mortgage, the less interest you'll pay. And so increasing your mortgage repayments by a little can have a big impact.

There are three steps you need to take at this point:

→ find out how far away you are from purchasing your second property
→ set up your bank accounts to use the Mortgage Buster strategy below, and
→ find a way to increase the extra payments you make.

Find out how far away you are from buying your second property

Making extra payments against your mortgage is going to mean sacrificing today (spending less and saving more) so you get a reward later (buying your next property). Making those extra repayments and making that sacrifice is going to be much easier if you know how far away you are from your next property. When you know how long you need to sacrifice for, it's easier to push through the pain.

The first step is to figure out how far away you are. This requires some number-crunching. So, as always, there is a spreadsheet for you to download. We call it the Portfolio Planner. Once you plug in your numbers it will tell you how far away you are from purchasing your next investment property. You can then test how much more quickly you could purchase a property if you attack your mortgage more aggressively. Download it at opespartners.co.nz/book. This spreadsheet has been downloaded so many times that it clearly meets a need. So much so that Catalyst Financial – our mortgage advisory business – identified the potential need for more support and guidance in this area, and started a service specifically to help future property investors put a plan in place to purchase that next property.

The Mortgage Buster strategy

To be successful with money, you need to get your behaviour right. And one of the most overlooked ways to change your behaviour is simply in how you set up your bank accounts. This is where the Mortgage Buster strategy comes in.

Using the Mortgage Buster, you split your mortgage into two parts: one that you'll pay down at the minimum rate, the other that you'll attack aggressively. It starts by fixing the bulk of your loan at a fixed-term interest rate (e.g. one year at 4 per cent). Then you'll set up the smaller part on either a revolving credit or an offset account, depending on what your bank offers.

Revolving credit vs offset accounts

Revolving credit and offset accounts are a type of mortgage product that is enormously useful for property investors and those in the starting blocks, providing flexibility in paying down a mortgage aggressively.

REVOLVING CREDIT

Think of a revolving credit like a massive overdraft. If you put money into your revolving credit, you reduce the interest you're charged. But, like an overdraft, you can also take that money out at any time. If you move across $10,000 of your mortgage as a revolving credit, initially it would look exactly like a $10,000 overdraft that is fully maxed-out, and you'll pay interest on the full $10,000. But if you then transfer $1,000 across from your everyday transaction account to this revolving credit, you will now only pay interest on $9,000. Crucially, with a revolving credit, you can withdraw that money at any time and spend it if needed. You can't do that with a regular mortgage. And if you ring up the bank and ask to make an extra payment against your regular mortgage, you'll need to make a full mortgage application to withdraw that extra payment again, even though it was voluntary. This isn't the case with a revolving credit, so it represents a significant advantage.

Revolving credits tend to be a good option for investors who are disciplined and can stop themselves from spending everything that's in their revolving credit.

OFFSET ACCOUNTS

An offset account works very similarly to a revolving credit, except there are two types of account. The first is the loan, which is set on a floating interest rate; the other is a standard account that you put money into. Crucially here, any money you put into that account is 'offset' against your mortgage. You only pay interest on the balance.

Using the same numbers above, you might have a $10,000 portion of your loan set up on a floating rate. If you then put $1,000 in the offset account, then you'll only pay interest on the remaining $9,000 balance.

In fact you can have up to 10 offset accounts. That means if you have one bank account to save for your holidays, and another for an emergency fund, and another for shoes, all of the money in these accounts can be used to pay less interest on your mortgage.

Offsets tend to work better for people who like to split their money up into different accounts so they can manage it better.

Using either a revolving credit or an offset account is not just useful when paying down your mortgage aggressively, as discussed below. It can also be useful when you have money squirrelled away into different accounts; $2,000 in an emergency fund or $5,000 saved for a holiday. Even if you don't pay this money off against your mortgage formally, you can still use it to help reduce the interest you pay by transferring it into your revolving credit or offset account before you use it. This helps to keep the interest you're paying as low as possible in the meantime.

Using the Mortgage Buster to pay down your mortgage

The purpose of the Mortgage Buster is to change your behaviour by giving you a set goal. While making minimum repayments on your main loan, you direct all extra money towards the revolving credit or offset. This does the following two things.

First, it gives you a very specific goal to work towards by dividing your mortgage into smaller chunks. Let's say you have a $500,000 mortgage. If you just increase your repayments after talking to the bank, you won't see the impact of those payments clearly. Pay an extra $5,000 off your mortgage, and the balance will have gone down to $495,000. It's only moved by 1 per cent. But put that same $5,000 into a $10,000 revolving credit and you're 50 per cent of the way towards paying it off.

Secondly, these types of accounts are flexible: if you put money in, you can still take it back out again. That gives you the ability to be really aggressive. You can challenge yourself to transfer more and more money into the account to decrease your mortgage, but if you overstretch yourself or have an emergency, the money is still available. This contrasts with if you had just increased your mortgage payments on one large mortgage – for instance, on a one-year fixed term – which would lock you into that higher repayment for the next 12 months *and* not give you the option to access that money in the future.

So you're pouring all your extra money into the revolving credit, what happens next? When it's time to re-fix your mortgage interest rate, you can pay off your mortgage by as much as you like. If you had accumulated all the money needed to pay off your mortgage, you could theoretically get rid of it all at that point. While you won't have enough money to do that just yet, you can still substantially pay it down now, using the money in your revolving credit. You transfer the money from your revolving credit or offset and make a bulk payment against that main mortgage. Now you're really starting to bust that mortgage. Of course, don't transfer across any emergency funds or savings you are planning to use for a holiday, car or something else.

To put this strategy into practice, you don't need to wait for your property to come off a fixed-term agreement to set this up. (Note that, especially in a period where interest rates are rising, there is unlikely to be a break fee if you are splitting off a portion of your mortgage as a revolving credit.) Ask your mortgage adviser to break off a portion of your loan and set it up as a revolving credit or offset. Alternatively, you can talk to your bank directly if you've got the confidence to. At Opes Partners, our property investment firm, we handle this for investors as part of our Investment Ready programme, which is specifically for investors who are at the starting blocks. Once the bank accounts are in place, set up an automatic payment that triggers the day you get paid and transfers the additional funds into the revolving credit.

How big should my revolving credit be?

Even if the bank would let you, which is unlikely, you don't want to set up your whole mortgage as a revolving credit or offset. Because these accounts are on a floating rate, you will typically pay a higher interest rate compared with your main mortgage. That means that these accounts tend to cost more money if paid down slowly, and it also means that the interest you need to pay will fluctuate as the bank can change the interest rate at any time.

This is why it's best to set up your revolving credit for the amount you want to save within a year. That means that you have a small, definable goal with a set timeframe of when you want to pay it off by. For instance, if you thought you could pay an extra $200 a week as part of the Mortgage Buster, then set up your revolving credit for $10,000. If you think you can do $100 a week, set it up to be $5,000.

Find ways to make additional payments

Once you've set up your mortgage accounts correctly, you'll have an idea of what your current payments are and how aggressively you are paying your mortgage off. If you want to kick things up a gear and go even harder, you only have two options to create more surplus cash. You can either increase what you earn or decrease what you spend.

For investors in their first home, there are three sources to increase your income. The most common at this stage is to get flatmates in. Let's say you're paying off your $450,000 mortgage, which is on a 30-year term at 4 per cent interest. Your minimum repayment will be $495 per week. But let's say you're a little more motivated, so you get a flatmate in. You charge them $200 a week, and you round up your mortgage repayments to $700. If you adjusted your repayments and kept that up for the life of your loan, you'd pay off your mortgage 13 years earlier, with the mortgage paid off in 17 years as opposed to 30. In addition, you'd also save $151,843 in interest over the life of your mortgage. But most importantly for investors wanting to grow a portfolio, as we'll see, you'll also get into your next property significantly faster.

Once you've got a flatmate in, your other options to increase your income are to either increase what you earn by doing your main job, through asking for pay rises, bonuses, or finding higher-income employment – or use side hustles, as we saw with Simrans's case study in the previous chapter.

If increasing your income isn't an option, then you've got to turn to decreasing what you spend through budgeting. While this isn't a book on how to budget, here is an amazing case study of what is possible by keeping a keen eye on your expenses.

CASE STUDY
How two average-wage earners saved $500,000 and got into the property race

For all those who reckon it's too hard to save to become investors, this story might just change your mind. We met Fred and Zoe, who saved a cash deposit – built over years – of around $500,000. Yes, *half a million dollars* – you read that right.

Did they earn $200k a year? Nope. Or were they the beneficiaries of a large inheritance? Nope again. They had the normal household income you'd expect for two people working office jobs. Given that, it seems impossible that anyone could have saved that much cash when faced with today's expenses – and yep, these two *do* live in the country's most expensive housing market: Auckland. But they both insist that anyone on a half-decent salary can save as much as they have, if they are prepared to make sacrifices now for the long-term good.

Fred states that at 30 he was single and in debt. Broke. In his own words: 'I was a loser.' But after he met Zoe, the two buckled down to a strict savings regimen by adjusting their lifestyle choices.

Both admit they live frugally, and currently rent a small room in a shared house, while still in their thirties. Zoe doesn't have a car and rides her bike everywhere, while Fred hasn't splurged on a new cellphone for at least a decade. Ask Zoe how much she lives on per week and she can tell you straight away down to the dollar ($425 by the way, including her part of the rent and saving for ski holidays). The pair insist they still have a nice life, but their hardcore saver attitude and strict budgeting has paid huge dividends in the form of money in the bank.

By 2020 the pair had saved up $500,000 over six years. Even after being this financially savvy, some investors don't know what to do next. Fred had worked in finance and had even been at a mortgage-broking firm – but still didn't have the confidence to take the first step into property investment. In fact, Fred says that all that knowledge was dangerous: he thought he could go it alone as he didn't/shouldn't need any help. But sometimes you need someone else to give you the push to break the inertia and get you over the line.

It's important to note that while investors tend to follow the general path from the starting blocks to running the race, each journey can look a bit different. Fred and Zoe, because they had such substantial savings, were in the position to leap straight into running the race, purchasing multiple properties at once. In this case, Andrew created a plan to put that money (but not all of it) into three different new-build properties, two in Auckland and one in Rolleston, near Christchurch.

From a standing start, the pair control a property portfolio worth over $2.2 million, yet have only used $222,000 of their cash deposit upfront (securing each property with a 10 per cent deposit).

By committing to a path of limiting their spending, Fred and Zoe have been able to save a substantial amount of money without having to massively increase their incomes. While most investors won't take on the sort of budgetary sacrifices this pair has, their example shows us what is possible.

Summary

One path to blast out of the starting blocks is to build equity through aggressively paying down debt using the Mortgage Buster strategy.

→ The first step is to **buy a low-maintenance property**, generally a new-build, that has been selected to take advantage of capital growth occurring naturally in the market.
→ Next, set up a **revolving credit or offset account** against your property. This becomes your savings goal for the year.
→ Once you get paid, **automatically transfer your intended savings** across to your revolving credit or offset account.
→ Once a year, **pay down debt** and decrease the size of your mortgage.

In Chapter 7 we'll run the numbers of how long you have to do this in order to get into your second property. But, before we get there, in the next chapter you'll learn the alternative pathway to that discussed in this chapter: renovating your property to increase equity.

Chapter 6

Renovate to add value

The alternative path to accelerate your way out of the starting blocks is to renovate your properties to increase their value. This will create more useable equity within your property that you can then use to purchase your next property.

When you come to selecting a property to renovate, you can't just buy anything and decide to 'do it up'. In any renovation you need to make sure that any money you spend gets a return. Exactly how much your property increases in value is more art than science. But generally, if you spend $1 renovating your property, you should aim to increase its value by a minimum of $2.

Spending $50,000 to renovate your property? Aim to increase its value by at least $100,000. When an investor spends money on a renovation and the property increases in value *by less than what was spent*, we say they have 'overcapitalised'. In some smaller parts of New Zealand where there is little demand for property, you can overcapitalise just by painting the mailbox.

In terms of the property you buy, if you're following this path you will likely invest in something completely different from what you would buy if you were following the strategy discussed in the previous chapter. For instance, there's nothing to renovate in a newly-built property. Any money you spend will likely result in overcapitalising since the developer has already built something up to modern expectations. Instead, if you're looking to build equity through renovating, you'll purchase an existing property that was likely built over 20 years ago and can be cost-effectively renovated.

To make sure that you get a return on your renovations, we use a six-step framework of the renovation activities that most cost-effectively increase the value of a property. They are also designed to increase the rent a property can generate, so that if you turn the property into a rental, or get flatmates in to help you pay the mortgage, you are maximising your income. We call this framework 'Cashflow Hacking', which was developed by property investor Ilse Wolfe, who runs our renovations-coaching business, Opes Accelerate.

Just before we jump into the framework, there are two clear warnings we need to give. First, when you're renovating, you need to keep a handle on costs as renovations can easily blow out. This particularly happens when first-time renovators start to undertake improvements on their own home which make it nicer for them to live in, but don't substantially increase the value of the property. When renovating your own home, adopt the mindset of 'I'm renovating it to increase its value', rather than 'I'm renovating the property because I want to live in a nicer place'. This means you don't need to splash out on Italian marble tiles when the hardware store ones will do the trick.

Secondly, if you already owned your own home before picking up this book – and didn't purchase a property that specifically could be renovated – you need to figure out whether a renovation project will be profitable. If you want to get a good idea of this, go to open homes in your area to compare properties that have recently been renovated with similar properties that have not. Ask yourself:

→ What are they selling for?
→ What's the price difference between the two?
→ How much would it cost to make my property like the ones that are worth more?

This isn't because you want to sell your house; it's just to give you a sense of whether the renovation project is worth doing.

Six steps to Cashflow Hacking your property

When choosing your property consider which of the Cashflow Hacking steps you could apply to the property.

Step 1: Add an extra bedroom within the existing floor plan

Adding an extra bedroom by rejigging the floor plan is the most cost-effective way to increase the value of a property. From our experience and the experience of the investors in the Opes Accelerate programme, the value of the property will increase usually by at least $20,000 by doing this alone. In addition, it typically increases the rent you can charge by 15 per cent, as a larger family can now rent the property.

However, for this to be cost-effective the bedroom must be added within the current floor plan. It shouldn't be built on as an extension, which requires council consent and is costly. This means that investors following this strategy need to purchase properties where the extra bedroom can be incorporated within the space already present. Properties built between 1960 and 1980 tend to do the trick. They often have superfluous floor space which can be repurposed into a bedroom. Think dining rooms, second lounges and separate kitchens.

But to get the increase in value and rent, the additional bedroom needs to feel like a genuine bedroom. It can't feel bolted on, or as if the lounge has been sacrificed to cram in an extra sleeping space. For instance, we once saw a one-bedroom property that had been 'converted' into a two-bedroom unit. Originally the property had a single double bedroom. The investor then built a wall to partition the double bedroom into two smaller bedrooms that could only fit a single bed in each. The layout didn't work, felt pokey, and wouldn't be viewed as legitimate by either a valuer or a prospective tenant.

To avoid these sorts of mistakes, you need to purchase a property that has enough space in the current floor plan. Use these basic guidelines when considering properties:

CONVERSION	MINIMUM FLOOR SPACE
2-bedroom converted into 3-bedroom	80 square metres
3-bedroom converted into 4-bedroom	95 square metres
4-bedroom converted into 5-bedroom	120 square metres

You can set your filters on TradeMe and Realestate.co.nz to specifically start to look for properties that meet this criteria.

In creating the extra bedroom there are four key things to consider: making an alteration that avoids the need for council consent; windows; wardrobes; and layout.

1. AVOIDING THE NEED FOR COUNCIL CONSENT

If you need to move a load-bearing wall, or need council consent for any other reason, your project will take more time and accrue more cost. When you are scoping where to put an extra bedroom (and potentially whether to buy a property to renovate), it is best practice to work with a licensed building practitioner (a builder who is certified to carry out certain building work). They can give you advice about the building structure and what would be involved with the property you are looking at.

2. WINDOWS

In selecting where to put the bedroom, you need to make sure it has access to natural light and windows. Under the current tenancy regulation every bedroom needs to have windows that open to the outside, which must measure 5 per cent of the floor area within the room. So you can't square off and make an internal bedroom that only has artificial electrical light, like you could if it were a study.

3. WARDROBE

For an extra bedroom to feel genuine, it needs a built-in wardrobe. This can be constructed or can be repurposed from a linen cupboard, pantry or hot-water cupboard where possible.

4. LAYOUT

Finally, you need to consider whether putting the bedroom in will impact the layout in a way that makes the property feel cumbersome or peculiar. An investor we know added a bedroom to a two-bedroom unit, but in doing so she had to carve so much space from the lounge that the front door would hit the couch when opened. Ultimately this meant that the property felt too small, was hard to rent, and tenants quickly moved on.

The most simple bedroom additions will typically cost $7,000–$8,000 and add at least $20,000 in value. They will also add to the rental potential.

Step 2: Turn it into a multi-income property

The next step, when applying the Cashflow Hacking framework to a rental property, is to see whether the property can be reconfigured so that it can be rented out to multiple tenants. This is called making it a multi-income property. For instance, you might adapt a dwelling so that it can be rented out room by room. Alternatively, you might have multiple dwellings (and tenants) on the same plot of land. This tends to increase the total rent you can charge.

The more achievable of these two options is to have multiple dwellings on the same plot of land. One investor you'll hear about on page 72 purchased a two-storey property in Hamilton, and then converted the house into two separate legal dwellings: one upstairs and one downstairs. While this required substantial construction and a renovation budget of $85,000, this step (along with the other Cashflow Hacking principles) increased the rent from $650 per week to $1,125 per week. A massive $475 difference.

Although this is a more advanced strategy and not typically used by investors on their first property, it can be attractive for investors at the starting blocks because then you can get income from people living in a completely separate part of your house. This makes it a good alternative for people who may not want to have flatmates in the same space – for instance, those with younger children.

Step 3: Upgrade the kitchen and bathroom

The next areas that will add significant value are the kitchen and bathroom. This will also make the property significantly easier to rent if you decide to turn it into a rental. When deciding what to change, it is generally best to keep the plumbing where it is to keep costs down. And don't get suckered into splurging on a $6,000 toilet. Nobody needs that amount of porcelain.

To keep costs down it is a good idea to reuse or repaint cabinetry instead of replacing it outright. This means replacing old-fashioned cupboard doorknobs and giving them a lick of paint.

While it doesn't sound like a lot, a cost-effective kitchen renovation should take an investment of $5,000–$10,000 and provide a two to three times return. Bathroom renovations should be cheaper, usually costing $2,000–$6,000 and usually returning two times your spend.

Step 4: Update the fixtures and fittings

Light switches, lamp shades, door handles and plug sockets are small details that implicitly change the value of the property. You might not notice them individually, but collectively old brown door knobs and yellowing lamp shades will quickly date a property, making it less attractive and therefore less valuable.

You could spend $1,000–$4,000 to upgrade the fittings and receive a return of up to $20,000 in terms of the property's value. Aesthetics make a massive difference.

Step 5: Refresh the interior walls

The inside of the property is what really counts, and many a property has been greatly improved by repainting the internal walls. A few fresh coats of white paint will lighten a room and make it feel significantly more modern. Neutral, 'safe' colours tend to hold the widest appeal. There's a reason why Dulux Ōkārito is a top-seller at the paint shop.[22]

Depending on whether you paint the internal walls yourself or hire a painter, you should expect to spend $1,000–$5,000, and generate a two to three times return on that spend.

Step 6: Replace the carpet

The sixth and final step of the Cashflow Hacking process is to replace the carpet within the home, but only if necessary. Another option, which is preferable, is to use a Rug Doctor or other carpet-cleaner to bring the flooring back to life. Cleaning on its own is a highly underrated method to increase the value of a property.

If you replace the carpet in your property it will cost from $4,000 depending on the size of the property. At the time of writing, an average DIY clean of a full house with a Rug Doctor will cost less than $100. Depending on the final result, you may receive a return of between $8,000 and $10,000.

Things to avoid in your renovations

When looking at renovations, there are also five important things to avoid. These are improvements that first-timers tend to spend money on that don't get a return:

1. Installing nicer letterboxes and screening fences.
2. Landscaping overgrown gardens (within limits).
3. Replacing carpets, if they could simply be cleaned.
4. Replacing curtains, when they could be dry-cleaned.
5. Removing overgrown trees, when they could just be trimmed.

You might see something like an overgrown garden and think 'that obviously needs fixing', and it may do, but it won't substantially increase the value of the property.

CASE STUDY
A Cashflow Hacker's story

As already mentioned, Ilse Wolfe runs Opes Accelerate, our renovations-coaching programme, and originally came up with the six steps that make up Cashflow Hacking. One of her recent renovation projects in Hamilton provides a good example of the principles in practice.

She initially bought the run-down Hamilton home having spotted it when driving between properties she was working on. The sign advertising the property for sale was faded – always a giveaway that a property has been on the market for a while without real interest. At the subsequent viewing with the agent, it became apparent that he was a bit new in his chosen profession and didn't realise the gold-mine he was selling. This meant he hadn't marketed it properly or shown investors what the opportunity really was.

After a bit of digging, Ilse found out that some of the building work undertaken on the property hadn't been consented. This means that the property had a defective title and some of the building work was illegal. This makes it harder to get insurance on a property, and can impact the ability to get a mortgage. This is clearly what had scared most prospective purchasers off. However, from Ilse's experience she knew that improving the building works, getting sign-off and rectifying the title weren't too difficult to achieve.

She negotiated the price down to $425,000, even though she reckons it was really worth $575,000 at the time, had it been marketed effectively. So she put down a 40 per cent deposit of $170,000, borrowed the rest of the money from the bank ($255,000), and got to work.

First, she turned the old separate kitchen into an additional bedroom. She then built a kitchen into the living-dining space to create an open-plan kitchen and living space – much better suited to twenty-first-century lives. She redecorated the bathrooms, repainted the walls, and got the illegal building work consented and improved.

The renovations cost $70,000 and were completed within seven weeks. So, all up, Ilse had put $495,000 into the property – her $170,000 deposit, the $70,000 in renovations, and the $255,000 she borrowed from the bank.

Ilse then had the property appraised by a registered valuer, who reported the property was worth an incredible $850,000. Yes, she made $355,000 profit in seven weeks through following the Cashflow Hacking steps described in this chapter. And since the property is now rented, it earns a healthy cashflow. Here's how the numbers worked:

Final value: $850,000
Purchase price: $425,000
Renovation cost: $70,000
Equity gained: $355,000

But best of all, because the property was worth more, Ilse could now borrow more against it. Remember, since it's an existing investment property Ilse could borrow up to 60 per cent of the final value – $850,000. That meant the bank would lend her up to $510,000 against this property. Her mortgage was already $255,000. So that meant there was an extra $255,000 the bank would lend to her. That's enough for her to borrow her deposit back out of the house as well as all the money she spent on the renovations. This is the refinancing part of the BRRRR strategy.

However, just before you run off and apply to become the star of the next season of *The Block*, remember that not every renovation turns out to be this profitable. Even so, there are ways to substantially increase the value of properties if you have the gumption, grit and get-up-and-go to find the right property, scope the renovations, and see them through to completion.

If you would like to learn more about Cashflow Hacking and renovations, we have recorded webinars and many episodes of the *Property Academy Podcast* with significantly more detail.

As a starting-blocks investor, if you are living in your home you won't need to go to the full extent that Ilse did. That's because she treated her property as an investment, which meant the bank would only lend her up to 60 per cent of the value of the property. But if you are treating your property as an owner-occupier you'll be able to borrow up to 80 per cent of the value. Put simply, that means you don't need to increase the value of your property to the same extent as Ilse had to in this example.

Do-up or lemon?

Naturally, not every investor gets it right on the first, second or even third try. Renovations-focused investors, in particular, are more likely to succumb to 'oddball' investments, or 'lemons', thinking that there is value to be added. Anything has the potential to be a lemon if you don't do your due diligence. But from an investment point of view there are specific types of properties that it's better to steer clear of – unless you're a confident investor and know what you're up against. This list applies to all investors in the starting blocks, whether you're taking the passive or the active approach.

Properties to avoid

- **Specific types of hotel rooms. The main reason here relates to how the agreement is set up with the hotel.** You might have a contract that states you get a percentage of any income/rent received. Sounds good in theory, but if the economy suffers or Covid hits, all of a sudden it doesn't generate any income.
- **Leasehold properties. These are cheap for a reason, and do not increase in value since you don't own the land.** The properties take a long time to sell, and are prone to ground-rent increases.
- **A leaky building.**
- Something where there might be **challenges lending against it** (e.g. a really small apartment). While banks' criteria vary, they might lend only 50 per cent on an apartment if it's less than 40 square metres. And they might drop this ratio if they get nervous about the economy. This takes more useable equity out of your portfolio.
- **Any studio apartments** – generally returning poor capital growth and requiring a high deposit for the same reasons as above.
- **Bare land.**
- Something that requires **very high maintenance costs**, such as an old property that will soon need the roof redone, or another maintenance issue that, if left, can cause major problems. See the following case study.
- **Holiday homes in off-the-grid or undesirable spots** that are too remote for anyone else to rent. You might think it's romantic, and you could hold out hoping for long-term capital gains – but in the meantime you're paying the mortgage without any supporting cashflow, and are likely to be going backwards into a financial black hole.
- Lastly, **a property in a very small town**, such as Manaia (population 1,000). In such a small community, it doesn't matter how good your property is, you'll have a limited pool of very few renters. Generally speaking, you should be aware that it may be unrealistic to find a tenant quickly.

Note that this is not a definitive list, but it's a good place to start. Another source of lemons is when investors take on a property to renovate, thinking that they will 'do something with it one day' and then that day never really comes. Our next case study is a clear example.

CASE STUDY
Andrew's biggest lemon

I'm a rich mine of what to do well – and what *not* to do at all if you can help it!

As I was coming off the starting blocks and moving towards running the race, I bought my parents' house in Christchurch (for all of you podcast listeners, this is the one on Wilsons Road). Looking back, I'd say it's probably the worst deal I've ever done.

No one was out of pocket; the purchase price of $200,000 was the market valuation. However, the 100-year-old home had been owned by my grandparents, who – followed by my parents – had, shall we say, not kept on top of necessary maintenance. Plus, it was in a fairly low socioeconomic part of town. A polite realtor might say it had 'untapped potential' or was 'a renovator's dream'!

Although I was getting tired of renovating for profit, I got stuck into some capital improvements, quickly realising that I could spend the next 100 years working to improve something of that age. Leaky hot-water cylinder, rickety foundations – every time I fixed something, it uncovered more issues. It was a money pit. I spent way more on it than I should have.

I owned the property for 12 years, only selling it recently. I'll never take on such a painful and expensive project again. The more time, energy and investment I poured into the house, the more I thought 'I'll make a return when I bowl it over and build six townhouses there. It'll happen one day.' That day never came.

Many investors at the starting blocks get stuck in this trap. This is often because of bank lending restrictions. Although the bank lent me the money to buy it, for the first 10 years of ownership I wouldn't have been able to get the money to develop.

At the time of sale, the property had only increased in value by an average of 2.3 per cent per year – not a lot compared with the rest of Christchurch. And while it generated a decent rental yield on paper, I failed to pick up on number seven in the 'properties to avoid' list above: buying a property where the maintenance costs are high. Replacing a hot-water cylinder is expensive.

As an investment it proved to be a dud, because I could have got a much better return had I bought something else. Buying it quickly on emotion – because my parents wanted to buy another house and they needed to sell quickly – cost me.

Another lesson to be learned from this case is that, as well as it being important to identify whether a property has potential, it is important to know whether you are in a position to realise that potential. Otherwise, you'll make my mistake and hold on to a dud property for 12 years.

Summary

Some investors will renovate properties to blast out of the starting blocks. To make sure that you sprint instead of stumble:

→ Direct your renovation efforts towards the **six Cashflow Hacking steps**:
  — adding a bedroom in the existing internal floor plan
  — maximising the rental options
  — focusing your efforts on bathrooms and kitchens
  — replacing fixtures and fittings
  — repainting internal walls
  — replacing the carpet (or cleaning it if possible).
→ **Avoid 'offbeat' investments** like hotel rooms, leasehold property, leaky buildings, studios and small apartments.
→ If you buy a property with potential, make sure you are in a position to **realise that potential today**, rather than at some unspecified time in the future.

In our next chapter we are going to round out the starting-blocks section by talking about how to figure out how much useable equity you need to build up, and the precise point at which you can move on to the second stage of investing – running the race.

Chapter 7

Getting out of the starting blocks

So you've bought your first house and it's either an investment property or an owner-occupier. You're either paying down your mortgage aggressively or renovating your property. Potentially a mixture of both. To transition out of the starting blocks and start running the race, you need to get financially ready to purchase your next property. The question you may be asking is: 'I know the strategies to use, but how do I know when I've reached that point?' That's what we're going to cover in this chapter.

What's the strategy to get out of the starting blocks?

To get out of the starting blocks and transition to running the race, you need to have enough useable equity within your own property to fund the deposit for your next one. Once you've amassed enough equity, you'll borrow the deposit for your new investment against your first property, and then get the rest of the money from the bank. This is the process we talked about earlier in the book when we said that most property investors don't use cash for the deposit for their investments.

To illustrate the mechanics of how this works, we'll use the example of buying a $750,000 new-build investment property, using your own home to get the deposit and using two banks. First, because you're buying a new-build investment, you'll need a 20 per cent deposit. Since the property you want to buy is worth $750,000, you'll need a $150,000 deposit.

We then use what we call the Lend Before You Leap strategy. This is where, before you've even found a property, you get the lending for the deposit set up against your own home. You'd go to your bank and get a $150,000 revolving credit set up against your first property. That means you can withdraw that money at any time, and then go to another bank to get the rest of the money for the investment property.

We've used two banks in this example, because (a) it makes it easier to understand, and (b) investors are usually better served if they use the 'Split-banking' strategy where they use multiple banks at once. More on this in Appendix B.

So the key steps as part of the Lend Before You Leap strategy are:

→ get the lending for the deposit approved from your main bank
→ find the investment property that you want to purchase
→ work with a second bank to get the rest of the money (80 per cent) approved for the rest of the investment mortgage.

Using this process means that you can buy an investment property, in effect, with 100 per cent borrowing. No cash put in. This is why as you grow your portfolio it becomes easier and easier to buy more properties from an equity or deposit perspective.

To be clear, it's not compulsory to use multiple banks. You can just go to your main bank to get the money for an investment. But, as you'll see many times throughout the book, using multiple banks is often better than using one.

And it's important to note, too, that equity is not the only factor banks look at. As your debt grows, the bank's income tests will generally start to bite.

How do I calculate useable equity?

Throughout the book, we've mentioned 'useable equity' in passing. Remember, this is how much you can borrow against your home for a deposit on an investment property. This is the most critical part of property investment. Up until you buy your second property, you don't need to think too carefully about this. But now that you're gearing up to blast out of the starting blocks, it's time to jump into the maths.

As mentioned, the bank will lend you up to 80 per cent of the value of your own home. That means at any time you need 20 per cent equity within your home before the bank will start lending you more money. So, if your mortgage is currently 60 per cent of the value of your home, you can borrow up to an extra 20 per cent against it.

Put in dollar terms, let's say you have a $1 million home. The bank will lend you up to $800,000 against the property. If your mortgage is currently $600,000, there is another $200,000 that you could borrow against this home for investment property deposits.

If you are borrowing against your own home for the deposit for an investment, use this formula:

Useable equity = (Property value × 80%) – Mortgage

If you are borrowing against an investment property for your deposit, then you can't borrow as much, since the bank will currently only lend you up to 60 per cent of the value of an investment property under the Reserve Bank's LVR restrictions. In that case, the formula is:

Useable equity = (Property value × 60%) – Mortgage

How do I know if I've got enough equity to transition out of the starting blocks?

The minimum useable equity you need will change as the market goes up. If property prices go up, you need a larger deposit and so will require more useable equity. You'll need to base the minimum amount required on what an entry-level investment property costs and the amount of deposit required as the market moves. At the time of writing, the minimum is about $120,000 of useable equity. That is based on the entry-level price of a new-build two-bedroom townhouse in Christchurch of $600,000, which would require a 20 per cent deposit. The way this is calculated is:

Property value × Deposit required = Useable equity needed

If you were purchasing an investment property to renovate in Auckland, you would need more. For instance, if you intend to renovate an existing property in South Auckland, it might cost $1 million and would require a 40 per cent deposit ($400,000 in useable equity), plus the money for any renovations.

Calculate your gap

Now that we know the bare minimum useable equity required and how to calculate it, it's time to see how far away you are from your second property. Let's say that you own a property worth $650,000 that you live in, and you have a mortgage of $450,000. You know you want to reach the $120,000 worth of useable equity needed as a minimum. So how close are you? And how much can you currently borrow against your home? Let's run it through the formula:

$$(\$650{,}000 \times 80\%) - \$450{,}000 = \$70{,}000$$

The bank will lend up to $520,000 against your property, since it's an owner-occupier. You already have $450,000 worth of mortgages, which leaves $70,000 over to invest in property. Remember the goal is $120,000 of useable equity, so that leaves a $50,000 gap. That's $50,000 of useable equity to find before you can get into that second property.

Fill the gap

As we have already seen, there are four ways to get the equity for your second property. Each will already be familiar from earlier parts of the book:

→ capital growth – the property increasing in value
→ paying off your mortgage aggressively
→ renovating the property to increase its value
→ using other people's equity / the Bank of Mum and Dad.*

Let's see how these strategies would apply in this situation to close the $50,000 gap, starting with capital growth. Every $1,000 your property goes up in value, you can borrow another $800 worth of useable equity for your deposit, which is up to an extra $4,000 you can spend on an investment property. For every $1,000 you pay off your mortgage, that's an extra $1,000 worth of useable equity for your deposit, which is up to an extra $5,000 you can spend on an investment property, assuming you already are at or under 80 per cent LVR.

To close the gap your property will naturally increase in value, and you will be making the minimum repayments on the mortgage. Based on the property increasing in value by 5 per cent a

---

* We talked a lot about the Bank of Mum and Dad in Chapter 4, so we won't spend time revisiting it; just be aware that it is an option, as is purchasing a property in conjunction with a friend or another relative to pool your equity.

year and making the minimum repayments on a 30-year mortgage at a 4 per cent interest rate, it will take you two years to build the extra $50,000 worth of useable equity needed.

However, this is where the two strategies we discussed in the previous two chapters come in. Let's examine the impact of each, starting with paying down the mortgage aggressively. Based on the above numbers, your weekly mortgage payment is $495 a week. Let's say you could get a flatmate into your property and charge them $200 a week. In addition, you think you could actually raise your own payment to $600 a week, putting in an extra $105 of your own money. Together with the rental income, this means you will be paying $800 a week against your mortgage. Adding in the capital growth, you'd be able to purchase your investment property in just over a year.

Let's say now that you decide that you don't want an extra flatmate, but you are willing to use the renovations strategy to increase the value of your property. You price up the job and decide you can spend $30,000 renovating your property, and you'll borrow this amount from the bank using a mortgage top-up. You use the 2:1 ratio, meaning that by spending this money you think the value of the property will increase by $60,000. Once the renovations are completed your useable equity would go up by $18,000. That's because while the value of your home has increased, your mortgage has also increased to fund the renovations. But you now have a more valuable asset increasing in value, so you'll get more capital growth.

Similar to the first strategy, you are projected to be able to fill that $50,000 equity gap in just over a year. As long as the bank approves you from an income perspective, you'll soon be in a position to purchase your first investment property.

Set a goal

Before you start pouring money into a revolving credit and ripping down walls to renovate, you've got to set a goal. Running the numbers to see how far away you are from having your second property means the goal can be very specific and targeted. This is important because if you're going to make a sacrifice to pay down your mortgage more quickly, for example by getting flatmates in, you're going to want to know that it's actually getting you closer to owning your investment property. Without a goal you're more likely to slacken off and not make that extra payment this week.

So you don't get overwhelmed by the maths, we've developed a spreadsheet, which you can download at opespartners.co.nz/book to run your numbers, set a goal and see how far away you are from bursting out of the starting blocks.

We had to end this section of the book with the truly inspirational story of an investor who sprinted out of the starting blocks, buying four properties by the time he was 21.

CASE STUDY
I did two jobs so I could afford to buy a house

This story is one of our favourites. We first met this investor when he became a fan of the *Property Academy Podcast* and came along to one of our in-person events. He's the sort of person who shouldn't really be listening to the show – he should be hosting it. He's the real deal.

For this investor, his dream of owning property and creating financial freedom has been driving all his decision-making since he was a teenager. Having cut his teeth on a paper run at 11, at 16 he got his first job at Burger King and began saving as much as he could. At 18, he was working full-time at Burger King in Wellington. He got promoted, got a small pay increase, and managed to save even more. He lived in a shared room with two other people, something many people would never consider doing. However, he said the lack of privacy didn't bother him because he was hardly ever home.

This dedicated investor spent all his spare time on financial education, drawing inspiration from books like *Rich Dad, Poor Dad* and *Mindset*, local experts like Graeme Fowler, online resources like *BiggerPockets*, and of course the *Property Academy Podcast*.

With plenty of savings under his belt and a decent chunk of money invested in shares, he soon went looking for his first property. Unfortunately, Wellington homes were just too far out of his price range. So he jumped on a plane and moved to Christchurch. 'I moved specifically to buy property, but I was single and I didn't have any kids, so I could easily move down there,' he says. 'I worked two jobs. I'd do a full shift at KFC, and then do the graveyard shift at Maccas. I got free food at work, which meant big savings.'

Eventually, after trying to secure a loan for many months, he found 'a really nice lady' at one of the major banks who helped him get approved for a mortgage. 'I told her the whole situation, and I think she felt sorry for me and pushed me over the line.' In 2019, he was able to buy his first property: a two-storey, three-bedroom, one-bathroom unit in Riccarton for $350,000. He then followed many of the strategies discussed so far. 'I added on an extra bedroom [a textbook Cashflow Hacking move], then lived in one and rented out the other rooms so I could pay the mortgage down faster,' he says. That income covered all his costs, and he says it felt good to be living in his own place.

'I was still working most of the time, but after a couple of months I went looking around for my next property. I had about $70,000 in shares, so I sold those at a very slight loss and bought my second house in late 2019. That was a three-bed, one-bath for $299,000 [in Shirley]. I moved into that and rented out all the rooms in the Riccarton house.'

The main banks wouldn't keep lending him money, so he turned to Resimac, a non-bank lender, for his subsequent borrowing. Non-bank lenders are often more lenient in their credit criteria, but will charge a higher interest rate. That's why many investors – ourselves included – turn to them as their ability to borrow becomes more limited.

In 2020 this investor was able to secure lending for a third property – a unit in Papanui. Once again, he used the strategy of adding a bedroom to boost the value.

If this level of drive to buy a house seems surprising in a teenager, that's because it wasn't just about owning a home. Our investor is driven by a desire for future financial freedom, and moving through from the starting blocks to eventually cross the finish line. That's the point where his wealth will grow: he'll build a passive income from property and shares, and can then choose whether he wants to work or not.

Now 21, he is no longer living in the house in Shirley. While working at KFC he met his partner, and after dating for a year they decided to buy their first house together in late 2020. That's property number four. It's in Sockburn, and it's already had an extra bedroom added. Luckily, his partner also has the renovating bug.

Summary

Once you own your own home and have decided which strategy to use to build your equity, it's time to:

→ calculate **how far away you are from being able to purchase** your first investment property
→ use the formulae to figure out **how much useable equity you will need**
→ use the **portfolio planning spreadsheet** (at opespartners.co.nz/book) to project how far away you are from getting into your second property
→ once you have this initial baseline, see whether you can **pay your mortgage down more quickly or renovate your property** to increase its value to get there more quickly.

Once you have enough equity to buy your second property you can blast out of the starting blocks and move into our second phase of investing in property – running the race. The next section of the book will deep-dive into exactly what you need to do in this second phase of investing, before heading towards crossing the finish line.

03

Running your race

Chapter 8

Calculating the length of your race

Once you're out of the starting blocks and have built a base of equity, you're ready to start running your own race. A heads-up: this section of the book is really the 'meat and potatoes' part, and the place we'll spend a lot of time.

There are three main steps. First, you learn how to acquire investment properties, including what to look out for and how to evaluate deals. You'll then learn how to be a landlord, so you can hold on to these properties over the long term. This includes knowing what you actually need to do, and what you can outsource to other people. Finally, you'll learn how to expand your portfolio over time, continually growing your assets and hitting your stride as a property investor.

While you're running your race, you'll likely loop through these steps. You'll buy a property, set it up, you'll max out your borrowing from the bank, and then it's a matter of building back equity before, at some point, it'll be time to expand your portfolio again. That's when you loop back to the first section and acquire another property.

You may have noticed we call it running 'your' race rather than running 'the' race. Frankly, using a racing analogy for this financial framework is a bit risky. It makes it sound like you need to compete with other people to get ahead. And that's not what we're suggesting at all. You don't need to 'keep up with the Joneses' or own more properties than the people you hang around the barbecue with.

All you need to do is keep up with your *own* goals and ambitions. You need to keep up with the pace that you set for yourself. That's why in this section you are going to define how long your race is and set a pathway for your individual property investment journey. Once you do that, it's a time trial: getting to the crossing the finish line stage with the wealth you want, in the time you want.

What's the point of the 'running your race' section?

This section will get you in the position where your assets and wealth produce an income to support you later in life. That's why in this investment stage you'll purchase multiple investment properties to grow your wealth.

To do that, you can keep using the renovations strategy discussed in Chapter 6, or any investment strategy championed by other financial commentators – whether that is property development, subdivision development, landbanking, commercial property or even investing in shares. After all, this is *your* race. However, this section champions using the passive buy-and-hold strategy, where investors purchase properties with the intention of holding on to them, primarily for capital growth.

The reason we suggest this passive approach is because your life priorities tend to change as the years tick by. Marriage, kids, holidays and day-to-day life start to take up more time. For other investors, work becomes the top priority. Their focus is on growing their career to support their family, or others might run their own business. In these cases, no matter your age, swinging a hammer and renovating an old dunger isn't necessarily at the top of your weekend to-do list. You might prefer to spend those hours building your business, progressing your career or spending time with the kids.

While this passive strategy isn't right for everyone, it is a legitimate strategy that works for investors who want a hands-off approach to property. It's also an approach often ignored by property investment authors and educators, who tend to favour a more active strategy. Nevertheless, it is an alternative – and legitimate – approach.

What properties should I buy?

Because running-your-race investors are focused on passive capital growth, they'll tend to seek out properties that are best positioned to take advantage of a market moving upwards. These days, that likely means investing in new or near-new standalone houses, or townhouses in high-growth areas, such as the main centres. These properties don't take up much headspace at the best of times, but the real benefit comes from their lower deposit requirements, which often means building a larger asset portfolio in a shorter timeframe.

While this strategy may mean that you're not manufacturing equity through renovation, that's okay. Think of it as being a bit more on autopilot. Rather than focusing on one or two properties as you may have while you were at the starting blocks, your growing equity base allows you to buy multiple investments.

CASE STUDY
When Andrew's strategy started to change

Although I see this three-step process (starting blocks – running your race – crossing the finish line) all the time with the investors I work with, it wasn't until I sat down to write this book that I realised my own journey has followed a similar path.

After that first (oh-so-successful) property, where I painted every wall a different colour, I continued in the starting blocks. I would buy a property at the lowest price possible, renovate it cheaply, and sell. This is your classic 'buy and flip' move.

When I bought and sold one of my first flips for a $30,000 profit, I was walking around thinking I was Sir Bob Jones. At the time, this was about my yearly salary. Of course, these were the good old days where you didn't have to pay any tax on that profit. Today, my silent business partner, the IRD, would take at least a third of that. It's less profitable now.

Chapter 8 Calculating the length of your race

> I kept doing this until the Christchurch earthquakes struck, when I was only 27. At that point I tapped into a new opportunity: buying earthquake-damaged houses and buildings that could be brought back up to code cheaply, and then resold. Today, this 'as-is' opportunity has almost passed.
>
> My point is that in my younger days I took the active approach, scouting for properties every weekend, becoming a regular at Bunnings and Mitre 10, burning the midnight oil with a paint brush in my hand.
>
> Now that I'm a wee bit older, my situation is different. My time in the starting blocks gave me the equity to invest more, but I've now got less time. Many investors will identify with this situation. I now have a fiancée. We're building a family, and, as you can probably tell, Opes takes up a lot of time. As all of these changes in circumstances unfolded, my property investment strategy started to change, too.
>
> So, after years in the property investment game, most of what I'm doing these days is investing in 'normal' new-build buy-and-holds, as we describe in this book. I've moved into a new phase, running my race, and having done that, now the finish line is not that far out of sight.

Setting the length of your race

You've probably been told to set goals since primary school.

But once you're 30 to 55 (maybe younger, maybe older; it's just a guideline) the goal-setting starts to become a bit more serious. You start to think about what happens in your financial future, how long you really want to keep working, and how you'll spend your days, and money, when you clock off and leave your full-time job for the last time. We call this goal-setting process 'setting the length of your race'. This is a very specific process for determining how much wealth you are going to need to build throughout this section of your property investment journey.

We stumbled across this specific process somewhat by accident. In 2019 we'd just started recording the *Property Academy Podcast*, where we release a new episode every day to keep Kiwis up to date about property. We were gaining traction, with a couple of hundred people starting to listen to the show regularly. By the time we were six months in, investors would email us asking about their personal financial situations and we started to realise something remarkable. So many of the situations were similar. People had invested in properties, built some wealth, and then were looking at how to use these properties to do one of two things: grow a passive income or retire comfortably.

We wanted to see if this was just a coincidence or whether something else was going on, so we started a survey of our podcast listeners, the investors we work with at Opes, and any other property investors we could find. We asked open-ended questions about how investors wanted their lives to be different after they'd invested in property, and what their overarching goals were. We found that there are in fact four distinct ways investors want their lives to be different through property investment. It goes to show that no matter how different we think we are from other people, most of us are aiming for one of the following, long term:

1 **to build a passive income**
2 **to live a comfortable retirement**
3 **to grow wealth**
4 **to achieve financial freedom / to have no money worries.**

In addition, across all of these four categories, investors consistently wanted to provide for their families and their children.

These four categories have become the bedrock for the goal-setting framework that we now use. Historically, when sitting across from Kiwis wanting advice on their financial situation and we'd ask 'What are your goals?', we'd be met with blank stares. A lot of people don't have set, written-down goals. Now, under this process, if you don't have a set goal, you can pick one based on what other Kiwis in similar situations are aiming for: to build a passive income, secure a comfortable retirement, build wealth, or have no money worries.

Once you have that locked in, you build a long-term strategy to make sure you get there. But first, let's dig a little deeper, because each of these goals has a very specific meaning. The table opposite, on the information gathered in the Internal Opes Partners research survey, was based on a sample of 21,519 property investors.

Chapter 8 Calculating the length of your race

Passive income	Of those surveyed, 36 per cent say their primary goal is to build a passive income. In financial terms, this is where you build up a base of assets, and then live off the income those assets produce. (For a full rundown of what this involves, you can skip ahead to Chapter 18 and read about the Golden Goose strategy.) For example, you have $1 million invested and get a 4 per cent net return. Your passive income is $40,000 per year.
Comfortable retirement	For 31 per cent, their retirement is their primary focus. You can achieve a comfortable retirement through the passive income strategy. However, in financial circles when we talk about retirement, it's about building a base of assets, selling them, and then gradually spending and living off that money until you pass away. (You'll learn more about this in Chapter 18, which explores the Nest Egg strategy.) For example, you plan to retire at 65 and live until you're 85. You want to live on $70,000 per year (including superannuation). To do so you'll need a ballpark $1 million at retirement.*
Growing wealth	A further 25 per cent of Kiwis say that growing their wealth is top of the list for them. This goal is most often chosen by younger investors who are 25 years or more away from retirement and who want to keep working for the foreseeable future. For them a passive income isn't necessary yet, and retirement is a bit far off. Again, in financial terms this has a definable meaning. For instance, you have a goal in mind ('I want to be worth $5 million in 20 years') and you then drive towards it.
No money worries	The smallest group – just 8 per cent – say their major goal is financial freedom.** They're sick of worrying about money and want headspace for more important things. This goal is unique compared with the others, because it's the only one that's *not* quantitative. It's subjective. It's a feeling as opposed to a goal that you can put a number on. This goal is often achieved by following one of the three pathways outlined above.

* Assuming post-tax income of $70,000 in today's money, $20,000 provided through superannuation and $50,000 provided through assets.
** Because the last goal – financial freedom – is both chosen by the fewest people and the only one that you can't put set numbers around, it doesn't feature in this goal-setting framework.

Within this Wealth Plan way of goal-setting, you'll choose one of the first three aspirations and put specific numbers around it to turn it into a goal. This goal then defines the length and speed of your property investment race.

To be clear, in reality you don't have to choose one of these three goals. Not every investor's dream is the same. Some investors choose something more specific, like putting their children through private school. To do this they might need assets of around $250,000 by the time their children turn 13. That's a great goal and an investor in this situation could likely achieve it through property using the principles in this book. However, the purpose of this prescriptive framework is to combat two things: (1) from our experience, most investors don't have set and defined goals; and (2) one of our top bugbears is when people tell you to set a goal without ever giving you a solid framework for how to do it. So if you don't have a goal in mind already, here are the four solid steps for setting the length of your property investment race.

Step 1: Identify the long-term goal

Start by choosing one of the top three most popular long-term goals that other Kiwi investors have: building a passive income, achieving a comfortable retirement, or growing your wealth.

Let's say you've picked passive income as your primary goal. Now you can put numbers around it. You need to know two things: when you want to start drawing on this passive income, and how much of it you want. Once you've decided on these two things, you have a specific, measurable goal with a deadline.

Let's say you're now 45 and want your passive income to start at 65, the current retirement age in New Zealand. You've got a 20-year goal. Now it's time to decide how much passive income you want.

Over the years we've sat across the table from hundreds of investors. What do you think is the most common level of passive income (in dollars) Kiwis want per year? If you said $100,000 you are correct. For whatever reason, this number comes up again and again. Probably because it's big, round and sounds like it would provide a good lifestyle.

Other figures investors often choose is their current household income; or more savvy investors will aim for their current income, minus any savings they currently make (since you often won't need to save in retirement), costs they won't pay anymore, like childcare or private school fees, and their mortgage if they're not going to have a mortgage once the passive income starts. This allows them to pinpoint the exact income they'll need to retain their current lifestyle. As that last calculation can all get a bit complex mathematically, we've built a simple calculator that allows you to figure out the cost of your current lifestyle, which you can then use as the basis of your goal. Find it at opespartners.co.nz/book.

EXAMPLE GOAL

I want to: build a passive income
By: the time I reach 65, in 20 years from today
I want it to be: $100,000 per year

All figures adjusted for inflation

Step 2: Calculate the level of wealth you need to achieve this goal

Each of these three goals requires building assets and increasing your wealth to achieve the goal. For instance, if you want a passive income, you need the assets to produce it. The trick is figuring out how many assets you'll need, and here the path diverges depending on the goal you've picked. Because the calculations differ. For instance, in the passive income goal, how many assets you need is based on how much income your assets will produce.

This is where the *rule of 4 per cent* comes in. This rule says that, on average, you can retire, invest your money in a managed fund or high-yield property, and get a pre-tax net (after costs) return of 4 per cent. In simple terms, if you have $1 million of assets, you can safely estimate that it will provide a return of $40,000 per year, before tax.

If your goal is to build a passive income of $100,000, then you're estimated to need $2.5 million of assets in today's money. We know what you're thinking: 'That's a LOT of assets. How am I ever going to build that?' We hear you. But it's important to note that you're likely to already be part of your way there, which is where we come to the next step.

Warning: We're about to get even more tied up in maths, but bear with us. And just to put you at ease, there is a calculator that you're going to get access to that will do all the number-crunching for you. You're not going to have to do this all by hand.

EXAMPLE GOAL

I want to: build a passive income
By: the time I reach 65, in 20 years from today
I want it to be: $100,000 per year
To do that I need: $2.5 million of assets

All figures adjusted for inflation

Step 3: Figure out how on track you are for achieving that goal

No matter which of the goals you have chosen, once you've run the numbers you're likely to have a scarily large number of assets you need to build. So many investors baulk at how much money they are going to need to achieve the levels of income they'd like to retire on or have available at some point in the future. It can be eyebrow-raising, but this is just the maths of it. And most people are not starting out from square one. So now it's time to figure out how far you are towards your goal already.

Now that you know you need $2.5 million of assets to achieve your goal in 20 years, it's time to see how on track you are for reaching that goal. We do this by looking at the six ways you may already be building your assets, and projecting forward what the value of these assets will be by the time you reach your goal date. There are six ways you may already be running towards this figure:

1. **KiwiSaver**. If you are an employee, chances are you are already putting away 3 per cent of your income, which is then matched by your employer. Depending on how long you've been contributing, this can get you a good way towards the big $2.5 million goal.

    Let's say you have $50,000 in your KiwiSaver right now and you are earning $80,000 a year at age 45. Assuming you put in 3 per cent of your income, matched by the employer contribution, get the government support and put your money into a growth fund, this could be worth just over $191,800 by the time you want your passive income.[23] That makes up 8 per cent of the $2.5 million goal.

    If you have a partner and they are in the same position, together that will make up 16 per cent of the goal.

2. **Savings schemes**. Many investors we now meet dabble in a savings or investment scheme. This could be through your employer, or more commonly through a Sharesies, Hatch, Stake or Kernel account that you're regularly contributing to.

    Let's say you currently have $5,000 in your Sharesies account – and you diligently contribute $100 per week. If the shares then increase by 7.5 per cent a year, by the time you reach your goal you'll have $165,840 (in today's money). That makes up another 7 per cent of your overall goal.

3. **Current investment properties**. Many of you reading this book may have a few investment properties already. Particularly if you're out of the starting blocks.

    Perhaps what you own is worth $600,000 now and has a $400,000 mortgage. If it increases at 5 per cent per year – the forecasting rate we usually use at Opes – and you pay off none of the mortgage, within 20 years it's forecast to produce $802,000 worth of equity, or 32 per cent of the assets you need.

4. **Downsizing**. Some property owners buy a big family home while the kids are growing and need the space. Over time, the property has most likely increased in value and they've paid off a lot of debt. If you plan to sell the property and buy a smaller house in the future, this downsizing can factor into your long-term investment plans.

    For instance, if you project that your property will be worth $1.25 million by the time you retire, and you downsize to a $1 million property, then there is $250,000 left over that can be used as part of the assets that are needed. (This is in today's money, and less sales costs.) In this case $250,000 provides 10 per cent of the assets needed to reach this passive income goal.

    Just make sure that you only include the money you'll actually receive. So if you sell a $1.25 million property and then you buy a $1 million property, only factor in $250,000, not the whole $1.25 million.

5. **Inheritance**. If you are lucky enough to know you have an inheritance coming your way, you can factor this in, so long as you are 80 per cent certain what the figure is and that you'll get it by retirement.

For example, if you know you will be inheriting $50,000, and are likely to receive it in 10 years, then factor it in. If you don't know how much it is and it's coming in 30 years, best not to include it since your goal is only 20 years away. (For the example below we haven't included an inheritance.)

6 **Superannuation. Finally, New Zealand Superannuation counts, but in a way that's a bit different to the others. The government's superannuation scheme makes up some of the income you'll have in retirement, which means you need fewer assets.**

For instance, if you want a $100,000 income and both you and you partner receive NZ Super, you'll get just shy of $40,000 per year from the government. That means your assets only need to produce the extra $60,000 of income, so you need to build $1.5 million in assets.

A wee word of warning, though: Kiwi superannuation is likely to change at some point in the future. We have an aging population, we're living longer and having fewer kids. That means there's fewer workers to support more retirees. At our age (we're in our thirties), we don't expect superannuation will look the same as it does today by the time we get to it. So if you're on the younger side, it's worthwhile leaning less on the government. But, if you're 50+, you're probably going to get Super close to its current form.

Once you add this all up, you'll see how close you are. For the case study we're building, let's assume the investor won't factor their superannuation into their calculations, but will treat it as a bonus instead. This is what their Wealth Plan looks like:

	AMOUNT	ASSET GOAL
KiwiSaver, Partner #1	$191,842	8 per cent
KiwiSaver, Partner #2	$191,842	8 per cent
Sharesies account	$165,840	7 per cent
Investment property	$802,167	32 per cent
Downsizing	$250,000	10 per cent
Total	**$1,601,691**	**65 per cent**

EXAMPLE GOAL

I want to: build a passive income
By: the time I reach 65, in 20 years from today
I want it to be: $100,000 per year
To do that I need: $2.5 million of assets
I am currently on track to build: $1.6 million of assets – 65 per cent of my goal

All figures adjusted for inflation

Step 4: Calculate the gap

The final step before we start talking about properties is to see how far from your goal you actually are. This investor needs $2.5 million of assets and through their current plan – which includes two KiwiSavers, a Sharesies account, an investment property and downsizing – they're on track for $1.6 million of assets. This makes up 65 per cent of their goal, but still leaves a $900,000 gap (35 per cent). They need to build these extra assets before they move into crossing the finish line.

EXAMPLE GOAL

I want to: build a passive income
By: the time I reach 65, in 20 years from today
I want it to be: $100,000 per year
To do that I need: $2.5 million of assets
I am currently on track to build: $1.88 million of assets – 75 per cent of my goal
So I need to build an extra: $616,000 of assets – 25 per cent of my goal

All figures adjusted for inflation

Now this is goal-setting. And this is the way you determine the length of your race. For this investor, their wealth gap was an extra $616,000 of assets that they need to build in the next 20 years. That's in addition to what they are already doing. And this is why we said you don't need to compete against everyone else, because the length of your race is going to be totally different from the person living next door to you or sitting next to you in your office.

If there is a gap – and 99 per cent of the time there is a gap – you then get to decide how to fill it. You don't have to invest in property, but you will need to do something.

Chapter 8 Calculating the length of your race

How to set goals the right way

Example

I want: ____Passive income / ~~to retire comfortably / to build wealth~~____

By / within: ____20 years____

I want: ____$100,000____ (per year / ~~in total~~)

To do that I need: ____$2.5 million____ in net assets

I'm currently on track for: ____$1.6 million____ in net assets

So I need to build: ____$900,000____ of extra net assets

→ Your wealth gap

Your turn

I want: ____Passive income / to retire comfortably / to build wealth____

By / within: _____

I want: _____ (per year / in total)

To do that I need: _____ in net assets

I'm currently on track for: _____ in net assets

So I need to build: _____ of extra net assets

→ Your wealth gap

How do I calculate this on my own?

At this point you are likely to be feeling a bit overwhelmed and hoping we have got a spreadsheet to help you out. We'll do you one better. As part of our financial advice, we've built a piece of software that runs all of these calculations, doing the heavy number-crunching for you. It figures it all out, and even factors in the questions around inflation (which, while important, are also very technical and boring – and that's Ed the economist speaking). This software is called MyWealth Plan. When we first built it, the idea was that we would have this super-special software and people would come and see us to use it. But, as part of launching this book, we're letting everyone use this financial goal-setting part for free. You can now use it for free at opespartners.co.nz/book.

Summary

You have to set a goal so you know whether you are on track financially for the future lifestyle you have in your head. This lets you know where the finish line is and the length of your race, so that you're not running aimlessly – or, worse, getting lost in the woods far off the track. Here's what to keep in mind:

→ **Goal-setting is often a bit intangible. You are told to come up with a goal that can be whatever you want it to be.**
→ **Our approach is much more directive. This gives you a logical pathway to figure out:**
   — **what you want** (e.g. passive income)
   — **how much of it you want** (e.g. $100,000 per year)
   — **when you want it by** (e.g. on retiring at age 65)
   — **how many assets you'll need** to make it happen (e.g. $2.5 million)
   — **how on track you are** projected to be to hit that goal (e.g. $1.6 million)
   — **the length of your race** to close the gap between where you are and your goal (e.g. $900,000).

The rest of this section is about how to close this gap and run your race using investment property. We'll cover how to find the properties, how to manage them as a landlord, and then how to expand your portfolio over time.

Chapter 9

The hunt for 'running your race' properties

Now that you've calculated the length of your race, it's time to go shopping for properties. The critical question at this stage is: 'What sort of properties should I buy?' This is the section that Ed, the economist, has been waiting for, because we are going to delve into the data to share our eight principles of properties that tend to grow in value more quickly.

You're also going to get a step-by-step process for setting buying criteria that will help you determine where to look for those investments. But before we do that, you need to know that there are two types of properties.

Growth vs yield properties

It's typically thought that there are two main types of properties: growth and yield. *Growth properties* are those that increase in value more quickly, but have a poorer or even negative cashflow week to week. On the other hand, *yield properties* tend to bring in more weekly income, but increase in value more slowly. So which type is better for investors who are running their own race?

Most first-time investors tend to initially gravitate towards yield properties. They think, 'Yeah, I want an extra $100 a week to play with. That sounds awesome.' However, these properties are generally a better fit for later on when you are crossing the finish line, not when you're trying to accelerate through your race.

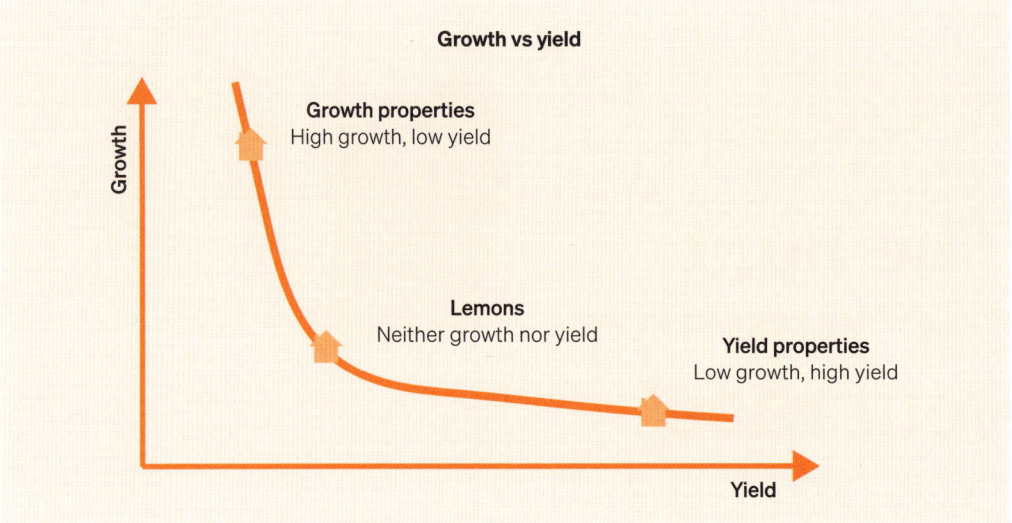

The purpose of running your race is to build your wealth to close the gap between where you are now and the goal you are chasing. Over the long term, most of the real wealth you create as a property investor is through capital gain: the property increasing in value. The properties that best do that are growth properties. Yield properties definitely have their place, but as you'll see they tend to be a more specific product – in more ways than one. So what do growth and yield properties tend to look like?

What is a growth property?

As you'll see in the evidence in a moment, a growth property tends to be a standalone house or townhouse in a relatively desirable area or neighbourhood – or one that is expected to become more desirable with time. Often they're the sort of properties owner-occupiers desire and will bid up the price for. This doesn't have to be your classic four-bedroom home on a quarter-acre section. It just needs to be something an owner-occupier would buy. For instance, a two-bedroom townhouse might be a good fit for a young couple looking for their first owner-occupier home.

It's traditionally thought that owner-occupiers make more emotionally-based buying decisions than investors, and, as such, they'll be prepared to pay more for their family home. Because of this, a growth property tends to be a single dwelling for one family to live in.

What is a yield property?

A yield property tends to be specifically configured to achieve higher rents. Room-by-room rentals are a classic example of a yield property. A room-by-room rental is a property where each room is rented to an individual tenant, rather than renting the whole property to a single person or a couple.

Because each room is rented out separately, there are multiple income streams, which tends to achieve a better yield. The sorts of properties that achieve particularly high yields are those that are specifically set up for this situation.

For instance, we once recommended a four-bedroom property to the investors we were working with. It was based in Hamilton and was being built close to the University of Waikato. Each room had its own ensuite and kitchenette, but the lounge and kitchen area was relatively small. The idea here is that the types of tenants renting this property were more likely to spend time either out of the house or in their rooms, rather than being in the communal living space. This would be the ideal rental set-up for students or professionals. Because the types of tenants who would live in this type of property are more interested in their own room, rather than the whole house, there is more bedroom space than living space. This creates the high yield for the investor.

However, no owner-occupier is going to move their family into this sort of property. Two-year-old Sally and four-year-old Jimmy don't each need their own studio apartment with a kitchenette in their bedrooms. It just wouldn't make sense. Owner-occupiers prefer more living space and more appropriately-sized bedrooms, rather than large bedrooms and a smaller living space.

That means that these rent-by-the-room sorts of properties are only ever going to be bought by investors for yield. As a result, the property's value tends to grow in line with rental increases rather than the market at large.

Which property gives a better return?

Which is better: growth or yield properties? It depends on where you are in your investment journey. If you are in your running the race phase, then your primary goal is to increase your wealth. Whereas if you are crossing the finish line you need to earn an income from your properties. Since we're in the running the race section of the book here, let's look at which will increase your assets and close your wealth gap the fastest – growth or yield?

A growth property will generally increase your wealth and help you speed through your property investment race faster. But there is a trade-off: these properties are frequently negatively geared in the medium term if you borrow all of the money from the bank to purchase them. That means the investor often has to contribute money towards expenses that aren't solely covered by a tenant's rent. Here's a look at how the numbers might stack up over a 15-year period if you are borrowing 100 per cent of the money to invest.

	GROWTH	YIELD
Purchase price	$750,000	$750,000
Growth rate	5%	3.5%
Cashflow per week	–$100	$100
Years	15	15
Total capital gain	$809,196	$506,512
Total cashflow	–$78,000	$78,000
Net gain	**$731,196**	**$584,512**
Difference	**$146,684**	

In this example, the growth property earned $146,684 (25 per cent) more than the yield property. Although the growth property lost $100 a week in cashflow, it made an average of $1,037 a week in capital growth – a net $937 gain per week.

In contrast, the yield property made $100 a week in cashflow, but only made an average of $649 a week in capital growth – a net $749 gain per week.

	GROWTH	YIELD
Average capital growth per week	$1,037	$649
Average cashflow per week	–$100	$100
Net gain	**$937**	**$749**

Although we've just said that growth properties tend to build wealth more quickly than yield properties, the truth is that most investors will purchase a mix of both over time. While growth properties accelerate your wealth, if they're negatively geared they require investment each week from the investor topping up the cashflow. That's why investors will often purchase a mix of assets to build a self-sustaining portfolio. This is where the concept of a wealth wheel comes in.

Building a wealth wheel

A wealth wheel is a balanced portfolio of properties that complement each other so that the investor doesn't need to contribute money towards the portfolio. While individual properties may be negatively geared, the portfolio itself can achieve neutral cashflow.

To keep things simple, let's say that you have the option to purchase two types of properties. The first is a growth property that grows in value quickly, but is negatively geared by $100 a week. The other is a yield property that grows in value more slowly but is positively geared by $200 a week.

An investor in this situation might purchase two growth properties followed by a yield property. The two growth properties might require investment of $200 a week in cashflow, but that is then paid for by the yield property. The positive $200 a week cashflow from the yield property means that the portfolio balances out: there's $200 a week coming in from the yield property and $200 a week going out from the growth properties.

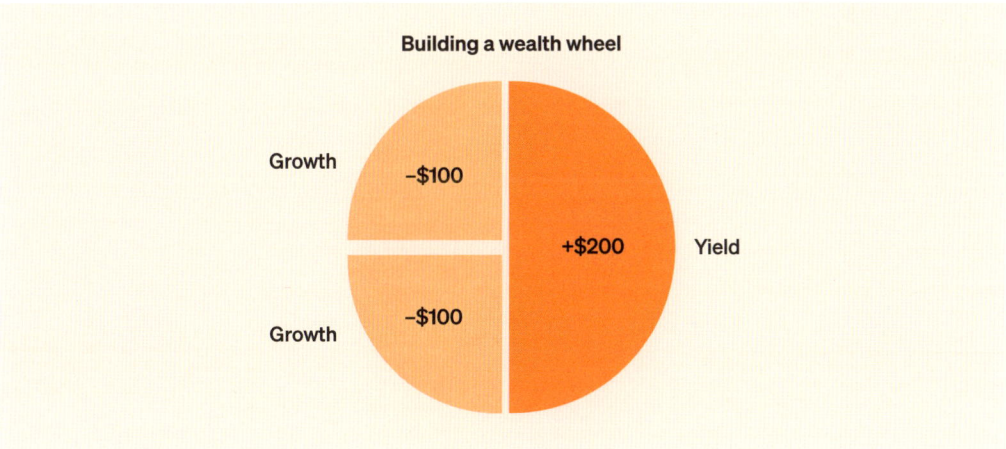

We call this a wealth wheel because your wealth primarily increases through the growth properties, whose required top-ups are paid for by the yield properties. Once these are set up – bank lending permitting – you can roll on to setting up another a wealth wheel that, again, starts to pay for itself.

When setting up these wealth wheels, it's often the right move to purchase your growth properties first. Why? Because this guards against the risk that bank policies change over time and later you can't obtain lending for additional properties. In this case, it's better to own your growth properties early, because they'll get you a better return over time, generating capital gain and equity which will help you make further investments. Investing in these first gives you more time holding them in the market.

How many properties do you really need?

It can be tempting to think you need to aim huge. Like, 'Sir Bob Jones' huge. However, you don't have to become a billionaire to hit your passive income or retirement goal. Nor do you need to own 48 properties, making up 12 wealth wheels. Investors who have set their goals in the way we showed in the previous chapter may need only three to five properties over the next 15 to 20 years in order to achieve their ambitions.

How do I find good growth properties?

You've calculated your goal, and you know you want to buy a growth property. How do you find them? And what do they look like? We've looked at the data from many different angles, both at Opes and through the *Property Academy Podcast*, aiming to understand what tends to grow in value the fastest. Through this research and subsequent number-crunching, we identified eight principles of capital growth. These are indicators of what tends to grow in value most quickly. Note, however, that they are *trends*; they are not necessarily hard-and-fast rules. We previewed these back in Chapter 5 (see page 59). Now, it's time to dig into the analysis to show you the evidence behind these principles.

Even so, we're going to move through these relatively quickly, with the focus on the principle and how to spot it. The evidence underpinning the principles can be found on our website, YouTube videos and podcasts for those of you who are really keen for detail.

The principles are arranged in the order of how you should go about looking for properties. We do this because you can't look at every property in the country. So you need a method to determine where to look for properties. This approach starts by looking at every region in New Zealand. Once you've found a target region or two, look at towns and cities within that region,

Chapter 9 The hunt for 'running your race' properties

then the suburbs. Once you've found the locations you want to target, you can then look at individual properties.

Regions nearer the bottom of their property cycle tend to increase in value faster

Property markets tend to work in cycles. They'll go through periods where prices rise rapidly, start to slow down, stay the same for a bit, drop back and, at some point in the future, boom again. Over the long term, the trend tends to be prices increasing, but there are sometimes long periods where prices will stay flat or even decline.

That said, all markets don't increase in value at the same time. Auckland property prices might be booming while prices in Taranaki are flat. At other times houses in Gisborne might be stagnant while Dunedin is pumping.

A good example is Wellington and Christchurch. These two cities are only an hour's flight away from each other, but their property markets have historically increased at different times. Between 2010 and 2015, house prices in the capital rose just 3.5 per cent, whereas Christchurch prices rose 30.6 per cent.[24] In the following five years (2015–2020), Wellington prices rose 70.2 per cent and Christchurch only 6.6 per cent.

	WELLINGTON CITY	CHRISTCHURCH CITY
2010–2015	3.5 per cent	30.6 per cent
2015–2020	70.2 per cent	6.6 per cent

Showing change in House Price Index

Now you might say 'Well that's because of the earthquakes in Canterbury', or 'Wellington needed to have properties restrengthened after the Kaikōura earthquake'. The exact causes don't matter; the point is that property prices across the country don't increase and decrease at exactly the same rate or at exactly the same time.

Because each region operates within its own property cycle, it makes sense that those areas that are in a lower point of their cycle haven't increased in value much recently and are more likely to experience 'catch-up growth' in the near to medium term (about five years) compared with those areas that have recently boomed. So how do you identify an area that is in a lower part of its cycle?

A good way to judge this is by looking at the house price within a region and comparing it with the New Zealand average house price. For instance, over the past 29 years, Auckland's median house price has been – on average – 1.40 times the overall New Zealand median house price. So if

105

the median house price in New Zealand was $1 million, we might expect Auckland's median house price to be $1.4 million. If, for instance, average Auckland house prices were in fact $1.25 million, then we would say Auckland is underpriced or undervalued by $150,000 (11 per cent). At the time of writing, Auckland house prices are sitting at 1.39 times the national median, so on par with where we might expect house prices to be. Here is a look at which regions appear to be the most under- or overvalued at the time of writing.

REGION	OVERVALUED/UNDERVALUED
Manawatū-Whanganui	12% overvalued
Gisborne	11% overvalued
Hawke's Bay	11% overvalued
Wellington	6% overvalued
Waikato	5% overvalued
Bay of Plenty	3% overvalued
Otago	3% overvalued
Southland	3% overvalued
Auckland	1% overvalued
Taranaki	−4% undervalued
Northland	−5% undervalued
Marlborough, Nelson, Tasman and West Coast	−10% undervalued
Canterbury	−18% undervalued

Source: Opes Partners analysis of REINZ data

This data continually changes as prices move. You can find the latest, up-to-date data on our website. At the time of writing, the Manawatū-Whanganui property market appears the most overpriced.[25] House prices there are 12 per cent above their long-term average. The most undervalued regions are Canterbury and those at the top of the South Island.

This is not a model without its faults, or one that tells you what's going to happen over the next 12 months. But it can give you a sense of the direction of travel. For instance, for years at Opes we – and many other commentators – have said that Christchurch and the surrounding districts were undervalued and due for catch-up growth.

Near the end of 2020 this model suggested that Christchurch was 25.4 per cent undervalued.[26] In 2021 house prices in the city increased 38 per cent,[27] higher than any other major or secondary city in the country over that timeframe. Christchurch is rapidly catching up, and at the time of writing is now 17.9 per cent undervalued.[28]

Cities with higher population growth tend to increase in value faster

Once you've considered a region that may be in a good part of its property cycle, start to look for regions, cities and towns with growing populations. An expanding population creates greater demand for housing. This intuitively suggests that prices should rise in regions where the population is growing and fall in areas where populations are shrinking.

While it is true that higher population growth areas have historically achieved higher house price growth, the trend isn't nearly as strong as you might think. For every 1 percentage point in population growth per year, house prices increased 0.4 percentage points faster per year.

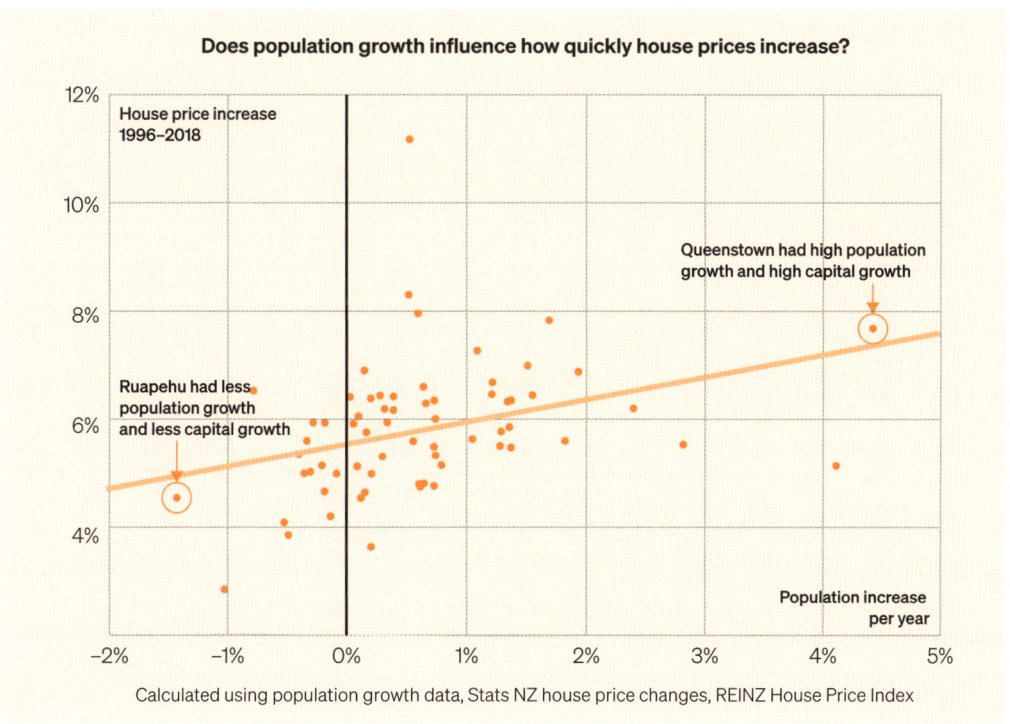

Calculated using population growth data, Stats NZ house price changes, REINZ House Price Index

What's interesting is that there are areas that have declining populations, but the house prices are still increasing. Take Ruapehu district, for example. On average the population shrank by 1.4 per cent every year between 1996 and 2018, according to Statistics New Zealand. Yet over the same period, the REINZ House Price Index shows that house prices grew by 4.7 per cent per year.

Why isn't the trend stronger, when the 'more people = higher house prices' story makes so much sense? It's because while more people means higher demand for properties, it also triggers what we call a 'supply response'. The increased demand for housing means more houses get built, which increases the supply of housing, helping to keep prices in check. So while choosing a high population growth area is an important factor, it's not the only factor to consider.

Cities and towns with larger populations tend to have more consistent capital growth
There is very little data to suggest that house prices in larger cities increase at a faster rate than cities with small populations. So why do some property investment experts recommend bigger cities? This is because while big cities don't increase in value faster than smaller population centres, they do increase in value more consistently.

In addition, property prices in larger cities tend to recover more quickly from economic downturns, as compared with smaller towns. Compare Canterbury house prices (a larger region) to Gisborne house prices (a smaller one) after the 2008 economic downturn. Canterbury house prices peaked in February 2008. Four years and two months later, Canterbury house prices recovered and surged past that previous peak. Gisborne house prices, on the other hand, took more than a decade – 10 years and nine months, in fact – to recover from their 2007 peak. Values in this smaller region were flat right through until mid-2018.[29]

Consistently, the regions with larger cities have recovered more quickly following an economic downturn than those filled with smaller towns. The top four fastest-recovering regions after the 2008 economic downturn were home to four of our five largest cities – Auckland, Canterbury (Christchurch), Bay of Plenty (Tauranga), and Waikato (Hamilton).

This consistency of capital growth is important because a steadily increasing house price creates equity that you can then use to increase your property portfolio. If your property's value stays flat for a long time, there's no additional equity to use to buy the next investment. So, it's all very well saying 'Invest in Gisborne, it's got the same capital growth as other regions over the long term', but it's not just the long term that matters. What happens to your investment property's value in the meantime will impact your ability to grow a portfolio.

This can be the case because the economy of a small town tends to be reliant on a few specialist industries, with the bulk of the town's population employed by those sectors. Think tourism in Queenstown, dairy and agriculture in South Taranaki, or aluminium in Invercargill. If these industries go through a downturn, it has a significant impact on employment in the town.

You don't see the same trend in larger cities. Instead, major metropolitan areas have diversified economies, which are based on multiple industries. If one industry goes through a rough patch, there are still employment opportunities in other sectors. That keeps demand for housing resilient, making it easier to find a tenant and have confidence in higher house prices remaining steady in the major cities.

Suburbs closer to the centre of the city tend to increase in value faster

The first three factors on this list are relevant to choosing a region and then a city. Once you narrow down your property search to a few regions or cities, you can take a closer look, deciding which suburb to look further into.

As a general rule, suburbs closer to the centre of a city tend to increase in value faster than those on the outskirts. For example, in Auckland, inner-city suburbs to the west of the CBD – Herne Bay, Westmere, St Mary's Bay and Grey Lynn – are among the top 10 per cent of suburbs for capital growth since the turn of the century. To the east of the city centre, Ōrākei, Greenlane, Remuera and Meadowbank are in the top 30 per cent of suburbs for capital growth over the same period.

In contrast, suburbs that are further away from the city centre grew in value more slowly. Albany, Hobsonville, Rosedale and Greenhithe to the north all saw average property values increase in the bottom 10 per cent of suburbs. This was also the case for suburbs like Totara Heights and Conifer Grove to the south.

Properties located in higher-end suburbs tend to increase in value faster than those in less desirable areas

Properties in higher-end suburbs generally – but not always – increase in value more quickly. This overlaps the point above, since higher-end suburbs also tend to be located nearer the city centre. However, Christchurch provides a good example of where high-end suburbs located away from the CBD also grow in value at a superior rate. As we would expect, the affluent inner-city suburbs of Fendalton, Strowan, Bryndwr and St Albans saw house price increases in the top 20 per cent of Christchurch suburbs. But even higher-end suburbs that are a 20-minute drive away, like Sumner, Scarborough and Clifton, grew in the top 10 per cent of suburbs. However, that doesn't mean that some lower-income suburbs like Addington, Sydenham and Spreydon didn't also do well.

Standalone houses and townhouses tend to increase in value faster than apartments

Having analysed the factors relating to the city and suburb, let's turn to factors about the specific property you buy. Houses and townhouses tend to increase in value faster than apartments. Since records began, the long-term, 10-year capital growth rate for Auckland dwellings (non-apartments) has always been higher than that for Auckland apartments.

On average, apartments grew at a rate of 6.1 per cent per year, while other properties (excluding apartments) grew at a rate of 8.9 per cent per year.[30] In Wellington, the trend is the same. Wellington dwellings increased in value on average 1.7 percentage points faster per year than apartments.[31] Interestingly, there were a few rare periods (2002–2005) where apartments did grow faster than other dwellings in the capital.

Although there is a clear and substantial difference in the rate that apartments increase in value versus houses and townhouses, the trend is less clear when it comes to houses versus townhouses.

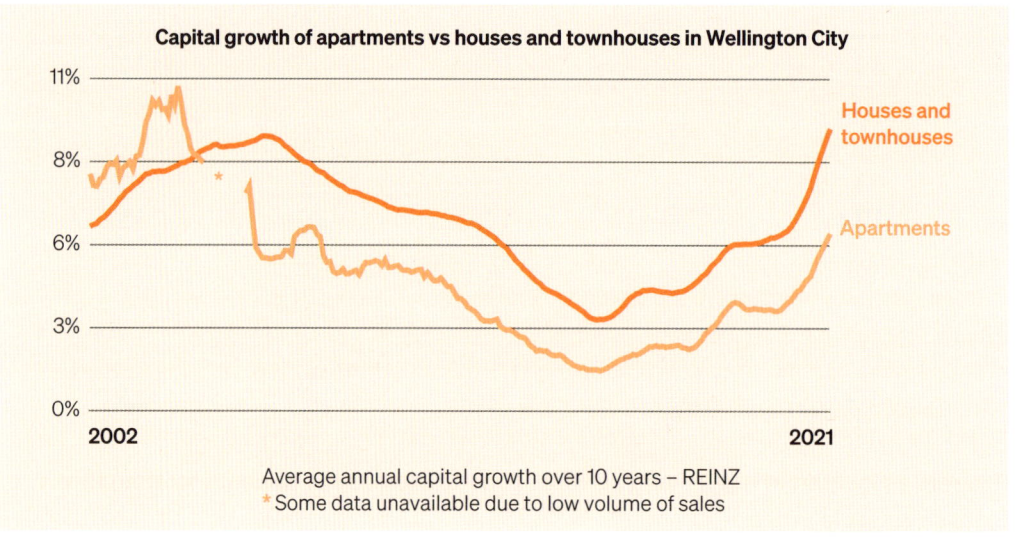

Capital growth of apartments vs houses and townhouses in Wellington City

Average annual capital growth over 10 years – REINZ
*Some data unavailable due to low volume of sales

The traditional thinking is that land increases in value, the building doesn't. So a property with more land should increase in value at a faster rate than properties with less land. Since standalone houses have more land, it's tempting to think that houses will appreciate substantially faster than townhouses. While it is true that houses have generally increased in price at a faster rate than townhouses, the margin is small. Despite the fact that there has been significant townhouse development in Christchurch, townhouses there lag only 0.5 per cent per year behind houses. In recent years the change in the price of a townhouse has been similar to that of houses.[32]

Chapter 9 The hunt for 'running your race' properties

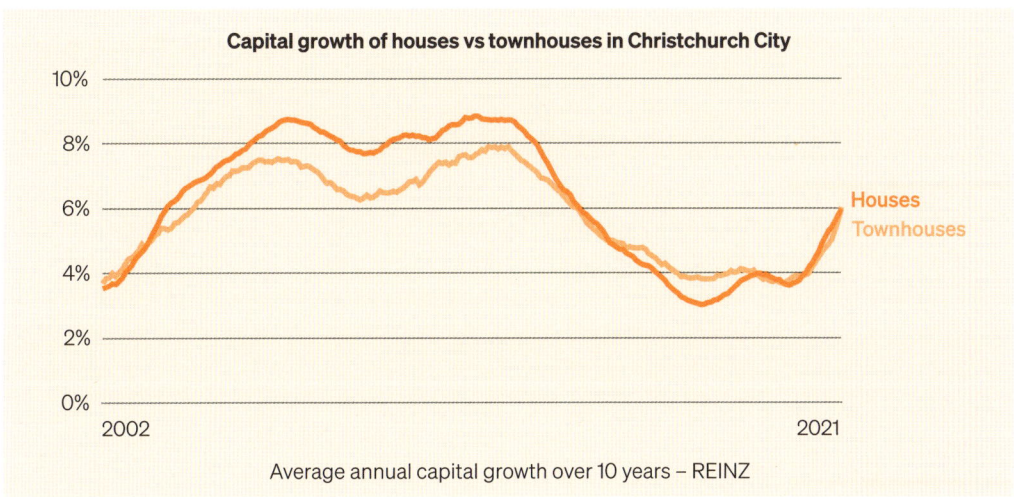

Of the three main property types, houses tend to increase in value the fastest, very closely followed by townhouses and units. Apartments then substantially lag behind the other two property types. This finding is not surprising given that apartments have tended to be thought of as a yield property, while the other two are considered growth properties.

Two- to four-bedroom properties tend to increase in value faster than one-bedroom properties

Single-bedroom properties grow in value at a noticeably slower rate than properties with more bedrooms. For each year between January 2000 and July 2020, two-bedroom apartments grew on average 1.77 per cent faster in Auckland, 1.33 per cent faster in Wellington and 1.04 per cent faster in Christchurch than one-bedroom apartments.[33] Looking at the same data over this time period for flats, townhouses and units, three-bedroom properties grew in value faster than those with only one bedroom in Auckland, Christchurch and Hamilton. Only in Wellington did one-bedroom flats sneak ahead. Therefore the trends are noticeably clear: one-bedroom properties tend to increase in value more slowly than those with more bedrooms. Once you get to two bedrooms or more there is not a clear difference in terms of capital growth.

Properties that are bought at or under valuation have more room to increase in value compared with those that are bought above valuation

The price you purchase a property at will also impact the percentage by which the property can increase in value. Just because property prices tend to increase in value over the long term doesn't mean you should take a deal that has a price tag that's higher than it should be in today's market.

If you overpay for a property by $10,000, then at the time you sell it that's $10,000 less capital growth if you sell at valuation.

How do I find a property with all these attributes?

It is highly unlikely that you will find a property with all of these attributes that is also both affordable and has an acceptable rental yield. The purpose of sharing these principles of capital growth isn't so you can find a property that fits all eight principles; it's to give you a list of attributes that you can look for to then narrow your search. Do the best you can. Don't wait to find the perfect unicorn property. They don't exist.

Summary

When it comes time to run your race, you want to purchase properties that can help close your wealth gap.

- There are two main types of properties: those that grow in value faster but have a poorer yield **(growth properties)**, and those that have higher yields but increase in value more slowly **(yield properties)**.
- Growth properties will tend to help you **grow your wealth faster** than yield properties, so are generally the focus when running your race.
- There are **eight principles of capital growth** to look for when choosing a property.
- Don't try to look for a property with all eight principles; **find one that you can afford** that exhibits as many of the principles as possible.

Now you are ready for **Step 3: Buy your first investment property**. You're going to learn how to evaluate an investment property when it comes time to purchase, including how to run a return-on-investment analysis.

Chapter 10

Evaluating properties

Once you've followed the process outlined in the previous chapter, you'll be looking at properties within specific areas of a city or town, and will start to look at individual properties. Once that happens, the obvious next question is: 'Which one should I buy?'

One approach is to think about how nice the local shops are, perhaps the colour of the backsplash in the kitchen, which one 'feels' the best, or whatever else. While these considerations aren't totally without merit, any investment needs to be based on the numbers.

Together we've spoken with literally thousands of investors, and we've never met one yet who disagrees with the statement 'you should invest based on the numbers'. In fact, you're probably nodding your head right now, agreeing with this. But then the big question becomes: 'Which numbers should I look at?'

Gross yields, net yields, annual cashflow. These are the traditional tools of the trade. And while they have their place, they're not great at analysing long-term hold investments. The reason for that is that they only measure a point in time: right now. For instance, it was easy to find a property that had positive annual cashflow in 2020 when interest rates fell to 2.19 per cent per year. Almost everything had positive cashflow. Did that make every property a good investment over the long term? Nope, because interest rates rose again, making the cashflow negative. You need to evaluate your properties over a 15-year period to see how they will perform.

To do this, we've developed our own model for evaluating properties. It's based on a basic accounting principle – the return-on-investment method. But we have developed it to apply to long-term buy-and-hold properties. It is strikingly simple, based on a spreadsheet that you can download for free and use yourself. But while simple, it is also strikingly powerful. Behind each sheet there are over 100 lines of formulae that power the calculations, and you can change any of the underlying assumptions to see how the numbers would work under almost any scenario you can think of. This spreadsheet has been downloaded more than 8,000 times by investors around the country, and is quickly becoming the standard way to compare properties. You can download this at opespartners.co.nz/book.

What does the return-on-investment method do?

There are three types of return you can get from your property once you decide you're going to hold on to it. The property can increase in value (capital growth), you can earn cashflow from the property, and you can get a return from paying down debt.

Similarly, there are two types of investment you can put *into* the property. Your initial deposit, and then any cashflow that you put in to top up the property. Even if you borrow the deposit for the property it's still an investment, since you are putting that money at risk by investing it.

The model then projects the cashflow, the potential capital growth and any other returns based on your assumptions, adjusts everything for inflation, and then gives you a single number: the estimated return on investment over that 15-year period.

What does that single number mean? Let's say the spreadsheet projects you'll receive a 323 per cent return on your investment. That means for all the money you put in – your deposit and any cash as top-ups – you get your money back and 3.23 times the money you put in.

Now of course these are just projections in a spreadsheet on your computer. The actual returns you get will differ, and all investment involves risk. For instance, inflation isn't going to be 2 per cent per year, every year. The property market won't always appreciate consistently at 5 per cent per year. Even so, basing your investment decision on detailed financial modelling and long-term forecasting will probably lead to a better decision than just eyeing up the colour of the backsplash in the kitchen.

What number should I aim for?

After running their prospective investments through the spreadsheet, many investors have emailed us asking what sort of return on investment they should aim for. 'What's a good number?' This is a good question, but one that is tough to answer because the market is frequently changing, and it depends what assumptions you put in.

One week, somewhere between 275 and 375 per cent could be good. But if interest rates change the following week, then the projected return can change. Rather than aiming for a specific number, it is more important to look at a range of properties using the same set of assumptions.

And that's because this way of analysing properties is *comparative*. It was never designed to tell you whether a property is a good investment or not; it is designed to tell you 'between the properties I am looking at, all using the same set of assumptions, which is projected to earn a higher return?'

It's easy to fluff your way to get a high return on investment. Just use an unrealistically high capital growth rate, in which case any property you run through the spreadsheet will look like a winner. The true test is: when you look at multiple properties under the same set of consistent assumptions, which comes out best?

One last tip: this sort of analysis is best used when looking at similar strategies. For instance, it's really good at comparing hold properties with one another. But not good at telling you whether you should develop a property or hold a property over the long term. In other words, it's good at comparing apples with apples, or oranges with oranges, but not good at comparing potatoes with celery.

The numbers are just a starting point

At the risk of contradicting what we said at the beginning of the chapter, although the numbers you get from the spreadsheet are important, there is definitely a place for judgement calls. The numbers aren't the whole deal.

Consider this example. Say you're purchasing a new-build and trying to make a decision between two properties. Just hypothetically: one has a projected return of 425 per cent, but the developer is a former bankrupt, who has run into trouble with the Financial Markets Authority and has a bombastic attitude on social media that suggests he's compensating for something. The other has a projected return of 415 per cent, from a developer with a long-standing brand and a reputation in the community for doing good work.

There is absolutely nothing wrong with deciding to work with the second developer if you perceive that they pose a lower risk, are likely to deliver a better-quality product, or are more likely to get the build completed. You can adjust your decision based on any qualitative factor you like. However, the process should start with the numbers and then adjust for other information you think is relevant. The numbers are there to inform your decision, not necessarily make the decision for you.

Evaluating properties case study

To give you a sense of how to use this model, let's look at two separate properties and see how they compare.

In this case, you've gone through the steps in the previous chapter and have decided you want to invest in Auckland. You've seen that it's one of the least overvalued areas in the country, you like its long-term population growth projections and the diversity in the economy. You've decided to invest out west, because it's historically had some good capital growth and properties are affordable. And you've narrowed your search down to two- to four-bedroom townhouses, because they're more affordable than standalone options and you want a property with two or more bedrooms.

From your search you've found two new-build townhouses (note: these are both real properties that were on the market in late 2021). The first is a two-bedroom townhouse in Henderson that is being sold by a large developer. The prices for these start from $915,000. The second property is a four-bedroom townhouse in Glen Eden, being built by a lesser-known developer, being sold for $979,000. Both are in West Auckland, not that far away from each other. You've been through the property information packs and run the numbers through the spreadsheet. Time to see which one is projected to make the better investment:

	HENDERSON TWO-BEDROOM	**GLEN EDEN FOUR-BEDROOM**
Price	$915,000	$979,000
Rent	$535 / week	$800 / week
Bedrooms	2	4
Bathrooms	2	2
Car parks	0	1
Estimated operating expenses (e.g. rates, insurance, maintenance . . .)	$10,203	$11,678

Looking at these numbers, which do you think will make the better investment? And what makes the difference? In this model, it's best to assume that similar properties – in this instance, townhouses in West Auckland – will attract the same rate of capital growth. That might not be what actually happens in practice, but it's a good assumption to test the properties on. That means that when you look at the return on investment, what really drives the final number is cashflow.

Analysing the first property

The first property, situated in Henderson, is expected to have negative cashflow over the life of the investment of $172,327 (in today's dollars). That means the investor is projected to need to top up the property by $221 per week. This is what the cashflow of their property would look like:

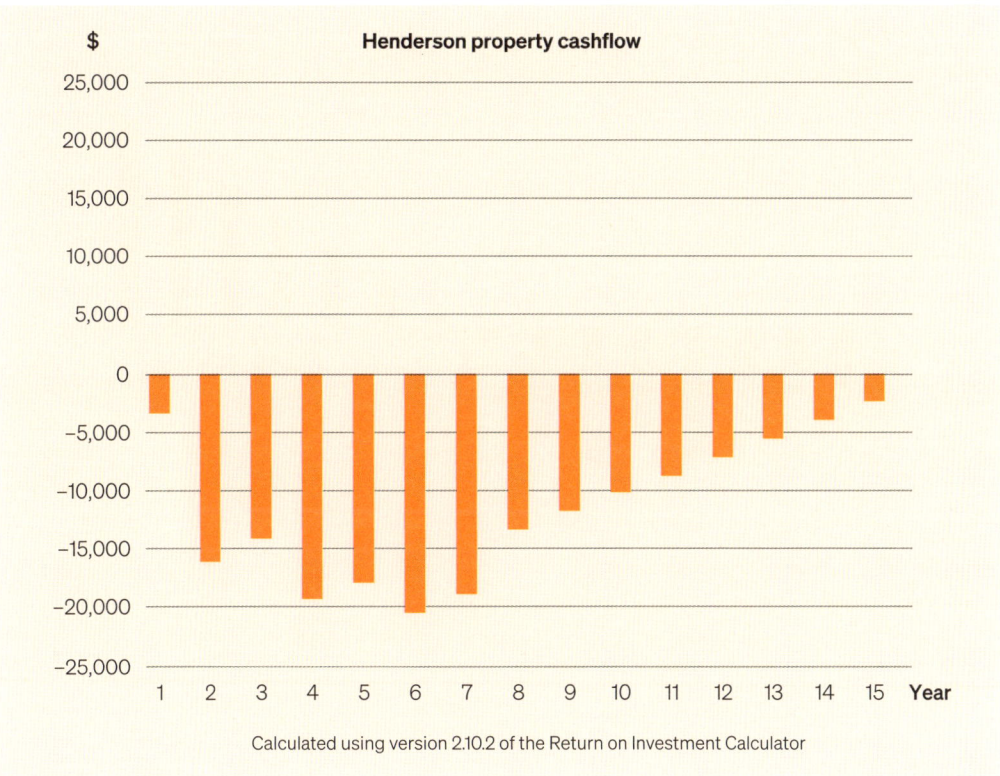

Bear in mind that at a 6 per cent capital growth rate, the investor is still getting a positive return.

Analysing the second property

The second property, situated in Glen Eden, is a good example of the principle that cashflow improves over time. It is projected to initially have negative cashflow, for the first eight years, before becoming positively geared. In fact, over the 15-year period the property is anticipated to receive more back in cashflow – $53,447 – than the investor had to put into the property – $43,886. However, you still need to consider the money the investor has to put in while the property is negatively geared as an investment. That's because even though the property will eventually pay that back, the investor still has to front with the cash initially.

Looking at it a different way, the property starts out requiring a top-up of – on average – $106 per week over the eight-year negatively-geared period, before the cashflow starts to turn. In the last seven years the property is projected to earn $147 per week on average.

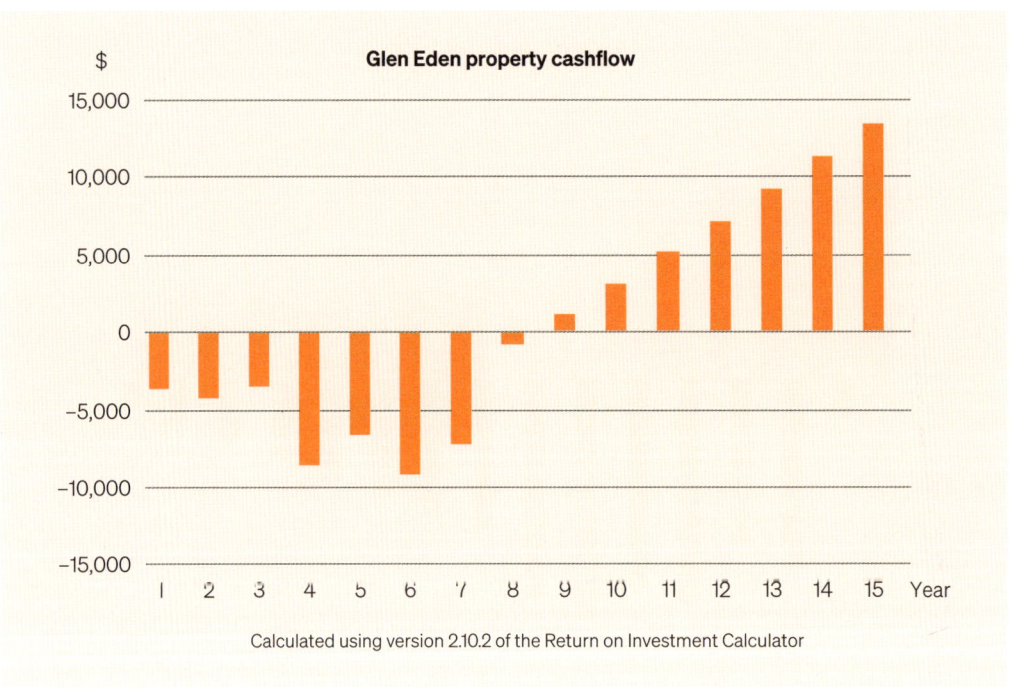

Calculated using version 2.10.2 of the Return on Investment Calculator

Which is the better investment?

Let's compare the returns from each.

	HENDERSON TWO-BEDROOM	GLEN EDEN FOUR-BEDROOM
Returns		
Capital gains	$949,462	$1,015,872
Cashflow gained	$0	$53,447
Debt repayments	$0	$0
Total returns	**$949,462**	**$1,069,319**
Investment		
Deposit (Borrowed)	$187,000	$199,800
Cashflow invested	$172,327	$43,886
Total investment	**$359,327**	**$243,686**
Return on investment	**264.2 per cent**	**438.8 per cent**

In this instance, the Glen Eden property is projected to give a 1.7 times higher return on investment than the Henderson property. This is such powerful analysis, but so few property investors run their numbers like this.

The reason that conducting such an analysis is important isn't just academic, or because we like spreadsheets. Running your numbers like this comes back to what we talked about in Chapter 8: your wealth gap. You're not just looking at properties for kicks, or just to get a good investment. You're looking at properties because you want to close your wealth gap, cross the finish line and sort out your financial future.

Which of the above two properties does that better? The Henderson property provides a lower total return and costs more money. The Glen Eden property provides a higher total return and costs less money. So which is going to close your wealth gap faster? Likely, the Glen Eden property. Firstly, it provides a higher total return. Secondly, you don't need to put as much money into it. That frees up money for you to put towards another investment property – further closing your wealth gap. Does that mean that you should definitely buy this specific property in Glen Eden? It depends on the other subjective factors you take into account – design, style, the developer, and location.

You've also got to consider whether you've looked at enough options. Remember, this model is primarily a comparative tool. It doesn't tell you what's a good investment and what's a bad investment, only if one is expected to return more than another. If you only put two 'bad investments' through the model, it won't tell you that they're both bad. Similarly, if you compare two good investments it won't tell you they're both good, only that one is better than the other.

This is why it is best to canvass the market. For instance, at Opes Partners we have relationships with 58 developers looking at new-build properties. Working with somebody with some market knowledge, or running the numbers on multiple investment properties yourself, will give you a good baseline of properties to either accept or reject, knowing that you've canvassed the market appropriately.

Which numbers are most important?

Looking at the second table you've just seen, what do you think are the two most important numbers? Yup, return on investment is important, that's going to inform the decision of what we buy, but there is one more crucial number. What do you think it is?

If you said 'total returns' you are correct. This is because total returns is the additional equity created through this property. This is what you have in assets once you hit the end of the 15-year period. That's important because that's the number you use to figure out how far this property will take you through your property investment race. It tells you how much of your wealth gap will be closed through this property.

Let's say that you ran through the process in Chapter 8 and realised you had a $2 million gap. That's the length of your race and the equity you need to generate through property, and in this example you've got 15 years to do it. The Glen Eden property in this instance is projected to give returns of $1.07 million. That's just over 50 per cent of your wealth gap. This one property is projected to get you halfway there.

It's not enough to just buy property; to run your race well you've got to tie it back to your goal, too. That's going to give you the comfort, when times get tough, that there's a reason you've invested in the property, and give you the motivation to soldier on.

What are the projections based on ?

You might be wondering what this model is based on. What does it factor in and what doesn't it? There are a number of assumptions, but the main ones you need to know are:

→ the rent increasing every year by the historical average
→ the costs of the property going up, like rates and insurance
→ interest rates rising to the rate that the Reserve Bank suggests is the long-term 'neutral' mortgage interest rate*
→ inflation, bringing everything back into today's dollars, rather than making you think 'what is the value of a dollar going to be in 15 years' time?' (Less than what it is worth today is the answer.)

Often you'll find that the cashflow of a property will be worse at the start of your ownership, but will improve over time. This is because your rent goes up as incomes rise. However, your biggest cost – your mortgage – is not impacted by inflation.

Summary

Investors usually agree that it's best to invest based on the numbers. Do the following to make that happen:

→ Pick a metric to base your property comparisons on; we suggest using **return on investment**.
→ **Download a copy of the spreadsheet**. (This is updated every few months, so always be sure to download the latest version at opespartners.co.nz/book.)
→ **Canvass the market to find a range of properties** to see how their return on investment compares.
→ Run your numbers, and then **tie back the total returns to your goal** to see how each property will get you through your race.

In the next chapter you'll round out this section on how to acquire investment properties by building a team of property investment advisers – a support team who can help you run your race.

---

* This is an Official Cash Rate (OCR) that neither expands nor contracts the economy. This would have the one-year fixed mortgage interest rate at around 4.5 to 5 per cent.

Chapter 11

Assembling your team

No élite athlete runs a race alone. No property investor should either. As Kiwis, we tend towards a culture of DIY. We get stuck in – boots and all – and don't always like to seek or pay for help. This can lead to the mentality of 'knowing the price of everything and the value of nothing'.

Some investors, for instance, will complain about paying $500 for a chattel valuation – 'Why do I need that?' they ask – not realising that this small outlay could save them over $15,000 in tax over the lifetime of their investment if the chattels are valued at $45,000.

Similarly, we've met several investors whose mortgage set-up means they can't borrow more. 'Nobody ever told me to split banks,' they say. That might be true, but if you didn't seek help from an expert mortgage adviser you can't absolve yourself entirely.

Looking at ways to save money is good. Being cheap and doing the wrong thing because you didn't talk to the right people is self-defeating. Investing in property is one of the largest financial decisions you'll make in your life. The cost of getting it wrong is high, so you need to find the right professionals to help you on your journey.

In this chapter you're going to look at the advisers you'll need, along with how they charge, what they cost, the benefits of using them, and, importantly, how to tell the difference between a quality adviser and one who is more mediocre. We're going to cover off the roles of:

- property advisers
- mortgage advisers
- property lawyers
- property managers, and
- property accountants.

The traditional advice when looking for advisers is to get a recommendation from someone who has used them before. This approach has two flaws. Firstly, it assumes that your friends or the person you are talking to can tell the difference between a good and a bad mortgage adviser/lawyer/other property adviser. Secondly, that advice doesn't help if you're starting from square one and don't know anyone who can give you a recommendation. That's why in this chapter you'll also learn what questions to ask each professional when hunting around for someone to advise you.

Property advisers, coaches and finders

There are a number of different businesses that help with formulating a property investment strategy and then finding a property. It's often confusing since they don't all offer the same services. Generally, there are three types: property advisers, property coaches, and property finders.

Property advisers help you create a property investment plan or strategy, and then find properties (generally new-builds) to fit with that plan. This makes property advisers a good fit for investors following the passive buy-and-hold strategy. They generally don't charge a fee to investors, as they earn a fee from the developer. Our company, Opes Partners, is an example of this type of adviser.

Property coaches are different. They will help you create a property investment strategy, but leave you to find and negotiate the property on your own, often with their support. These businesses focus on the BRRRR or active buy-and-hold approach, and are the right fit for investors who want to renovate their properties. They typically will charge a fee of between $8,000 and $25,000 (+ GST), depending on the company you decide to work with. We also offer this service at Opes through our Opes Accelerate programme. Other similar companies include Property Apprentice, Wealth Mentor and AssetLab.

Finally, a property finder will – you guessed it – find you a property to invest in, but they don't create a plan or strategy for you, or guide you on the journey. They typically focus on existing properties that you can renovate and add value to. This can make them a good complement to a property coach, since one advises on strategy and one finds the property for you. They typically charge you a fee of between $10,000 and $25,000 (+ GST) for finding the property.

What to ask them

QUESTION	ANSWER
Most important: **'Which strategy is your service the right fit for?'** **'Which strategy is your service the wrong fit for?'**	If they reply 'It works for everyone . . .' you know they're full of it. By definition, no one can 'specialise' in working with everyone. What you want is a clear indication of which of the two strategies discussed in Chapter 5 – the passive buy-and-hold, the BRRRR / renovations-focused strategy – the company is the best fit for.

'What sort of services do you provide? Do you find properties? Do you advise on strategy?'	These questions are designed to help you figure out which of the three categories the company falls into: are they a property adviser, coach, or finder?
	     Just be careful. Because there are no set definitions, some people who we define as property advisers will call themselves property coaches. Similarly, some property finders will call themselves property advisers. That's not because they're ill-willed or dodgy; there are just no set defined terms.
	     But if you can figure out which category the business falls into, you can determine whether they're the right fit for you.

'What does it cost, and how are you paid?'	This is important to ask, because some property advisers provide their services for free (as they are remunerated by the property seller instead), while others charge up to $25,000 + GST. Make sure you ask how the company you're working with charges, and whether what they offer will work for the strategy you want to pursue.

After you've ascertained price and what services they offer by asking the questions above, it's then a judgement call based on who you trust the most to deliver the strategy you want to pursue, and to find the properties that fit with that strategy. The questions you need to ask yourself are: 'After reading and listening to everything put out there by each company in the industry, who do I trust the most? Who do I think will work for what I want to do?'

Mortgage advisers

As banks' lending policies become more complex and the rules more technical, mortgage advisers have become vital for property investors to help get their lending approved. But not only that, a mortgage adviser will help you set it up and structure it the right way.

A mortgage adviser will act as your representative to the banks and other lenders. Good mortgage advisers study the banks' policies and rules, aiming to understand which banks will lend to what types of people, and on what properties. They then negotiate with the banks to ensure that you get both the best lending and the best interest rate possible. But, arguably more importantly, they help you manage your mortgages and set them up the right way so you can keep borrowing in the future.

Sure, you can go it alone, using the banks' various mortgage calculators to try to figure out which bank will lend you the most money. However, the pitfall here is that there are bank policies behind the scenes that you won't have access to. A bank will share their full lending guidelines with an adviser – all 100+ pages per bank – but does not release them to the general public.

As an example, a good mortgage adviser will know that one bank has policies that are kinder to couples expecting a child compared with other lenders. Similarly, advisers will know which bank currently accepts more bonus and commission income in their calculations, making them a better bank for flight attendants, salespeople and the like.

This level of detail will help you get your mortgage application over the line when your income or equity is looking tight. If you don't use a (skilled) mortgage adviser, you may end up wasting your time talking to banks who won't lend to you, and this could jeopardise your chances overall as other banks may not lend to you because they can see from your credit report that you've already been denied finance.

Will I get a cheaper interest rate if I use a mortgage adviser?

You are unlikely to get a substantially cheaper interest rate when using a mortgage adviser. Often you will get the same or a similar rate if you approach the bank directly. The real benefit of using a mortgage adviser is getting the money in the first place – and then setting up your mortgages either to pay them off more quickly or to put you in a position to grow your portfolio faster in the future.

Some investors don't want to use a mortgage adviser because they don't want to spend the money, but, generally, mortgage advisers don't cost you anything. They're paid a commission by the banks when they successfully get you the lending you want. There are times when an adviser will charge you a fee directly. However, only a minority of advisers do this, and you will know about this upfront. Ask the question if you want to be extra sure.

How to find a good mortgage adviser

Not all mortgage advisers are created equal. Like any industry there are going to be people who are world class, and others who are not as capable. That's life. The trouble with financial services is that it's hard to tell whether someone is good or not. It's a bit like a mechanic. They know lots about cars, and you (or at least we) don't. So when they start mentioning jargon like axles and carburettors, we're going to think they know their stuff – even if they're actually a bit shonky. You need to understand how to evaluate whether a mortgage adviser has the goods.

A bad adviser is someone only interested in getting the lending approved so they get paid a commission. They look for 'easy' clients, the ones who will sail through the bank's assessors. On the other hand, a good mortgage adviser is somebody who's willing to go in to bat for you. They look for ways to get your mortgage approved, rather than just accepting your initial application at face value. A good broker will challenge the interpretation and application of the bank's own policies; for instance, if there are no genuine policy grounds for a certain loan to be turned down.

Andrew would do this all the time when he was a mortgage broker. If a bank assessor was hesitant to approve an interest-only loan period, in some cases he'd ask accountants to write letters to the bank. The letter might state that going interest-only was the right thing for the investor to do from a tax perspective. Outlining the facts and being forthright can make the difference in getting your lending over the line.

What to ask them

Here are the questions to ask a mortage adviser when interviewing them, along with how to evaluate what they say.

QUESTION	ANSWER
Most important: 'Are you a property investor, and what sort of properties do you invest in?'	If you're dealing with a fellow investor, they should know the strategies of how to secure and structure investment debt. The advice an investor or investor-focused adviser will give is different from someone who primarily works with first-home buyers.
'How active are you in the property investment community?'	If your adviser isn't an existing property investor, but is active in the investment community, they might be a good fit. For instance, if you're talking to a young adviser who isn't ready to invest yet, but they specialise in working with investors, go to every property investors' conference, contribute to the *NZ Property Investor* mag and continually educate themselves, we'd still feel comfortable giving them a go. (This was Andrew when he started at the bank.)

QUESTION	ANSWER
'Which lenders do you work with? And how many lenders do you work with?'	Some advisers don't work with that many banks. For instance, NZ Home Loans – while a good mortgage advisory firm – at present only works with two banks. So, if you own, or plan to own, more than two or three properties, then how they answer this question may encourage you to find someone who has a wider, more diverse range of lender contacts, and so is more likely to get you more, and better-structured, lending. And you can find this out on each mortgage adviser's website. Legally each mortgage adviser needs a page on their website – often headed up 'important information' or 'disclosure statement' – where they state which lenders they have relationships with.

Next, we have a series of 10 questions that you can choose from. These questions are technical. You may not know whether what the adviser says is accurate or not – after all, they're the expert. But you can get a sense of the adviser's willingness to answer your questions by the level of detail they can go into. These questions are also designed to prod the adviser to give you advice. If they weren't going to talk to you about loan structure anyway, you've now put it on the table. And if they've not thought about how to increase your borrowing, you've now asked them to give it thought.

1 How much can I borrow? How does that amount change across the different banks and lenders?
2 If I'm not ready now, what can I do to get ready?
3 What can I do to increase my borrowing?
4 What options are there outside of the main banks?
5 Which properties in my portfolio should I have on interest-only, which should I have on P&I (principal and interest; i.e. a table mortgage)?
6 Should I be fixing my interest rate for the short term or long term?
7 How can I use a revolving credit to help me pay off debt faster?
8 Should I keep my credit cards, close them, or simply lower the limit?
9 Are there any clever ways to access more of my equity?
10 Is my current loan structure the best for me? How should I be structuring things moving forward?

Note how these questions aren't the obvious ones you might initially think you should ask when picking a provider: 'How many years have you been a mortgage adviser?' or 'How long have you been in business?' Answers to these 'obvious' questions won't actually give you a sense of whether the adviser is any good or not. A motivated young-gun who's been in the industry for a year and commits to studying hard will give better advice than a sluggish adviser who's got 10 years of poor experience.

Property lawyers

You can't purchase a property without a lawyer to handle the paperwork and transfer the money from you and the bank to the person selling the property. They'll also manage the title of the property: that's the legal description of the property e.g. 'Lot51 DP11261, Otorohanga'. They'll transfer the title into your name and register the mortgage against the title.

Beyond these basics, a good lawyer will do a few other things. First, they'll help you make sure that it's the right property. That starts by looking over your sale and purchase agreement. This is the contract you use to purchase the property. They'll make sure you have all the right clauses within your contracts so you are protected. A good lawyer will also look over the LIM (Land Information Memorandum) Report, which is a complex document from your local council containing pertinent information about the property such as zoning and things like flood risk.

If you don't get a quality lawyer, you may end up buying a property you don't fully understand (e.g. legally what happens if there is a shared driveway or a cross-lease). You may also accidentally agree to clauses which aren't in your best interests. And, if they don't pick up issues like a deck being unconsented, you can run into problems getting a mortgage approved from a bank.

Finally, a lawyer will also make sure you have the right ownership structure in place. For instance, if you are self-employed, using a trust could be a good fit for you to protect your assets, since you're more likely to get sued if you run your own company.

Lawyers charge a direct fee for their services. As a general rule, budget between $2,000 and $4,000 (including GST).

Like the other players on the team, not all lawyers are created equal. Some will be more familiar with some parts of property conveyancing than others. For example, if you are building your investment property – whether by hiring a builder yourself or purchasing off a developer – you'll be best served by working with a lawyer who specialises in build contracts.

CASE STUDY
I would have had to pay hundreds of thousands more

To give you an example of why a lawyer who specialises in build contracts is necessary when negotiating for a new-build, think about sunset clauses. These are a common clause used when purchasing new-builds from a developer. Under this clause, you can cancel a contract if the developer hasn't completed the build on time.

If the builder plans for the development to be finished in 12 months, your sunset clause might allow you to cancel the contract if the build is not completed within 24 months of signing. That allows you to get your deposit back and invest somewhere else.

Sounds great, so what's the issue? One of the listeners of the *Property Academy Podcast* provides a good example. He bought into a development in West Auckland as his second home. His neighbours had signed a contract in July 2020, which had a 15-month sunset clause. However, both the developer and the purchaser could use this clause to cancel the contract.

What happened? By the time the property was built, two things had happened: (1) there had been build delays due to the Covid-19 pandemic, because builders weren't allowed on-site and materials had become scarce due to supply-chain issues; and (2) property prices had risen dramatically.

So the developer used the sunset clause to cancel the contracts. He then offered to sell the now-completed properties back to the purchasers at a significantly increased price. Every single one of this listener's neighbours were faced with paying hundreds of thousands of dollars extra. But not our savvy listener.

After learning about sunset clauses from the podcast, he had worked with his lawyer to push the sunset clause date out when negotiating the original contract. So instead of having a 15-month sunset clause, he had a 27-month sunset clause. That meant the project would have to be delayed by another year before the developer could cancel the contract.

Because this listener knew the risks of sunset clauses, and had worked with a lawyer who understood build contracts, he was the only one of his neighbours to settle at the original price they'd signed up for. Sadly, everyone else in the development either had to cough up an extra six figures or walk away from the deal.

You don't have to understand the nitty-gritty of the contract yourself. But you do need to understand that these contractual matters are technical and complex. The devil is most certainly in the detail. But it's also true that *the quality is in the contract*. So you want your lawyer to advise you correctly, and negotiate a quality contract.

Usually investors don't hunt around for lawyers like they might for a mortgage adviser, an accountant or a property manager. Typically, they'll use the same person they've used for a while, or their parents' old golfing buddy. While that person might well be a competent lawyer in their area of expertise, there is a danger that they don't have the specialist knowledge in property and investment that will give you the right amount of protection.

What to ask them

If you are buying a new-build, here are some questions to ask to prod your solicitor to give you the right advice:

- In what instances can the developer cancel the contract and sell the property at a higher price?
- In what instances can the price of this contract change? Can the developer/builder increase the price?
- How can we tighten up this contract so that the developer can't increase the price or cancel the contract?

A wee word of warning here. Many lawyers are conservative by nature: if they see risk in the contract, they flag it and make sure you know about it. One of the most important things in property is not to lose a good deal. It is better to have a great deal with okay terms in the contract, than an okay deal with great terms. While you want to be aware of the legal risks you're accepting, you don't want to let an overly conservative lawyer talk you out of taking action on a profitable opportunity.

Property managers

Property managers look after your investment so you don't have to. They'll find a tenant, make sure the tenant pays the rent on time and looks after the property, organise maintenance, and regularly inspect the property. In our view, every property investor should use a property manager. If you don't, you'll have a lot more worries about your properties and tenants. You'll spend more time dealing with your properties, which often causes stress and may result in you limiting the size of your portfolio.

This is the difference between being a landlord and being an investor. A landlord focuses on managing the property they have and takes on the job of looking after the house. An investor, on the other hand, keeps their eye on the overall portfolio and delegates the 'job' of looking after the property to a property manager.

Some property investors are reluctant to pay for a property manager. They might think 'It's only down the road, I can look after it myself', or 'I've known (tenant) Jim for years, he'll be okay'. Famous last words.

If you do decide to forgo a property manager, you've got to be fully aware of the additional responsibilities that you are taking on. Take property inspections as an example. Most property investors know they need to do regular inspections, but many fail to do so. However, if you don't inspect your property every three months you'll have broken the terms of your insurance. This means that if something goes wrong – e.g. a leaking pipe that causes hidden damage – you'll likely need to foot the bill yourself.

Expanding regulation is also increasing the time needed to manage a property, with new legislation like the Healthy Homes Act, lease agreements, bonds, tenancy disputes, and more. For peace of mind alone, it's well worth outsourcing the management to a specialist company. They are familiar with what is required and when.

A (good) property manager will also help you set the rent and keep it up with market rates.

Property managers generally charge two types of fees. The first is a percentage of the rent that you get paid. This is typically somewhere between 7 per cent (+ GST) and 10 per cent (+ GST). For a property that charges weekly rent of $500, that's about $40 to $58 per week, or $2,000 to $2,900 a year (factoring in two weeks for the property being empty).

Most property managers then charge a tenant-sourcing fee every time they need to find a new tenant for the property. This is to advertise the property, find a tenant, and get that tenant to move in. This is typically one week's rent + GST, which for a $500-a-week property is $575.

To be fair, finding a property manager is often a bit lower-stakes than finding a good mortgage adviser or lawyer. That's because there is an advisory relationship between mortgage advisers, lawyers, property advisers and investors. While you want your property manager to make sure you're following the right rules and regulations, you're not relying on them for property investment advice. It's also relatively easy to switch property management companies if you need to.

So instead of going through a list of what to ask a property manager, let's go through a couple of things you should keep on your property manager's case about.

- **Raising the rent:** **In our experience, property managers are often too conservative at reviewing rents.** In Chapter 13 we'll introduce the RightRent system to help keep you on top of this.
- **Healthy Homes Inspection:** **If your property manager hasn't had a Healthy Homes Inspection completed and given the paperwork to the tenant, you're the one copping the fine.** Ask to see the report from the Healthy Homes Inspection.

→ **Credit, reference and affordability checks: The most important job of a property manager is finding the right tenant.** So before accepting a tenant's application, ask your property manager what credit and reference checks they have done. Also ask how they know that the tenant will be able to afford the rent.

Property accountants

Using a general-practice accountant to guide your property tax strategy is like going to the GP for brain surgery. The long-term outlook isn't great, and in the meantime you're left with a whacking big headache. So when you look for an accountant, make sure they are a specialist in property.

This is a money-saving exercise. Any accountant can file your tax returns. But a property specialist will advise you on how to minimise the tax you have to pay. We often come across property investors who pay more tax than they legally need to. This could be because:

→ **they're not claiming all the legally-allowed expenses against their income** (e.g. home office, a portion of their telephone and internet and travel costs)
→ **they're holding assets in entities that have higher tax rates** (e.g. in their own names as opposed to a trust or a look-through company, if appropriate) – more about look-through companies in Chapter 14
→ **the ownership of those entities requires more tax to be paid compared with if the ownership was set up properly at the start** (e.g. if the shares within a look-through company haven't been optimally allocated)
→ **they have a mix of assets (positively geared and negatively geared) that are held in different entities.**

Right now, that might all sound like a whole heap of accounting jargon to you. Don't fret, you'll learn what this all means in Chapter 14.

What to ask them

QUESTION	ANSWER
Most important: 'Are you a property investor, and what sort of properties do you invest in?'	It's a good sign if your property accountant also invests. That way they have a vested interest in knowing the tax code back-to-front, and how to minimise the amount of tax you have to pay.
'What sort of properties are your clients investing in? And what strategies do they use?'	It's important to understand whether your accountant only specialises in one type of strategy, as opposed to a range of strategies. Some accountants will give advice on whether they think the property you're investing in makes sense or not financially. In weighing up their advice, it is useful to know what they do and 'where they are coming from'. We were working with one investor who was considering investing in a new-build. Their accountant was only interested in renovation projects, which this investor wasn't interested in. After seeking the accountant's advice the investor decided not to go ahead with the purchase, and instead decided not to invest at all. Over the past 24 months they have missed out on approximately $245,000 worth of capital gains they could have made. To be clear, you should listen to your accountant's advice. But you need to work with an accountant who is aligned with the strategy you're pursuing. Otherwise they might talk you out of a deal without giving you a credible alternative.
'What sort of accounting do you specialise in?'	As with mortgage advisers, it can be hard to sort the most competent property accountants from the less able. That's why this question is so important. After you ask which area they specialise in, you need to shut your mouth, say nothing more, and don't mention property. If they don't mention property or residential property accounting, head for the lift. They're not right for this assignment. You need a property specialist.

While the fees charged by property accountants differ from firm to firm, it's safe to budget between $1,000 and $2,000 (including GST) per year when starting out. This will increase as your portfolio becomes more complex.

The savvy investor is using a property accountant now more than ever, due to the fact that there is so much complexity around property tax. Where once you could go it alone, now you probably shouldn't try.

CASE STUDY
What can you do that I can't do?

Sometimes it's the most educated investors who decide not to use people to help them in their journey. Although we've just talked about property accountants, here's a good example of a highly intelligent investor, Jun, who decided not to get advice from a mortgage adviser. Jun is highly educated and very motivated. Initially she wasn't keen on using a mortgage adviser. Here is her story in her own words.

'As someone who has been working on my own and quite proud of my achievements, the first sentences to my new mortgage adviser were "Tell me what value you can provide. What is it that you can do that I cannot do by myself?"

'Now one month later, the facts are that if I had come to him earlier:

- I could have purchased more properties in the 2020 market when prices were lower. This would have saved me money and meant that I'd received more capital growth.
- I could have had sufficient time for restructuring. I could have put my most expensive new-build purchase under lower new-build interest rates. That change alone would have saved me $6,000+ per year for three years. Now that I've put my mortgage somewhere else, that option isn't available.
- I could have fixed the last two mortgages at a lower interest rate.

'I know there are others like me who listen to the podcast and think "I can just extract the information and work on my own." Well, in my case, my arrogance has basically cost me at least $30,000.'

Now, to be fair, Jun is very successful. She's smart, she's motivated, and she'll be fine. This is just to show that using property experts can help you grow your portfolio further and faster, while saving on things like tax.

Chapter 11 Assemble your team

Summary

There are five professionals who you should use:

- **A property adviser** to help create your financial strategy and find the right properties for you.
- **A mortgage adviser** to help get your lending approved, and make sure it is structured in the right way.
- **A property lawyer** to transact your property deal and make sure your contracts are secure.
- **A property manager** to take day-to-day management off your plate.
- **A property accountant** to minimise the amount of tax you have to pay.

Now that you've assembled your property investment team, you'll be in a position to acquire properties and then get ready to manage them. In this next chapter we're going to talk through **Step 4: How to manage your properties**, including how to set up your bank accounts and financials for your property effectively.

Chapter 12

Setting up your financials effectively

For your long-term property investment strategy to work, there is one key ingredient: time. You need to hold these properties for as long as possible to give the market time to appreciate. This is the same for any investment, whether it's shares, KiwiSaver, another type of fund, or property.

But you're not going to be able to give your portfolio time if you can't manage the cashflow, or if your bank accounts are a mess, or your tenants are so bad that you're encouraged to sell. That's why the next step in your property investment journey is to set up your properties to be able to manage them. Property investment is a business, and these next five chapters are your guide to how to operate your property investment business.

The first lesson is to set up your property investment bank accounts to manage cashflow the right way. If your properties end up costing you way more than planned and you're chronically losing money, your portfolio is probably not going to last. You'll end up selling and will potentially miss out on the capital gains that come with long-term ownership.

And it's also important for your tenants. Nothing turns a good tenant bad more surely than reporting maintenance issues to their property manager month after month, only to have the defect ignored by the landlord.

And why do you reckon such landlords ignore property managers' requests for maintenance? If you're guessing it's because the money isn't in the property's bank account and the landlord has to pay for it from their own pocket, you are correct. This is why you must set up your bank accounts effectively from the get-go. So let's crack into how to do just that.

Managing your bank accounts

A huge part of property investment is managing your bank accounts and cashflow – the money coming in and the expenses going out. You must keep an eye on your banking app so you don't go into an unarranged overdraft or miss an important mortgage payment. Thankfully, this can often be solved by setting up your bank accounts correctly. Once set up this will seem incredibly simple, but it is powerful all the same.

Smart property investors will set up one main bank account for all of their properties owned within the same structure or entity. Put simply, let's say you've got two properties in a trust and three in a look-through company. You'll have one bank account for your trust and another for the look-through company. This means that all rent for the properties held in the trust will come into the trust's account. And all expenses for those properties will be paid from that account, too. The same applies to the look-through company's properties and account.

Setting up your bank accounts in this way means that your properties begin to support one another and create the wealth wheel we referenced earlier. For instance, one property within an entity might be cashflow-positive, whereas another might be cashflow-negative. So the money coming in from the cashflow-positive property can straight away supplement the cashflow of the negatively-geared one. This means you're not having to transfer money around every time one of your properties needs to meet a mortgage payment.

The cashflow of your properties will also differ. For example, over the course of a year your properties might look like they are positive on average $20 a week. However, depending on when those expenses fall, there may be times when the property needs you to top up the bank account. Having one account makes it easier to juggle what money you do have, keeping on top of any outgoings or automatic payments. So, if one property happens to have lower expenses and another has a one-off higher expense (e.g. maintenance or a big body corporate bill), then the cash is there to spend. You're not having to move money around. It's simpler, it's safer, and it means the risk is spread.

Say you have four rental properties. Ideally, set up one account and have all four rents paid into this, and all expenses paid out of there. That means that all four mortgages are paid from the same place, as well as all rates, insurance, and any other expenses, too. Some investors prefer to scrutinise each property in more detail, and so keep them separate. You certainly can do it this way, but it causes a bit more admin.

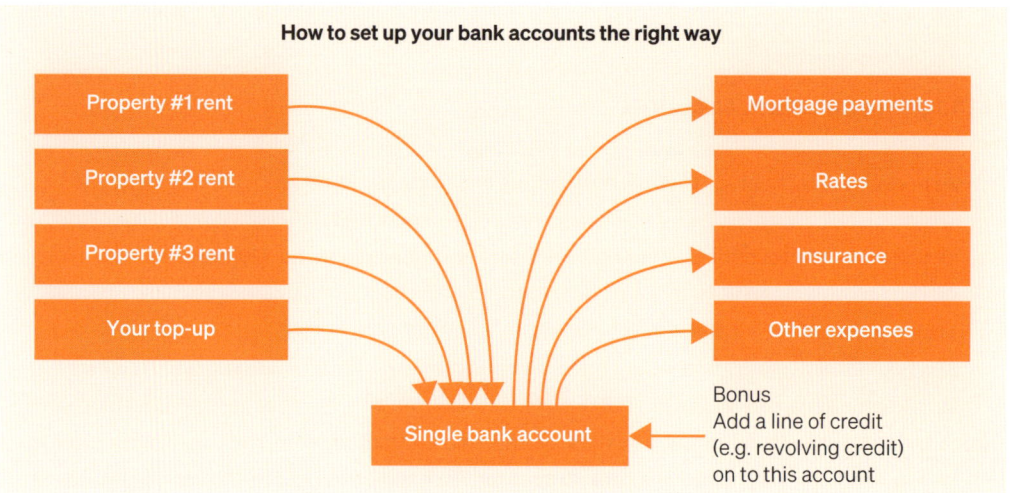

In addition to the rent coming into this account, you'll also automatically transfer your top-up into the bank account as well. So if one property is negatively geared by $50 a week and another by $80 a week, your portfolio requires you to contribute $130 per week to keep them solvent. So you transfer across $130 a week as an automatic payment. If you are paid fortnightly or monthly, increase the size of your payment accordingly and have it transferred out the day you're paid. If you're struggling to figure out what you need to contribute to your properties per week, remember this is fully calculated for you in the spreadsheet discussed in Chapter 10.

On top of this, we also recommend setting up an undrawn revolving credit on your rental accounts, say with a $10,000 limit. This acts as an overdraft and gives you flexibility if you lose your job or your properties go through a period where cashflow is tight.

Once you've set all this up, check your bank accounts once a week to make sure that the rents have gone in and are in line with what you are expecting. While your property manager will send you a monthly statement, it's important to double-check that the money actually came in. If they miss a payment or miscalculate (which can happen occasionally) and you aren't keeping an eye on things, the only other way you're going to find out is when your bank calls you to tell you that you've defaulted on your loan. This is not a call you want to receive. And it's one that Andrew has had.

Chapter 12 Setting up your financials effectively

> **CASE STUDY**
> **Missed mortgage payments, missing rent and the missing property manager**

Another notch on my property belt is the cautionary case of the missed mortgage payments. After trying to manage my properties myself, my next step was to go to a '5-percenter'. These are low-cost property managers who charge under the market rate, and cost substantially less than other property managers. Unfortunately, in these situations you often get what you pay for.

All went fine for a couple of months before *ring ring, ring ring* – it's Westpac calling. 'Mr Nicol, your mortgage account is in arrears.' That's a fancy way of saying that I'd missed my mortgage payment. This was surprising, since the rent was meant to cover all of the mortgage payments, and the property manager hadn't mentioned any issues with the tenant not paying. In fact, I hadn't heard from the property manager at all, so I had assumed that all was well.

Imagine my further surprise when I looked at the bank account and discovered that no rent had hit my account in the previous two months. I jumped in my car and drove over to the property manager's office – he was nowhere to be found.

I later learned that the property manager had succumbed to a drug problem and skipped town along with two months' worth of my rent – and probably the rent of quite a few other landlords as well. Suffice to say the missed mortgage payments left a hole in my personal bank account, because I had to cover the costs since the missing money wasn't recoverable. I never tracked him down.

The moral of the story? While it wasn't my fault that rent hadn't been put into the account, it was my responsibility to (a) check that it had been deposited, and (b) ensure there was enough money in the bank account to cover the mortgage payment.

Even though we now own property management firm Venture Management as part of the Opes Group, I religiously check that the money is in the bank account. You never know what is going on in someone else's life, and difficult circumstances can indeed create dodgy dealers. If you can spot these situations early, you can limit the damage.

Because I've set up my bank accounts so all the rent from the properties comes into the same account, my portfolio of 40+ properties runs like a well-oiled machine. On an average week I spend only a few minutes on it. That means it's one less thing (or 40 less things, really) to worry about.

But what about Split-banking?

If you're an avid fan of the *Property Academy Podcast*, you're probably tearing your hair out now, thinking: 'But you guys keep telling me to use different banks, and now you're telling me to have one bank account . . . What's the deal?' Fair call. That can be confusing.

If you're new to the concept of Split-banking, this is where you use multiple banks to fund your investment properties. You might take out the loan for your deposit from your main bank and then get the rest of the loan from another (read more about this in Appendix B). While we still suggest you set up your lending with multiple banks, for the purposes of *managing the cashflow* it's best to have one bank account for your properties' rent and expenses. Then you set up automatic payments from that rental account to pay the various bank mortgages for those rental properties.

For example, one of Andrew's main banks is the BNZ, where his personal account is. This is the main bank he logs in to every day. He uses an account with the BNZ as his rental account, and it has a revolving credit facility attached. From this primary account, he has set up a series of automatic payments to the banks he has the various properties' loans with, to pay the interest. All of the general expenses (rates, insurance, etc.) come out of the (main) BNZ account.

Managing cashflow

One other way to manage cashflow is by limiting your fixed expenses, so that when times get tough you still have flexibility. In practice this means selecting the right type of mortgage, and deciding whether to make principal and interest payments, or go interest-only.

As a general rule, we recommend paying down only one mortgage at a time. If you then have extra cashflow to pay down debt, direct it towards the mortgage you are trying to pay down first.

Some property investors with multiple mortgages will have all their home loans on principal and interest. This is usually not the right structure, for two reasons:

→ Not all home loans are created equal: some are tax-deductible, some are not. It's best to pay down the non-tax-deductible ones first.
→ More importantly, having only one property on principal and interest at a time helps to manage cashflow.

We'll go through that first point about interest deductibility in depth in Chapter 14, so let's just deal with the cashflow question right now.

Paying down debt is good. Being locked into paying down debt is not so good. Consider this example.

Let's say you have three mortgages that are all $600,000. One is for your own home, the other two are for two separate investment properties. If you pay them all down over 30 years at a 4 per cent interest rate, your weekly payment will be $660 a week per property. All up that is $1,980 of debt repayments a week (remember you'd have rent coming in to help you pay this). But if, on the other hand, you moved both of your investment mortgages to interest-only, your investment property mortgages would now only cost $462 a week. That's $198 less per property per week.

This might seem counterintuitive, given that not paying down debt means paying more in interest. The key to this strategy, though, isn't keeping the debt for as long as possible, but freeing up the cashflow so you are in control and can make decisions yourself.

In this instance, a savvy investor might use the Mortgage Buster strategy (discussed in Chapter 5), set up a revolving credit and direct the money they've now freed up from their investments to go back into their personal home loan. The rationale behind this is that there are two types of debt: debt that reduces the tax you pay (tax-deductible debt), and debt that doesn't reduce your tax (non-tax-deductible debt). Up until recently, investment debt reduced your tax, while the debt on your own home did not. So you had an incentive to pay down your personal mortgage before tackling the investments.

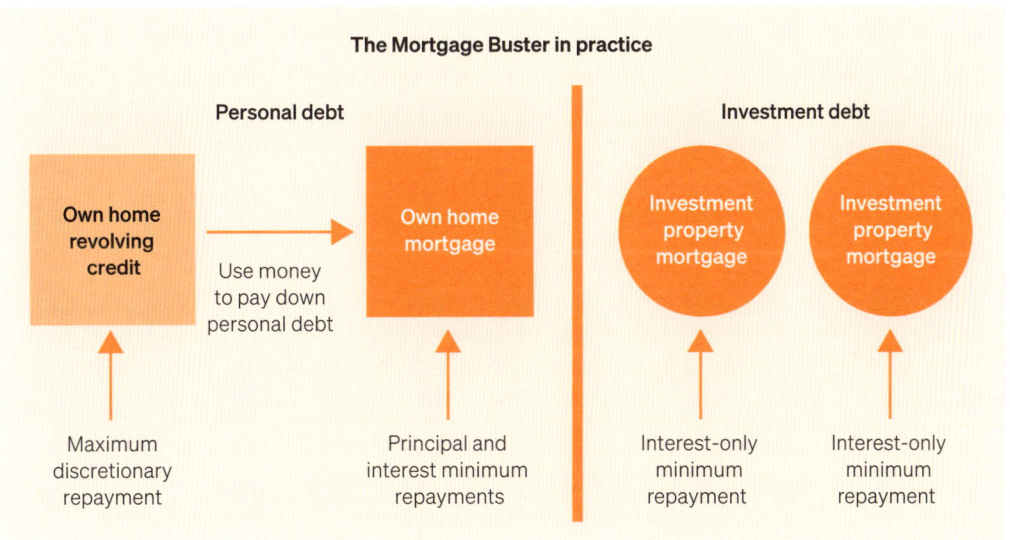

When you set up your mortgages in this way, you'll still pay down debt but the payments will be voluntary. That becomes important when interest rates rise, if you're made redundant, or when economic times aren't as good.

MORTGAGE STRUCTURE	ALL PRINCIPAL AND INTEREST (LESS IDEAL)	INVESTMENTS ON INTEREST-ONLY (IDEAL)
Interest rate	4%	4%
Own home: $600,000	$660	$660
Investment property #1: $600,000	$660	$462
Investment property #2: $600,000	$660	$462
Total committed mortgage payments per week	$1980	$1584
	$396 difference per week	

Assuming all mortgages are 30-year terms. Shows minimum weekly repayments.

To put this all in context, let's meet our next investor who was set back several years simply because of the way they managed their mortgages and cashflow.

> **CASE STUDY**
>
> **Starting out and making mistakes – it's all part of the journey**
> While the success stories are great, property investors love a good war story – where nothing quite went right. Earlier in the chapter, we mentioned that if you don't contain your fixed expenses, your cashflow could suffer and you might be forced to sell early, missing out on capital gains. That's exactly what happened to our next investor, Tim.
>
> Like many entering the property market at the starting blocks, Tim had to go for the classic 'do-up' as his first home. Fresh back from overseas and in his mid- to late twenties, it was around 2006 when Tim scored a run-down house in Spreydon, one of the cheaper suburbs of Christchurch at the time. It was seemingly a steal at $200,000. Tim put down a

10 per cent deposit and got stuck in to some much-needed renovations, in the tried-and-true tradition of roping in a few mates (as well as hiring the odd builder).

Over his first year, off the back of a rising market, Tim's equity in the house grew $50,000, enough at the time to get out of the starting blocks and start running his race. This allowed him to buy another property, this time in St Albans, a higher-end suburb in Christchurch. Two more off-the-plan properties followed, and it seemed Tim was on to a winner, investing more widely and gaining equity. That is, until interest rates skyrocketed and his mortgage payments ballooned . . .

Despite getting equity-rich from his portfolio in just two to three years and now owning four properties, Tim's portfolio was heavily negatively geared. It's not that the properties weren't sound investments, but his mortgage payments were all set on principal-and-interest, as opposed to having all but one on interest-only. That meant that as interest rates started to spike to 9 per cent and over, Tim could no longer afford the mortgages or to continue topping up his rental properties. It was unsustainable.

He got another shock when the 2008 global financial crisis kicked in shortly after. The banks severely clamped down on lending, and house prices in the Garden City plunged 12.4 per cent at their worst.[34]

Because he could no longer afford the cashflow, Tim sold three of his properties in one hit. It wasn't a great time to sell, but he had to at this point because of his unaffordable loan repayments.

'Looking back, if I'd got it right, and managed the payments I was making, I wouldn't have had to sell those properties. I could have held them, and today they'd be worth more than 2.5 times what I sold them for,' Tim says. 'Had I spoken to a good mortgage adviser and sorted out the structure, I could have held on to them rather than having to start again.'

This is a good example of how you can get the properties right, the timing right and have the right attitude, but failing to manage the cashflow will crash the whole plan. Now to be fair, all was not lost. Tim made a significant profit on the back of rising house prices. However, he lost the opportunity to hold the properties, and had to start his portfolio again.

Summary

Your investment portfolio needs *one key ingredient: time*. To make sure you can afford to hold on to your properties you need to manage your cashflow. Here's how:

→ Set up **one bank account per entity** that you hold your properties in (e.g. one per trust or look-through company).
→ Have all rent paid into that one bank account, and expenses paid from there. This allows the **cashflow of properties to cover one another**.
→ **Check your accounts once per week** to make sure they are in surplus.
→ **Set up a small revolving credit** to cover any temporary cashflow shortfall when there are multiple property expenses that fall at once.
→ Have a maximum of **one property at a time set to paying principal and interest**, and use the **Mortgage Buster strategy** to then pay down debt more quickly.

Now that you've got your cashflow and bank accounts sorted, let's turn to talking about tenants. Property investors have a responsibility, and a need, to be good landlords. So let's look at how you can deliver a good service to your tenants while protecting your investment at the same time.

Chapter 13

Being a good landlord and getting the rent right

If you're a landlord, you're in business – the business of providing rental accommodation. As a fledgling business owner, you've potentially got $2 million to $3 million worth of assets under your control. That's bigger than most small businesses, even if your property portfolio is relatively small.

In this chapter you'll learn how to have a successful relationship with your customers – the tenants. To teach you that, you might be expecting us to go through the Residential Tenancies Act – the main law governing landlords and tenants in New Zealand – with all of the details about the letters you need to send when inspecting the property or changing the rent. While complying with these regulations is important, you can find out most of the details online. And if you're using a property manager – and you will be, right? – they'll handle this level of compliance for you.

Instead, in this chapter you'll learn what passive property investors need to know when dealing with tenants. We'll start with our definition of a 'good' landlord, then we'll give you the exact process to use when 'pricing' your property and setting rent.

Being a 'good' landlord

No one could possibly disagree with the idea that landlords should be 'good'. Where people will disagree is in the definition of what a 'good' landlord is or does. For us, there are three key principles that landlords should follow. Each of these is based on the core belief (of both us and the IRD) that landlords are in fact business owners, and that your tenant is your customer. They pay you money, and in return you provide both a product *and* a service.

Your product is the property itself, and the service is responding to the tenants' maintenance requests or providing 'customer support' when issues arise. To keep your tenants happy and continue charging the same level of rent, you need to treat your customers the right way. That's where these principles come in.

It's your house, but the tenant's home

While you own the house, once your tenant moves in they're paying you for it to be their home. So it's best to leave the tenants alone and let them get on with their lives, rather than intruding. You don't need to continually drive past 'just to keep an eye on it', and it doesn't really matter if the lawns are longer than you personally would have them. You'll have the chance to keep an eye on the property every three months when your property manager conducts an inspection. But in the meantime, leave your tenant to it. We call this adopting a hands-off but informed approach.

After your property manager completes their quarterly inspection, you'll receive a report with photos of the property. This will include photos of the lounge and bedrooms, featuring the tenant's belongings. This can be a bit disconcerting, like you're intruding on the tenant's privacy. Whatever you think when looking at the photos, it's important not to judge a tenant if the place isn't spotless. We're not all Marie Kondo. It's their right to live however they want to live – after all, it's their home.

But where you can step in is if the way the tenant is living is damaging the property. That's the 'your house, their home' mentality coming back in. A good example of where tenants might be unintentionally damaging the property is when they are not opening the windows. This is especially common in newer properties. New-builds are so weather-tight that they need the windows opened to ventilate the rooms. If this isn't done, mould can start to grow, even in a new property. If this happens and you can see it in the photos, ask the property manager to contact the tenant to let them know that they need to open the windows more often.

Another common situation is appliances. If they're not wiped down or looked after they can start to become irreparably dirty. If you own the appliances, you can take the same course of action: ask the property manager to kindly have a word with the tenants so they can rectify the situation.

Keep the 'product' in good nick

Through Venture Management, our property management firm, we deal with hundreds of properties, and a range of tenants and landlords. What do you think is the number one thing tenants complain to property managers about? Without hesitation we can tell you: it's unanswered maintenance requests. A property manager often has the authority to spend small amounts of the investor's money on maintenance, taking it out of the rent. However, for anything over a few hundred dollars, the property investor needs to approve the spend.

If there's a leak in the roof, or the dishwasher's stopped working, and the landlord hasn't approved the money to get it fixed, tenants tend to feel angry and ignored. The product they're buying has become defective, but they're still paying the same amount of rent.

This sort of behaviour by some landlords has created a hostile feeling about property investors in the media. We're all painted with the same brush by the actions of a few. That is why a 'good' landlord does two things to keep the product in good nick:

→ **They are fiscally responsible and budget for maintenance.** The reason that some landlords ignore maintenance requests is because they don't have the cash at hand. The rent's come in, but it's been used to pay the mortgage or subsidise another property. Budgeting for maintenance and having the cash on hand allows you to quickly approve such requests as they come through.

→ **The second is to use a property manager, who can then provide customer service to the tenant.** If you're stuck at work or busy with life and can't respond to tenants quickly, that's a problem.

To be clear, this does not mean that you need to approve every single little maintenance request that comes through. In some rare circumstances, tenants will take the mickey. For instance, Andrew bought a brand-new house to rent out to tenants near one of New Zealand's larger cities. This brand-new house had never been lived in before, so it was strange that within weeks the maintenance requests started to come in.

First, the tenants asked him to 'spider-proof' the property. This is where a house-washer sprays chemicals around the building's perimeter to prevent spiders making it inside. It seemed a bit of (literal) overkill and cost $500 – over a week's rent – but he approved it to kick the relationship off right.

The next week the tenants called back because the toilet-roll holder was 'wobbly'. That was another $80 to get someone out to have a look at it. The week after, the tenants had broken a knob off the brand-new stove that was included within the house. A call-out fee and the cost of a new knob later, and these maintenance requests were beginning to become costly. It seemed endless, and in the end Andrew felt that the tenants were being unreasonable. After all, continually calling out a handyman to a house for small jobs starts to add up. He told the tenants that this was an unreasonably and unusually high number of maintenance requests. He also mentioned that these appeared to be in the realm of minor annoyances, rather than genuinely needed maintenance.

It's unusual for this to be the situation – usually it's the other way around, with landlords not responding to maintenance requests. However, if you do find yourself in this situation, you should first ask your property manager to let the tenant know that you won't immediately approve the maintenance request. Next, ask the property manager to check out the issue when they do their next inspection, and make a judgement call about whether it is a genuine concern that needs to be fixed, or whether it is unreasonable. For small niggles it's cheaper for multiple issues to be fixed all in one go by a handyman, rather than calling someone out every time the toilet-roll holder gets a bit wobbly.

Getting the rent right every single time

Many property investors ask: 'How do I make sure my rent is set at the right level?' It's often an emotional topic, especially when it comes to rental increases, which a property investor is able to review every 12 months. One of the reasons for this emotion is that property managers and investors alike often take a 'finger in the air' approach, or set the rent based on the costs they face.

Basing your rent on the costs you face is a mug's game. If all investors did this, identical properties sitting next to each other would have different levels of rent, since some investors will have high mortgage costs and others will have low mortgage costs based on the sizes of their home loans.

The customer doesn't care how much it costs you to run the property; they care what they pay per week and whether they can get a better deal elsewhere. This is why you need to ground your decision in the market reality, hence our development of the RightRent process. This is the system you can use to determine the correct level of rent, every single time.

We've developed this process because in our experience some property managers are timid when it comes to rental rises. Sure, as we said in Chapter 11, a good property manager will help you with rental rises. But not all property managers take a realistic approach to setting the rent. Instead they defer rental rises, on the basis that a rise in rent might risk losing the tenant, and then perhaps having weeks where the property sits empty. Safer and better to not rock the boat, and stick with the same, lower rent, they conclude.

However, that argument only works once. Because every year you delay raising the rent, you get further and further behind the market level, and the shortfall begins to compound. This is why we developed the RightRent system, so that property managers, investors and tenants are all clear on how the rent has been set.

The RightRent system adapts the process that a registered valuer uses when assessing what your property is worth. So what happens when a valuer steps in to put a price on your property? They start by comparing your property with other similar properties that have recently sold in the area, using a structured table.

They will then use this data to create a range for what they think your property is worth. The following is a stylised example of the sort of table a registered valuer might create:

ADDRESS*	SALE PRICE	FLOOR PLAN (m²)	ASSESSMENT
123 Queens Quay	$950,000	200	Superior. Newly refurbished interior
42 Kings Crescent	$800,000	160	Inferior. Smaller internal floor plan
93 Princes Place	$890,000	180	Similar. Same size floor plan and condition
2 Saint Street	$860,000	185	Similar. Larger floor plan, but poorer condition

* Fictional addresses have been used.

If all of these properties were comparable to your property, the valuer might say that your property is worth between $800,000 and $950,000 (the highest figure and the lowest figure). But since the Princes Place and Saint Street properties are similar to yours, your property is likely to be worth between $860,000 and $890,000. The valuer will then make a judgement call and might say that the value of the property is $880,000.

You might look at this process and think it's pretty simple. It's true, all they have done is look at what similar properties have sold for. But they have done it in a structured way to come to a fact-based decision. That's exactly what you'll do under the RightRent system.

Unfortunately, there is no online rental database equivalent to the house sales databases Homes.co.nz or OneRoof.co.nz, where you can easily see what properties rented for. So instead you will need to look at the rental prices being advertised and use them as a guide. The first step is to go to the likes of TradeMe, where you can see properties advertised for rent. You then create the same sort of table the valuer made, looking at what similar properties to yours are advertised for, along with which are superior (better) or inferior (worse).

Here is the exact table Ed created when assessing the rent of a two-bedroom, one-bathroom, two-car-park apartment in Christchurch. It had been rented for $405 per week; however, he knew it was severely under-rented and needed to assess what the new rent should be.

PROPERTY	RENT	SUPERIOR / INFERIOR
211 Peterborough Street	$450	Inferior New 2 bathrooms No car parks
2/15 Peterborough Street	$450	Inferior 1 car park Smaller kitchen Smaller deck
103/36C Welles Street	$560 (likely would rent for $500 without furniture)	Superior Better location Smaller floor plan, but newer Fully furnished Only 1 car park
14/41–43 Cambridge Terrace	$490	Mildly superior Has washer-dryer 1 car park Better location Right next to Hagley Park and Botanic Gardens
3/231 Madras Street	$490	Superior 1 car park Better location Newer

* Fictional addresses have been used.

Based on this data, two-bedroom properties in the Garden City rent for between $450 and $500 per week. However, setting the rent for his property at $450 would be too low, since the two inferior apartments on Peterborough Street were being advertised for $450 a week.

On the other hand, setting the rent at $490 or above would be too high. A tenant could simply choose one of the other three superior properties at that price. So the rent will likely fall within the $460–$480 range. Wanting to minimise vacancy and find a tenant quickly, Ed decided to set the rent at the lower end of that range, settling on $460.

This process is simple. It's what you're doing already: looking at the market and setting the rent. However, it is looking with more precision. Instead of making a judgement call by looking at properties' rental prices alone, you need to look at what's on offer for those prices: the size of the floor plan, whether it's got car parks, the quality of the property, and the location. Once you have made an assessment of your property compared with others on the market, you can set the rent in a systematic way.

You can then send this analysis to your property manager to let them know the research you have done in setting the rent, which then helps them understand why you've reached that decision.

One important tip. Having done this multiple times, one flaw is that TradeMe rental listings often expire quickly. This means that if you send your property manager a bunch of links to TradeMe, by the time they click on the link to look at the photos the listing may be gone. That's why it's useful to actually download the photos, or put them into your Word document. That way you won't lose them.

CASE STUDY
It would take them 21 years to pay me back

Early on in my property investing days, I started to diversify my portfolio outside of Christchurch, purchasing a property in Tauranga. It was a newish place that I hoped would attract good tenants. Even though I was a two-hour flight away, I still decided to manage it myself, from a distance. Because it was a new-build, I wanted to set the rent at an aggressive price, which really meant advertising the property above the market rate. (This was before we created the RightRent system.)

Because I set the rent at such a high rate, there wasn't a lot of interest, so I said 'yes' to the first person who came along. No credit or reference checks. The tenants quickly got behind on the rent. By the time we got to the Tenancy Tribunal, the tenants owed me $5,500. I won the case, and looked forward to receiving the money that was owed. To serve the judgment from the Tribunal (known as an order), I needed to give the Tenancy Tribunal an address for the tenants. Unfortunately by this time the tenants had scarpered, and I had no idea where they'd gone. The order couldn't be served, so there was no chance of getting the money back.

What did the 'Prince of Property' do? Something I hope I never have to do again. The tenants had left some of their belongings in the garage, so I called them and asked them to come over to collect their stuff. Meanwhile I hired a local private investigator to discreetly follow the tenants home to confirm their new address. Once I had the address, I informed the Tenancy Tribunal to get the order served.

In many ways this was a bit sad; nobody wants to have to get to the point where someone gets followed. However, the tenants had already broken their tenancy agreement, racked up large rent arrears, and then were deliberately avoiding our country's legal process for settling disputes. So they'd left me with the option of either walking away and being out of pocket by $5,500 – and knowing that the tenants could do the same to another property investor the next week (because if the order wasn't served the details couldn't become public) – or hiring an expert to help me track the tenants down. I called a PI, and got the order served.

But the story doesn't end there. Even after all of this, they didn't pay. In the end the tenants were means-tested through the Tribunal. The missing rent would still be paid back – but at a rate of $5 a week. It would take them 21 years to pay back all $5,500.

I'm not telling you this story to play the victim. In fact the moral of the story is that it was my fault: I should have hired a property manager in Tauranga to look after the property. That would have meant that the proper credit, background and reference checks were completed, and the rental application from these tenants wouldn't have then been accepted.

In addition, I should have been more realistic with the rent. Now, using the RightRent process, I would be able to price it properly. That would mean I could attract quality tenants to the property, not just those who don't have another option.

Summary

To make sure you keep yourself, your tenant and your property manager happy, remember to follow these principles:

- Your tenants pay you to **provide both a product** (housing) **and a service** (maintaining the property and answering questions).
- **While it is your house, remember that it is the tenants' home.** It is best to leave your tenants to enjoy the property and check in only at the quarterly inspections.
- It's your job to **keep the product in good nick**, approving reasonable maintenance requests quickly. Make sure that **maintenance is budgeted for** so that the cash is there to be used.
- **Use the RightRent system** to set the rent based on the market reality, and position it realistically for your tenants.

The next chapter – the third in the series of how to manage your properties – is about tax. You'll often hear the words 'tax minimisation', and we're going to talk through what this is and the principles you can use to make sure you don't overpay your tax.

Chapter 14

Taxing times

Tax. Does the word strike fear, loathing and resentment into your heart all at the same time? Don't skip ahead, thinking you might ignore this chapter because it's going to be about as dry and unpalatable as six WeetBix with no milk. This part of the book contains some of the most crucial knowledge you'll need to take with you on your property investment journey, especially after recent tax law changes. And crucially, you're going to learn exactly how property investors minimise the amount of tax they need to pay.

Now this comes with a necessary disclaimer: over time this chapter will become horrendously out of date, especially with the speed that new tax changes are being introduced. To combat that, we'll start by talking about the main new taxes property investors need to know about today: interest deductibility. Then we'll talk about how to minimise your tax in general, before touching on the bright line test. While the details of the specific taxes will likely change, the principles about minimising your tax and how to respond to tax changes will not.

Interest deductibility

In March 2021, New Zealand's government made some significant changes to the tax that property investors will soon have to pay. While the reforms didn't change the tax rate, they did change how property investors' profits are calculated. Some investment properties will be taxed as if they don't have a mortgage – despite the fact that they do. Because the profit is calculated without interest costs being taken into account, the properties appear more profitable. That's why some investors will need to pay more tax.

So how does this tax change work? Soon the interest expenses you pay on your property's mortgage won't count when you calculate your investment's taxable profit. Let's go through an example to see how this actually works.

Assume an investor has owned a property for a few years. They purchased it three years ago for $500,000 as an investment, borrowing all the money and putting it on an interest-only mortgage. While the rent and the value have increased, the mortgage has stayed the same: $500,000. The property now rents for $500 a week, so will earn $25,000 per year (making the standard allowance for two weeks' vacancy). The property also has operating costs of $10,000 per year, which accounts for rates, maintenance and insurance. And because the mortgage is interest-only and fixed at 4 per cent, it attracts interest costs of $20,000.

Under the previous rules, the property had negative cashflow. The property earns $25,000 but there are $30,000 worth of expenses ($20,000 from the mortgage interest, $10,000 in operating costs). The property has a cashflow of –$5,000 and there is no taxable profit. No tax to be paid.

Rent	$25,000
Mortgage interest costs	$20,000
Operating costs (e.g. rates and maintenance)	$10,000
Taxable profit	**–$5,000**
Tax	$0
Cashflow	**–$5,000**

The numbers look drastically different under the new rules. The mortgage costs won't be deductible when calculating tax. In simple terms, that means that *investors will soon be taxed as if they have already paid off their mortgages, despite the obvious fact that they still have their mortgages.* So while the investor still has to pay the mortgage interest costs, the IRD will view their property as having a $15,000 taxable profit ($25,000 of rent − $10,000 of operating costs).

Rent	$25,000
Operating costs (e.g. rates and maintenance)	$10,000
Taxable profit	**$15,000**
Tax	$4,950
Mortgage interest costs	$20,000
Cashflow	**−$9,950**

If the investor structured this property in a trust they'll pay 33 per cent in tax on the property, which is $4,950 paid to the government. But then of course the trust still has to pay its mortgage costs. So now instead of cashflow of −$5,000 per year, the property has cashflow of −$9,950 annually. That means that instead of topping up the property by $96 per week before the changes, they now need to invest $191 per week. The rent is the same, the operating costs are the same, and the interest costs are the same. What's changed is the tax bill. That increase is entirely going towards paying tax.

A simple way to estimate the cost of the full changes is to multiply your interest rate by 1.5. For instance, if you currently pay a 4 per cent interest rate, the effect of the full changes will be roughly the same as paying a 6 per cent interest rate under the old rules (4 x 1.5 = 6). These new tax rules started to be phased in from 1 October 2021. At the time of writing, you can still deduct 75 per cent of your interest costs on any properties you owned before 27 March 2021. This drops to 50 per cent from April 2023, then to 25 per cent in April 2024. From April 2025, no existing properties will be able to claim this deduction. The rules are even tougher for any recent properties you'll have acquired. If you bought a property on or after 27 March 2021, you can't deduct any interest costs after 1 October 2021.

Note that the 1.5 multiplication factor only works if your tax rate is 33 per cent. If you're on a different tax rate, here's what you multiply your interest rate by:

TAX RATE	MULTIPLY YOUR INTEREST RATE BY	WHO PAYS THIS RATE
0%	1 ×	Renting to social housing, or new-build
10.5%	1.1 ×	Annual income: < $14,000
17.5%	1.2 ×	Annual income: $14,001–$48,000
30%	1.4 ×	Annual income: $48,001–$70,000
33%	1.5 ×	Annual income: $70,001–$180,000 (or trusts)
39%	1.65 ×	Annual income: $180,001+

This can all be a bit scary, and property investors will baulk at the prospect of paying more tax even when their properties are potentially cashflow-negative. However, not all property investors will be impacted equally and there are some exemptions.

Knowing all of this, you're probably wondering how you should respond as a property investor. No, it's not time to come up with protest slogans or create a new chant. There are three steps you need to take:

1 Understand how your properties will be impacted by the rules.
2 See if you can fit your property under one of the exemptions.
3 Find ways to minimise the tax that you have to pay.

Who will be most impacted by these changes?

As we've said, not all property investors are impacted equally. There are five groups of people who will be impacted the most harshly:

→ **People who invest in existing properties (not new-builds).**
→ **People who are on higher interest rates.** If you multiply a high interest rate by 1.5 it has more of an effect than if you multiply a lower interest rate by that same number.

- **People who are highly leveraged and invest with 100 per cent borrowing.** Higher mortgages naturally have higher interest costs.
- **People who buy an existing property and don't conduct significant renovations.** People who renovate tend to have higher cashflow so can better absorb the additional cost of the taxes.
- **People who purchase lower-yield but higher-growth properties.** There is less rent available to cover the additional costs.

On the other side, some investors will be less impacted:

- **People who invest in new-builds.** Their properties will be exempt depending on when they purchase and when the Code Compliance Certificate is issued (more opposite).
- **People who have low mortgages, whether because they purchased when properties were cheaper, they have historically paid their mortgages down, or they used a cash deposit.** In this case they have lower mortgages and therefore lower interest costs.
- **People who invest in higher-yielding properties.** There is more rent available to cover the additional taxes.
- **People who have managed their interest rate risk and are on lower interest rates.** Because 1.5 times a low interest rate is less scary than 1.5 times a high interest rate.
- **People who purchase existing properties to renovate.** They increase the property's value and cashflow to absorb the taxes; the Cashflow Hacking strategy we love. (Go back to Chapter 6 for a refresher.)

As an investor, your properties are likely to have features that appear in both lists. The true test is to run a 15-year projection to understand how your property may perform over time.

The best way to do this is using the Return on Investment spreadsheet we introduced in Chapter 10. You can download this for free at opespartners.co.nz/book. If you find that you are significantly impacted, it's time to see whether you can come under one of the exemptions to the rules.

Exemptions to the new tax rules

As it stands now, there are three major exemptions to the latest tax rules. The main one is that new-builds get to stick with the old rules. Their mortgage costs will be taken into account when calculating profit, and they'll pay the same amount of tax as before. Next are properties that are rented out as social or community housing. Finally, there are a number of specific exemptions for properties that are not good substitutes for residential housing.

Chapter 14 Taxing times

All of these are discussed in more detail below. As you're reading through these, consider whether your properties may either already come under these definitions, or could be adapted to come under them.

NEW-BUILDS

Whether your property is considered a new-build or not depends on when the Code Compliance Certificate (CCC) was issued. This is the legal sign-off that councils give to say that a property complies with its building and resource consents.

If the CCC was issued on or after 27 March 2020, then your property is considered a new-build, and can stick with the old way of calculating tax for 20 years. Conversely, even if you bought a new-build directly off a developer but it received its CCC on 26 March 2020 or before, it will not be considered a new-build under this tax definition. It all feels somewhat arbitrary, but them's the rules.

Note, though, that some properties can be adapted to come under this definition and be classed as a new-build. For instance, if you use a house-mover to relocate an existing building on to your property or land, that's a new-build. If you carve up an existing larger home into two smaller legally-consented buildings, those are both considered new-builds also. If you add a minor dwelling on to the back of your property, the debt associated with that will be treated as a new-build.

SOCIAL HOUSING

The next exemption is for properties rented out as social housing. According to the Ministry of Social Development, as of June 2022, 26,664 New Zealanders were waiting for a property provided through social housing.[35] These numbers provide a huge incentive for central government to try to increase the supply of houses for those who are worse off financially, so they've responded with a massive tax incentive.

As a landlord you can receive this tax benefit by renting your property either through Kāinga Ora or through a registered community housing provider. Some of these organisations are well known, like Auckland City Mission and the Salvation Army. Check the Community Housing Regulatory Authority for the list of who to approach.

The properties that tend to be most in demand for the social sector are one-bedroom properties, followed by two-bedroom properties, both in the major cities. Among social housing tenants 48.4 per cent need a property with only one bedroom, and together one- and two-bedroom properties make up 80 per cent of the properties needed.[36] If your property fits these categories, there is a very good chance you can receive this exemption, provided you are happy that you have no say over who your tenants are, since it's up to the social housing provider to decide.

PROPERTIES THAT CAN'T BE USED AS RENTAL ACCOMMODATION

The third major area where investors can still operate under the previous tax calculation is by purchasing properties that can't be used as standard rental accommodation. Boarding houses, hotel rooms, commercial property, employee and student accommodation all come with exemptions, and tax is calculated the same way it always has been.

If your property isn't currently used as rental accommodation, but could be – holiday homes and properties rented as short-term accommodation on Airbnb are prime examples – then you don't fall under this exemption. Your property will be taxed as if it was rented out as standard residential investment property, and as if your mortgage was fully paid off.

Tax minimisation

If after reading this you still find yourself up for paying significantly more tax , the next step is to see whether you're paying more than you need to be. This is called 'tax minimisation' or 'tax efficiency'. Here, you set up your affairs to make sure you are not paying more tax than the tax rules specify you have to. To be clear, we're not suggesting you move your properties into a blind trust headquartered in the British Virgin Islands, or that you pay less than your fair share. We're simply saying: don't pay *more* than your fair share.

So how do you minimise your tax? Remember, we're not property accountants, and smarter people than us could write whole textbooks about tax minimisation. However, we believe that the clues for minimising your tax tend to come from how it's calculated.

Take a look at the formula, below. What would you do to lower the amount of tax paid?

$$\text{Tax} = \text{Taxable profit} \times \text{Tax rate}$$

There are only two options: either lower your taxable profit or reduce your tax rate. Let's briefly cover each.

Reducing taxable profit

You might wonder why anyone would want to reduce their profits. After all, doesn't that mean making *less* money? But reducing your *taxable* profit does not necessarily mean accepting a lower-cashflow property. Often there are costs that investors pay for anyway that could be counted as a legitimate business expense. If you then claim these expenses, you can reduce the taxable profit and therefore your tax bill. Here are some concrete examples to show what we mean:

- **Chattel depreciation**: Claiming that the value of everything not bolted down to the building is decreasing in value over time, such as your driveway, pergolas, curtains, carpets, appliances, and even your mailbox.
- **Home office expenses**: You run your property investment business from home, so a portion of your home's mortgage interest, rates and insurance can be claimed as a legitimate business expense. (This is usually calculated on the proportion of your home's overall floor area that your office space takes.)
- **Telephone and internet**: Again these are expenses you likely already pay, but since you also use them for your property investment business, a portion of the cost is deductible.
- **Travel expenses**: If you travel to your property for whatever reason, a portion of your fuel costs and the depreciation on your car is deductible.
- **Subscriptions**: Costs related to professional development can be claimed, such as a subscription to *NZ Property Investor* or *Informed Investor* magazine, or tickets to property investment conferences, since these are related to property.

To reiterate, you're likely paying for all of these costs anyway, so claiming these expenses will not impact your cashflow but will reduce the tax you pay.

The biggest opportunity from the list above is chattel depreciation. Chattels wear out over time and need to be replaced. You can claim that wear and tear (depreciation) as a legitimate business expense per year. If your chattels are worth $45,000 at the time you buy the property, assuming a 39 per cent tax rate, you can save up to $17,550 in tax over the lifetime of the property. But this applies only if you organise a chattel valuation and ask your accountant to start including these in your tax return right away. If you don't use them, you'll lose them.

Reducing tax rate

If your portfolio is already fully optimised and your taxable profit is as low as it can be, then it's time to see if you can reduce your tax rate. You can sometimes do this by changing the ownership structure of your properties. Here is how this usually works.

Let's say you earn a very high income from your job – $200,000 a year. Every extra dollar you earn is taxed at 39 per cent. So if you buy a property that earns a taxable profit of $10,000 a year, you'll pay $3,900 in tax.

However, while your personal tax rate in this example is 39 per cent, the trust tax rate is currently 33 per cent. If you changed the ownership of your property from your own name to your *trust*, then your tax rate would fall 6 per cent. That means you'd only pay $3,300 in tax, saving $600 a year.

Another option is to use a look-through company. These work like regular companies except that tax is paid at the shareholder's personal tax rates. This works well if you are investing with your partner and you are on different tax rates. It often happens that one partner earns a high income and pays a high tax rate, and the other is on a low income and pays a low tax rate. Here is a good example of how this works.

> **CASE STUDY**
> **Managing a targeted tax rate**
>
> For one couple we work with, the wife is a partner at a professional services firm. She earns a high income and pays 39 per cent tax on anything extra she earns. The husband, on the other hand, stays home and looks after the children. He doesn't earn an income, and therefore his tax rate is 10.5 per cent. It therefore makes sense to skew the ownership of their properties towards the husband since he has the lower tax rate.
>
> A common way to do this is by using the look-through company structure. These useful entities take on the tax rates of the people who hold the shares. For this couple, if 67 per cent of the shares were held in the husband's name and 33 per cent in the wife's, then two-thirds of the profits would be taxed at his lower tax rate and one-third at her higher tax rate.
>
> In practice, the split used in these circumstances is often 99 per cent to 1 per cent (i.e. 99 per cent of the shares are owned by the person with the lower tax rate, and 1 per cent by the person with a higher tax rate). This means that the majority of any profit earned is taxed at a lower rate.
>
> Digging back into the numbers, let's say this couple earns a $10,000 taxable profit on their property. If they own the property in their own names with no tax structure, then it will be 50:50. Half will be taxed at each partner's tax rate. That's $5,000 taxed at 10.5 per cent, and $5,000 taxed at 39 per cent. That means $2,475 of tax paid, effectively a 24.8 per cent tax rate.
>
> But let's look at what would have happened if the couple had talked to a property accountant and used the 99:1 look-through company tax structure. Then, only $100 of the taxable profit would be taxed at 39 per cent. The bulk– $9,900 – would be taxed at 10.5 per cent. That means only paying $1,079 worth of tax, an effective tax rate of 10.8 per cent.
>
> By simply using a different ownership structure of the property, this couple could save $1,396 per year in tax and lower the tax they pay on the property from just under 25 per cent to just under 11 per cent.*

* Seek legal advice as there may be other considerations, such as the Property (Relationships) Act.

While these tactics are powerful, changing the ownership structure of a property can't be done by everyone. For example, there's not much additional tax benefit that a single person on a lower income can gain from tax structuring, as they already pay a low marginal tax rate. But for those on higher incomes, or in situations where one partner is on a high income and the other doesn't work or only works part-time, there are potentially tax savings to be made by consciously deciding how to split the ownership.

Warning: Don't try and do this on your own at home. You can't just decide to change the ownership structure of your property and decide to pay less tax. That's illegal and would attract a visit from your friend, the IRD investigator. To do this the right way you may need to sell the property from one entity to another.

Whatever you do, make sure to get professional accounting advice that is suitable for your specific situation, because what works for one person can differ from what works for the next. These are simply examples of the process to work through to see if there are ways to improve the position of your properties.

The bright line test

This is New Zealand's version of a capital gains tax (CGT). Although not called a CGT, the impact is to tax some capital gains that occur from property ownership. At the time of writing, the rule says that if you sell a property (bought from March 2021 onwards) that you've owned for less than 10 years, you have to pay tax on the profit you make when selling. There are some exceptions:

- It doesn't apply to the home you live in.
- The bright line test only lasts five years for new-builds.

The amount of tax you actually pay depends on what you earn. Say you sold a property within the bright line test period and had to pay tax on $100,000 of capital gains. If you currently earn $50,000 you'll pay $32,400 in tax (32.4 per cent). On the other hand, say you earn a very high income of $200,000, then you'll pay $39,000 in tax on that gain (39 per cent). All governments are prone to tinkering with these thresholds, so these taxes are most certainly subject to ongoing change.

The bright line test is not really an issue for long-term, passive buy-and-hold property investors who are likely to hold on to their properties for more than 10 years anyway.

Nevertheless, there are still fishhooks to avoid. For instance, if you show a pattern of buying and flipping your own residence or home, then you will be taxed on those transactions. If you buy your own home, then move cities (for work or to travel) and rent it out, after 12 months out of your home you'll be treated as a property investor and can't fully rely on the exemption provided for main homes. You'll then pay tax on the period you did not live in it.

However, the main fishhook you need to avoid is if you're restructuring your properties to change the debt or ownership structure. Historically, if you wanted to move a property from your own names into a look-through company, as described in the preceding case study, you needed to sell the property from your own names into the look-through company. That's right: you'd sell it to yourself in order to change the tax rate. The issue that has crept up over the past four years is that doing so triggers the bright line test.

In practice that means that if you sell the property as part of a restructure for tax purposes, you'll need to pay tax on any gains within the property; to avoid this, you'll have to wait to restructure until the bright line period has ended. There is yet another fishhook, though. Let's say you sell a new-build property from your own name into a look-through company. You'd waited for the bright line period of five years to end so that doing so wouldn't mean paying tax on your gains. But once you do so the bright line period starts again, and this time for the longer year period of 10 years as it is no longer considered a new-build.

Are new taxes the end of property investment in New Zealand?

When Finance Minister Grant Robertson first announced the interest-deductibility tax changes in March 2021, it was like a bomb went off. The fundamental rules and norms of tax and calculating profit changed. Shortly after the announcements, many long-time listeners of the *Property Academy Podcast* messaged in to ask whether this was the end of property investment as we knew it. Would house prices stop going up? Would it lead to a mass sell-off? Would prices start to level? All fair questions to ask.

No taxes – whether the ones we're addressing in this chapter or ones that could be introduced in the future – will be the end of property investment. There will continue to be Kiwis who need to plan for retirement and see property as the way to get there. And one of the key reasons people invest in property is because they can use the wealth in their residential home to get started. So until people don't need to plan for retirement and people can't borrow against their homes, property investment will form the backbone of many Kiwis' wealth-building strategies. And these Kiwis will adapt their strategy over time to fit the environment. They may change what they buy (e.g. purchasing new-builds in this case), or change what they do with their properties (e.g. renovating to increase cashflow). But interest in property will likely remain.

Summary

The tax rules have substantially changed and investors can respond in multiple ways:

- → **Investors need to consider how they will personally be affected by the changes**, by running a 15-years cashflow forecast using our Return on Investment spreadsheet.
- → **Next, consider whether your properties can fall under any of the exemptions to still play under the old tax rules (e.g. new-builds or social housing).**
- → **Failing this, consider ways you can decrease your taxable profit using non-cash costs, things like chattel depreciation, or claiming back portions of home office expenses or phone and internet costs.**
- → **Consider ways to lower your tax rate by changing the ownership structure, whether through a trust or a look-through company.**

So far in the managing your properties section of the book we've discussed managing your finances, dealing with your tenants and managing your tax. Now we turn to one of the most important subjects in property investment: keeping your emotions in check.

Chapter 15

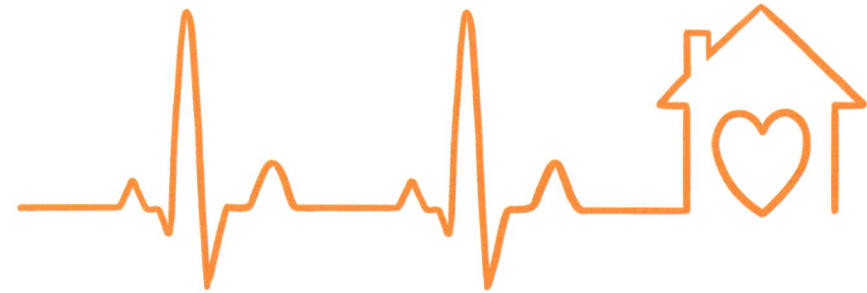

The emotions of property investing

One of the most common reasons people get cold feet and stumble at the first hurdle in their property race is emotions. You might get to that place where logic tells you that 'yes, property investment makes sense'... BUT (and it's a big but), there's something in the back of your mind holding you back.

Too many Kiwis have talked themselves out of improving their financial situation out of fear. This book is not intended to sugar-coat property investment and convince you that it's all a breeze and that the path is straightforward. But we *are* trying to say that you've got to manage your emotions and think through your fears so you can make a rational decision.

When you hold the pen, poised to sign your first contract to buy an investment property for $800,000, it's normal to think: 'What happens if I suddenly lose my job?' 'Are there "safer" options?' 'What happens if I don't have a tenant for a long time?' 'What if something else bad happens?'

These are valid fears. Because you could lose your job, or you could find that you don't have a tenant for a time. Instead of trying to convince yourself that these definitely won't happen, our approach is to mitigate the risk that unfortunate things happen, and set up your situation so that if bad things do happen you'll be protected.

> **CASE STUDY**
> **Don't give up at the first hurdle**
>
> One Auckland doctor found out first-hand how basing property decisions on emotional reactions can come back to bite. After deciding to purchase an investment property in Torbay in the early 2000s for just over $300,000, he quickly discovered that managing a property was far harder than he'd anticipated.
>
> He had found tenants, but they moved out after two and a half months, which left him scrambling to find new ones. Because he led a busy life, finding new tenants wasn't a priority, which left him with weeks of vacancy – and no money coming in.
>
> Because he had bought an older house, when he did eventually find tenants the cost of repairs started to stack up. It turned out that the roof was leaking, and the dishwasher needed to be replaced. He was frustrated with having to spend more time on the property than he'd ever thought was needed, and the property was losing money each week. He felt like he'd made completely the wrong call in buying the place. Dealing with all of this was way outside of his comfort zone.
>
> Within a few months of buying, the property was back on the market and, after the rental losses, and real estate agent and lawyer fees, he made a $15,000 loss. The real loss, though, was what he missed out on. Over the years since, the average property value in Torbay increased by 382.35 per cent.[37] Had he held on, he would have made about $847,050 in equity in the property.

Now to be fair, the doctor's fears and losses at the time were real. What he'd missed was how to set his property up to deal with these worst-case scenarios, which is where our top five tactics come in.

1. It's all in the property selection

The first place our doctor went wrong was in the property selection. He's a busy person who needs to focus on his job and business. He wanted to take a passive strategy, but in purchasing an older house he selected a property that wouldn't attract high-quality tenants, and was also high-maintenance. It was the right strategy, but the wrong property. If he'd got the property selection right, he might have purchased a newer home that was attractive to tenants and would therefore rent more quickly, and also have lower maintenance concerns.

2. Everyone on the same page

Another question investors often ask is: 'How do I get my wife/husband/dad/sister to invest with me?' Sometimes one party is dead keen to purchase property, while the other is gun-shy.

The best way we've found to get your significant other on board is to start listening, watching and reading the same things. Often it's not that they're totally opposed to the idea, rather that they have many genuine questions and concerns. The same as you likely did before jumping on YouTube or reading a book like this.

Consuming more of the same info about property investment saves you from feeling one of the most frustrating feelings in the world: trying to explain something, but not being able to get your point across. You think investing is a good idea because you've listened to a podcast or read a book. It all seems to make sense and you're convinced. But then your description might be less convincing.

For instance, if after reading this book you think 'maybe there is something in this investing thing' but your partner is less keen, it's much easier to give him or her the book to read rather than try to explain it all yourself. Afterwards you can have a discussion about what you've both read and what concerns you really have left over.

3. Set up a buffer account with a line of credit

One of the main concerns from the doctor in the previous case study was that he had a tough time with tenants, meaning that the money coming in to the property was sporadic. But then – double whammy – he also had high expenses because of all the maintenance issues. That means one thing: cashflow issues.

Other first-time property investors often share this fear: 'What happens if I receive a large expense on my property?' or 'What happens if I don't earn income because I don't have a tenant for a while?'

That's where a buffer account with a line of credit comes in. Put simply, this is a bank account with a large overdraft attached, which the bank secures against one of your properties. Many property investors will have a $20,000–$50,000 undrawn overdraft in case times get tough.

One investor we met, a woman in her seventies who owned 12 rental properties, had an undrawn overdraft of $500,000, just in case times got tough or she wanted to use some of it as a deposit for another property. This becomes really useful if, let's say, you're made redundant or you become unable to earn an income. You might initially think: 'I need to sell my investment property because I can no longer afford it.' But the line of credit can see you through those tough times.

Chapter 15 The emotions of property investing

While selling your investment property earlier than expected *might* ease some short-term pressure, it means losing out on future capital gains which will help you achieve your long-term goals. Let's say you are able to borrow a maximum of $200,000 against your own property right now and you want to buy an investment property. You might borrow $125,000 for the deposit for the investment property and set up an additional $25,000 of lending as a revolving credit or overdraft that is available when you need it, but only for emergencies. Because you would only use that line of credit when you need it, you won't pay any interest on it until you have to dip into it.

This sort of buffer account in some ways is the cheapest form of 'insurance'. When you're not using the funds, you don't pay interest. And you then only pay interest on what you actually use.

A word of caution: if you use this tactic, you must be diligent and not spend the line of credit on other things you might want to buy. This is a buffer account for emergencies only. A new car or handbag, or concert tickets, aren't emergencies.

4. Get the right type of insurance in place

Simple policies like house, fire and contents will protect you in the event that you are impacted by major unexpected events. But beyond that, it's also a good idea to get landlords insurance. This covers you for specific situations that impact property investors, like large hidden maintenance issues or bad tenants.

Each insurance company offers different policies – and they don't all cover the same thing. However, when you're shopping around, make sure you buy a policy that covers you for 'loss of rent'. That covers you in two main scenarios:

→ **If you have to evict your tenants because they aren't paying rent, or if they leave without notice, the insurance company will then pay their rent for you.** While tenants aren't 'allowed' to just up and leave, it does happen. And while you might be able to claw back some of your lost rent through the Tenancy Tribunal, that's going to take time. The insurance company will pay you cash now while you find a new tenant.
→ **Most companies will also pay the rent to you if your house is damaged and your tenant has to move out.** This was particularly useful for anyone after the Canterbury earthquakes. Many rental properties were uninhabitable and the tenants had to move out. So some landlords were left with no income but a mortgage still to pay. But the insurance companies would continue to pay rent for between six weeks and 12 months for investors who were covered for 'loss of rent'.

There are some other areas where this type of landlords insurance is useful. For instance, if your tenant accidentally damages the property. Legally, the tenant doesn't have to pay the cost to fix accidental damage. Landlords insurance will have you covered. In some policies, insurance will also cover any meth contamination, or hidden gradual damage, like rot caused by a leaking pipe that you didn't know about.

While landlords insurance is low-cost – perhaps an extra $8 a week – not every property investor necessarily needs this type of insurance. If you are aware of the risks and can pay the costs if the risk eventuates, then you might not need to pay for the policy. If on the other hand you are gravely worried about the prospect of your tenant up and leaving, and it's stopping you from investing, then having this sort of safety net could give you confidence to take your first steps and purchase your next property.

> **CASE STUDY**
> ### Why a good insurance adviser is a must
> Investors Kathy and Alun have had first-hand experience of what happens when you don't have the right insurances in place and things go wrong. Kathy explains.
>
> 'Previously we had poor experiences with insurance advisers, and so decided to go to the insurer directly when we took out homeowners and landlords insurance on our investment properties. We have always had our insurance on auto-renew. But when we set up our insurance ourselves, we didn't realise we hadn't asked for our policies to renew automatically. So the insurance company sent us a letter asking whether we wanted to renew. Unfortunately my father had passed away, so we were in South Africa and we missed the posted letter. So the insurances on both investment properties lapsed.
>
> 'At the same time we discovered this, our property manager warned us that the tenant had not paid rent. Even though there had been no issues at the recent inspection, it was unusual that they hadn't paid. The property manager went over and found the property abandoned with damage. There had been a relationship break-up and both parties had left the property without telling us.
>
> 'It was on the eve of the Easter long weekend that the insurance company told us that we weren't covered and our insurance policy had lapsed. So there we are, in South Africa, it's about to be the long weekend, our rental property is damaged and not covered by insurance, and uninsured if anything else should happen over the long weekend.
>
> 'Our first step was to get insurance on the properties. After a few panicked calls, we found a new adviser, who within the hour organised insurance for our properties late Thursday

> before the Easter long weekend. We have now moved all our insurances over to this adviser, who has provided us with exceptional service ever since.
>
> 'But for us the key lesson is not just to get the right insurance in place, but also to make sure you keep it there. That's why we now swear by using an insurance adviser. Every time something has gone wrong in our investment portfolio, it's been our fault. Either we've not listened to advice, or we've tried to do it on our own.'

5. Remove the emotion and focus on what you need to

Successful property investment is less about the 'property' and more about the 'investment'. So as an investor it's best not to focus on managing the property itself, but instead look after the whole portfolio. Your 'unknowns' right now might be to do with the property – what it'll end up looking like (if you're buying off the plans), or whether you'll get on with your tenants. In many ways, none of that actually matters. The reason you became interested in property investment was probably because you wanted a 'good' investment that builds a passive income, grows your wealth, or provides for your financial future. You don't have to be best buds with your tenant for the property to increase in value.

If you look at the Property Investors Chat Group NZ on Facebook[38] – a popular New Zealand Facebook group for landlords – you'll see people asking how to fix a leaky tap, what colour they should paint a wall, or how to deal with a tenant issue. None of that should be a property investor's primary concern. A successful property investor should spend their time looking at their overall portfolio, not focusing on the individual properties. That means picking the right investments, then leaving your team of professionals to manage the property, sort the tenants, and conduct maintenance.

There's always a way to respond

When bad things happen there is always a way to respond. One investor we were working with was terrified about the risk of vacancy. She was worried that if she couldn't find a tenant, she and her husband would be paying two mortgages at once, which they definitely couldn't afford.

To help her work through her fear, we asked: 'What would happen if you couldn't find a tenant?' The answer: temporarily drop the rent. Advertise the property at $50 less per week, get a tenant, and take the short-term cash hit. After 12 months, put the rent up to the market level. It's simple, it's obvious, and for this investor it was enough to give her the comfort to proceed with her investment.

RUNNING YOUR RACE

Once the property was built, and she settled the property, her tenants moved in the very next day. She's had only one day's vacancy over the past four years of ownership. During that time she's made over $200,000 worth of capital gains.

No investment is without its risks. But what's important is to first understand the risks, figure which ones you're really worried about, and then mitigate them. That way, you're entering the property race with your eyes wide open.

CASE STUDY
I lost my job, I need to sell

I received a phone call from one of my long-time investors. He was in a panic saying that he wanted to sell his most recent investment property. The investor was topping up the property's bank account diligently by $100 a week. He was living in Wellington and had just been made redundant – enough to throw anybody into a panic. He said he couldn't afford to put $100 a week into the rental property anymore, so he needed to sell.

I said, 'Mate, you've got a $50,000 revolving credit sitting right there. It'll cover the top-up for at least nine and a half years.' It's not that the investor had forgotten about the revolving credit, it's that he was in genuine emotional panic. Anyone in the same situation would be. But although it was an unfortunate situation, all was not lost.

In addition to being able to cover his investment property costs through the revolving credit, he also was able to use that line of credit to cover any short-term costs. Through work he also received a redundancy package that would see him right for the next six months. Working in IT, he started a new job within the next three.

Revolving credit in action

Income — $450 per week rent → Balance: $0 Available: $50,000 → Expenses — $500 per week expenses

Line of credit can cover shortfall for 1,000 weeks (19.23 years)*

* Assuming no interest to keep the maths simple

> My point here isn't that bad stuff doesn't happen. It's more that it's hard to see what's right in front of you when you're in the eye of the storm. Having somebody on the other end of the phone to help you set the game plan can both give you the reassurance to carry on and get you back on the right path.
>
> Now one thing that's important to point out is that had the investor applied for the line of credit once he was made redundant, he wouldn't have had it approved. The bank isn't going to approve a $50,000 overdraft for someone who soon won't have any income. It was vitally important to this story that he already had this in place. It's like insurance. You can't apply for insurance once something bad happens. You need to have your policy in place first.
>
> The moral of this story is that you need to apply for this line of credit when your employment is secure and you don't yet need it. Chances are that if you reach a situation where you do actually need the line of credit in place, it's too late.

Summary

You can't escape that there will be emotional times in property investment. You will be worried about things going wrong, and at some point something will go wrong. Sometimes you need to feel the fear and do it anyway. At other times the best course of action is to mitigate your fears by avoiding the potential risk through:

- choosing a **property that matches your risk tolerance**
- setting up a **buffer account** with a line of credit and
- getting **landlords insurance**.

In addition:

- Start watching, listening or reading the same things as your partner so you both get educated and **get on the same page**.
- **Focus on the portfolio rather than the property.** Property investment is more about the 'investment' than the 'property'.

We are almost at the end of what you need to know as a passive property investor when managing your properties and your portfolio. In the final two chapters in this section, we are going to talk through what a year in property looks like and then how to expand your portfolio further.

Chapter 16

A year in property

Even though we advocate a passive approach when it comes time for running your race, that doesn't mean you can just check out and forget about your properties for the next 15 years.

Even when you pull your team around you, there's still some oversight you need to give to your portfolio. So in this chapter, we'll pull it all together in a loose timeline of some of the things you'll encounter during a year in property investment.

The set-up

- → **Acquire your property.** Congratulations! You've done the due diligence, your finance is approved, and in a few weeks – or when the property is built – you'll be handed the keys to take possession of your investment property. Before you even get the keys for the property it's time to engage the services of a property manager to get the place tenanted. Ideally you want your tenant moving in the day you settle the property and are handed the keys.
- → **Set up your finances.** Confirm with your bank or lender that your mortgage account is active. By now you should have your cashflow spreadsheet up and running. Work out if you're topping up

the account, and, if so, set up a direct transfer from your personal account into the mortgage account. Do this in conjunction with your pay cycle.

Weekly

→ **Scan your bank accounts to make sure that you have enough money in your accounts for your mortgage and other payments.** A little time spent here can help avoid any unfortunate calls from the bank saying that you've missed a mortgage payment.

Twice-monthly

→ **Check your rent payments. In most instances your property manager will pass on your rent twice a month.** Most property managers pay on the 1st and 15th. Therefore we recommend that your mortgage payment goes out monthly on the 2nd, so you have two rent payments each time to cover your costs. If there's a public holiday or a long weekend that might delay payments, you need to keep on top of that. Remember that your property management fees (and any maintenance they have organised to be done) are deducted at the time of rent collection. Therefore, you need to check each rent payment, because, despite there being a set amount, any deductions for maintenance can skew your expected cashflow.

→ **Make sure you actually check that the rent comes in as expected.** Don't just look at the statement they've sent you. You need to see the money hitting your account.

Monthly

→ **Set up your other payments, such as insurance, rates, body corporate fees and water, to go out once a month.** Many of these are often billed yearly or quarterly, but by setting up smaller, incremental payments you can hopefully avoid big, one-off expenses and possible financial shocks. This will help to smooth your cashflow.

Quarterly

→ **Carry out a property inspection.** These have to happen every three months, otherwise your insurance will become void. That means if something goes wrong, the insurance company may not pay you out. If you're using a property manager, this service is often built into their fee – but not always, so check – and you will receive a written report after each inspection. They can also forewarn you of any maintenance that is required today, or maintenance that could be required in the near future. The inspections provide a good chance to make sure your property is being looked after – and give you the opportunity to pass feedback on to the tenant.

→ **Make sure you actually read these reports and look at the photos.** If the appliances aren't as clean as you could reasonably expect, then raise this. Remember your property manager might be looking after 50 to 100 properties, but you may only have one or two. Some property managers may let something slide if they get particularly busy. It's your house, so take a few minutes to scan the report and flick off an email if something looks amiss.

Annually

→ **Attend or get the information from your property manager about your body corporate's AGM (if you have one). Factor any fee changes into your annual costs.** Your property manager will sometimes represent you at the annual general meeting, especially if they look after multiple units within the complex.

→ **You and your property manager should also set a rent review each year using the RightRent system (see Chapter 13).** Our view is that if you put up prices incrementally and regularly, based on what similar properties are renting for in your area – say by $20 to $30 per week each time – tenants will accept these. It's the big jumps that cause the horses to bolt. The median rent in New Zealand has increased by 4.82 per cent per year for the past 20 years.[39]

→ **File your tax return with the help of your property accountant.** If you keep your accounts up to date in a system like Xero and you have your trusty Return on Investment spreadsheet, this will make life much easier. What you actually use will depend on your property accountant.

→ **Review your interest rate and lending set-up.** It's good practice to speak with your mortgage adviser each year to review your portfolio. This means seeing whether you're now in the position to purchase your next property, and ensuring that you've got the right interest rate set up (e.g. two years fixed at 4 per cent).

→ **Review your portfolio with a property adviser.** This is where you can have wider financial discussions about which properties to buy and which ones to sell, and ask any questions about your next move.

Summary

Although property is primarily a passive asset, there is still stuff you need to do:

- **managing the cash and bank accounts** for your properties
- **reviewing the property inspection reports** from your property manager
- **reviewing and resetting the rent** every year
- **managing your tax**
- **deciding when and where to expand your portfolio**.

That last point becomes the focus for the next chapter, where you'll learn about the next step on your property investment journey.

Chapter 17

Expanding your portfolio

At some point in your property investment journey the bank will start to bite and it'll be harder to get the money to continue to invest. Early on in your property investment journey the trouble is often equity: you don't have enough savings or useable equity for another deposit. As you acquire a few properties, the issue often turns to income: the bank says you don't have enough money to afford another mortgage.

Once the bank starts to say 'no' it's time to show your resolve. Because this is where you have to get creative. In this chapter you'll learn the strategies to continue growing your portfolio over time.

Equity strategies

There are six main equity strategies you can use to find the deposit to continually expand your rental portfolio. The first three we've already discussed throughout the book and are simple; the last three are generally used for investors who have an investment property or two already in their portfolio.

The waiting game – wait for capital growth

The first strategy is to wait for capital growth. You might look at that and laugh us out the door. After all, we're talking about sitting on your hands and waiting. (And this, during a supposed race!) Yet while it is simple, it is the most common way investors grow their portfolios – because it works.

The 12 months to November 2021 are a good example. According to the REINZ House Price Index, over that time property prices rose 27.2 per cent.[40] That created significant equity within both owner-occupiers' and investors' homes that can be used to fund the deposits for expanding their rental properties.

Paying down debt

Another simple but effective strategy is paying off debt more aggressively, as we explored in depth in Chapter 5 using the Mortgage Buster strategy.

Investing in new-builds

The third strategy is to invest in properties that don't have strict deposit requirements. One of the key reasons to invest in new-builds, other than their tax incentives, is the fact that they require only half the deposit required for an existing property. Put another way: because you only need a 20 per cent deposit for a new-build, you can purchase twice the number of new-builds with the same amount of deposit required for a single existing property, as long as you still meet the bank's servicing criteria.

Split-banking

One of the common issues that stops people continuing to invest in new-builds when growing their portfolio is how quickly a new-build is no longer a new-build in the bank's eyes. This has implications for future borrowing. However, as we shall see, both the problem and the solution lie in the structure of their lending. Remember, you purchase a new-build using a 20 per cent deposit, but the day it settles it becomes an existing property, and at that point it's treated as needing a 40 per cent deposit in bank calculations. All of which soon has an often unexpected knock-on effect. The following example illustrates all this, before we see how Split-banking can offer a solution.

Say you are buying a $1 million new-build. Initially, the bank lends you up to $800,000 for it, which means you only need a $200,000 deposit, which can be funded from equity in your main home. But the very next day after you pay for the property – bam! – they'll only lend you $600,000 against it. This is because it is now considered an existing property and has a 60 per cent LVR. That puts you in the situation where instead of using $200,000 of the useable equity in your personal home, it's now using $400,000 of that useable equity. If the mortgages are with the same bank, this means that when you go back to the bank for a loan to buy your next investment property, this new-build won't have as much lending secured against it, so you can't borrow as much. And on it goes, in ever-diminishing quantities, until you soon find that your race comes to an unwanted halt.

But if you use multiple banks rather than just the one, this shift in status from new-build to existing property doesn't have the same effect. The maths of this is technical, so we'll put it in Appendix B at the end of the book to dive into if you are really keen. But for those of you who are less passionate about the intricacies of maths, the simple message is: if you are investing in new-builds, you can often borrow more if you play the banking field rather than practise bank-monogamy.

There are also some instances where if you have a lot of equity (e.g. if you have a $2 million house with no mortgage), you might start with one bank and then move to multiple banks later on. This is a technical strategy and is worth talking with an adviser about if you do have a lot of equity and are not constrained by the deposit side of the equation.

BRRRR

If you are following a more active strategy, focused on renovations, then continually growing your portfolio is baked into the strategy name: Buy, Renovate, Rent, Refinace, *Repeat*. By renovating your property, you'll increase its value. You can then borrow against this higher value for your next property. Some investors call this 'recycling your deposit'.

Here's an example of a perfect scenario, where an investor would be able to recycle their full deposit. You purchase an existing property for $600,000. You need to put in a deposit of $240,000 (40 per cent). You do so and borrow the rest of the money – $360,000 – to purchase the property. You then renovate the property, increasing its value to $1 million.

As the property is an 'existing' one, the maximum amount you can borrow against it is 60 per cent. Remember, this comes from the LVR rules set by the Reserve Bank. That means you can now borrow up to $600,000 (60 per cent) against this property since it's now worth $1 million. But because you already have a $360,000 mortgage, you can only borrow the difference between the new allowable borrowing and what you have already borrowed ($600,000 – $360,000). That's $240,000 – the size of your initial deposit. So in effect you're able to borrow your deposit back from this property and use it as the deposit for your next investment property. For simplicity, we've left out renovation costs from this example.

Chapter 17 Expanding your portfolio

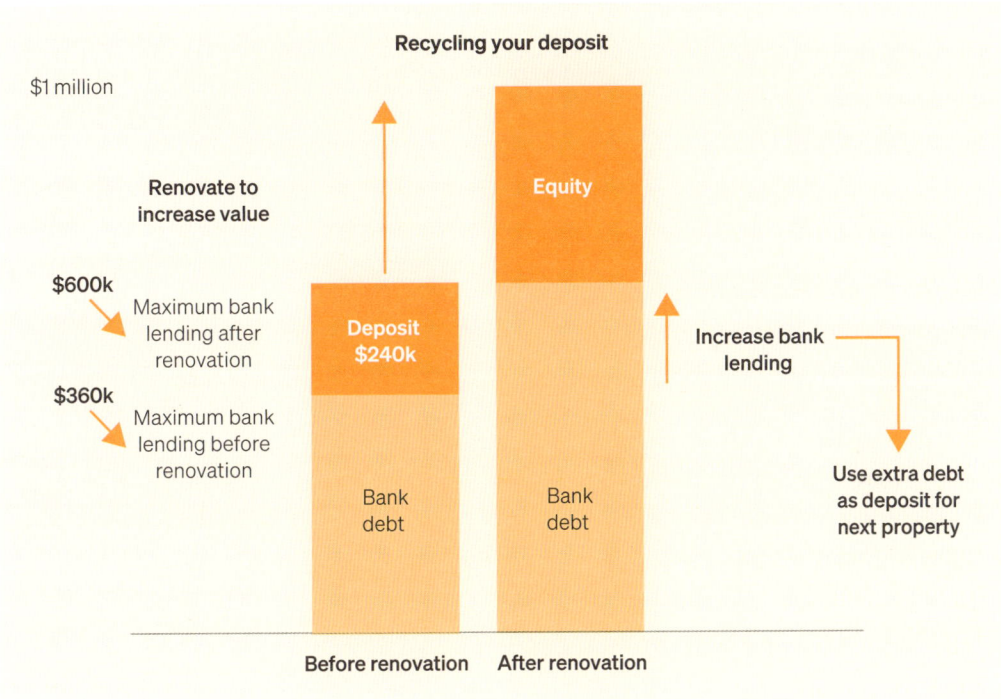

To do this with today's LVR restrictions, you need to renovate the property and increase its value by two-thirds to pull out your entire deposit again. In simple terms that means multiplying your property's purchase price by 1.66 times. This won't be achievable in every scenario, since that is a large uplift, and we haven't even accounted for the renovation costs yet, which can also be borrowed against the value of a property if you have enough equity. But as we saw in the case study on page 72, it is still possible.

Sell one to buy two

The last strategy, which is the most advanced – and arguably the most interesting – is selling one property to buy two or more. This can happen in three main situations.

First, you would be surprised how many New Zealanders own properties that suck. And by 'suck' we mean suck up more equity than they're worth. Bare land, hotel rooms and some small apartments all require 50 per cent LVRs, which are set by the banks rather than by government regulation.

That means that if you own a hotel room or a piece of land worth $400,000, you need at least $200,000 worth of equity within the property. So you've invested $200,000, which allows you to own $400,000 worth of assets. But if you sold the land – ignoring sale costs – you could take that $200,000 of equity and buy up to $1 million worth of new-builds. It's the same amount of equity invested, but it allows you to buy a greater level of assets. So the first strategy is to sell properties that banks don't like to lend against, to buy a property that you can borrow more for.

The second strategy is to sell off poor-quality, low-yielding or underperforming properties where the interest soon won't be deductible. The same maths applies from above. If you have an existing property worth $750,000, it needs at least $300,000 worth of equity. Sure you could buy one $750,000 property. But the alternative is to sell this one, take the equity and purchase up to $1.5 million worth of new rental properties, as long as your servicing is approved.

Third are holiday homes, especially if they are located in isolated or off-the-beaten-track areas that are unlikely to increase in value. This typically does not free up substantial lending, since holiday homes require a 20 per cent deposit, the same as new-builds. But it can help you purchase a better-quality asset, can make the interest on the property deductible, and can help with servicing the debt. On top of that, if you turn it into a rental property you'll receive a new stream of rental income, which can help get your lending approved.

If you are going to sell a property to purchase another, you'll want to ensure you get the best price possible for the property you are selling. In the next section of the book, Chapter 20, you'll learn what you need to do to make your property attractive to the market.

Servicing strategies

Once you start to build a bigger portfolio, you will likely find that servicing becomes the issue for you, as the bank may think you don't have enough income to service the mortgage.

When the bank looks over your mortgage application, they'll run it through a series of stress tests. For your property to earn enough income to fully cover the stressed mortgage costs, it would need to earn a gross yield of 10.8 per cent – assuming you're borrowing all of the money.

That is simply unachievable in today's market, where the gross yield the average Auckland City investor accepts on a $1 million property is 3.33 per cent.[41] That's why the bank will look at your income to see if you can make up for the shortfall through your salary, wages or business income.

But the amount of money that any of us earns is finite. We don't earn unlimited amounts of money, so we can't buy unlimited numbers of investment properties. This is why investors eventually start to struggle growing further.

Use a non-bank lender

So what happens when the bank starts to bite? The first strategy is to turn to non-bank lenders. These are businesses that lend money to buy residential property, but aren't banks. They don't offer credit cards, term deposits, transaction accounts or anything like a bank usually does – they just do mortgages.

Because they are smaller and focus on lending money, they tend to take a more case-by-case approach. Rather than having specific calculations that your mortgage has to pass through, they'll often make a judgement call about whether to lend the money or not. In practice this means investors are more likely to get money to invest through a non-bank lender than a traditional bank. Arguably, by following more flexible lending practices they are taking on greater risk, and so, because of that, they'll often (but not always) charge a higher interest rate for these loans.

CASE STUDY
We wouldn't have been able to invest otherwise

We were working with a pair of investors who were well into running their race. They were in their thirties and were your typical rent-vestors. While they owned four rental properties, they decided to rent instead of living in one of the properties they owned. All up they had $1.7 million worth of debt spread across their four properties, and earned $180,000 between the two of them from their salaries and wages. They wanted to borrow another $800,000 to purchase their fifth rental property.

When their adviser initially ran the numbers, all four of the major bank lenders would have approved the $800,000 mortgage. In fact, one was willing to lend up to $850,000. They had also approached a non-bank lender, who was willing to offer the investors up to $840,000.

But then the lending rules changed. The Credit Contracts and Consumer Finance Act 2003 (CCCFA) was updated and the banks changed their calculations when assessing mortgages. One bank introduced a debt-to-income ratio (DTI), and the investors needed to reapply under these new criteria. Running the investors' numbers through the new bank calculations – which are only available to advisers – showed that only one of the main banks was likely to still approve the mortgage for their fifth property.

Only the non-bank lender was still willing to lend the same amount as before: $840,000. In the end, these investors chose to go with the non-bank lender, and for that they paid a 0.1 per cent higher interest rate to get the money.

The next strategy to combat tight servicing requirements is to increase your income. You might think 'That's all well and good, how am I going to do that?', forgetting that over time your income naturally increases. Over the last 20 years, on average, median household incomes have risen by 4.12 per cent per year.[42] A combination of your income rising and rents increasing over time gradually raises the income needed to service investment property mortgages. So to some degree it can turn into a waiting game. In addition to that, you might advance in your career, or you'll get a new job and negotiate a higher salary or wages.

Having said that, this doesn't mean you have to sit around and wait. One option is to get boarders or flatmates in, both to pay down your mortgage more aggressively, which improves servicing in itself, and to increase the income you have to service other mortgages. If you got a flatmate paying you $150 a week in rent, which the bank tested as acceptable income, that could mean an extra $192,871 borrowing for a rental property.* While you may not want to continually have flatmates forever, at times they can help to nudge you over the line for an extra investment property.

Another option is to increase the number of hours you work. One investor we've recently worked with at Opes Partners will increase their hours from four days to five a week. This will increase their income and allow them to get the mortgage for an investment property approved. If they then decide to change their circumstances and go back to four days a week in the future, that is an option.

But while increasing income is an option, many investors try to decrease their fixed expenses in order to increase their servicing. Not every strategy is appropriate for every borrower, and this book does not offer personalised financial advice. However, the following are the strategies that some investors will use.

Cancel credit cards

The first is to cancel your credit cards, or reduce their limits. Even if you don't use your credit card, the bank will still test your mortgage as if it was fully maxed-out and you were making the minimum repayments. After all, once you've used the loan, you still have the ability to go on a spending spree at Kmart. A $10,000 unused credit card can limit your borrowing for investment properties by just over $89,000.

Extending mortgage terms

Next is investors extending their mortgage terms. If you have 15 years left on your mortgage, the bank will look at your mortgage payments over 15 years. If you decide instead to extend your

---

* This is based on the bank accepting $150 a week as serviceable income, a 4 per cent gross rental yield on your new property with 75 per cent rental shading, a 30-year mortgage term and a 5.8 per cent servicing-test interest rate.

mortgage term to 30 years, your tested mortgage payments will go down, allowing you to increase your potential borrowing. You can then use the Mortgage Buster strategy (see Chapter 5) to still pay the debt off over 15 years. If we applied these numbers to a $400,000 mortgage, the investor could potentially borrow an extra $292,600.

You might wonder 'How does this even work?' It works because, even though you have lowered your committed payments on paper, you can still make the same payments as you were previously, if setting up your mortgage under the Mortgage Buster strategy. What changes is that the previously committed payments become voluntary. That means you can continue to pay off your personal mortgage at the same rate, but now have more ability to borrow from the bank. Your committed payments have gone down, so your income can support more lending. This tends to work well for investors who have owned their own home for a while and have a shorter term. Lengthening the mortgage term from 28 years to 30 won't have as much impact as going from 10 years to 30.

Review KiwiSaver

Some investors who make KiwiSaver contributions above and beyond the required minimums find they can borrow more if they reduce their KiwiSaver contributions to the minimum 3 per cent requirements to receive their 3 per cent employer contribution. There are no additional tax or contribution incentives to invest above the minimums.

Because the money for KiwiSaver contributions is automatically deducted from your pay, the money never hits your bank account. For some investors this is an advantage – they don't want the temptation to spend it. However, the trade-off is that these voluntary savings aren't treated as potential income in the banks' assessments. An investor on an $80,000 income moving from a 10 per cent contribution down to 3 per cent can potentially borrow almost $138,600 more.

Just before the legal and compliance teams (rightly) jump down our neck, we have to add a warning that you have to be careful in this situation. Because if you follow this strategy you'll be stopping one type of investment in order to be able to take on more investment debt. That might not be the right financial decision based on your circumstances. And there could be a very good reason to continue paying into KiwiSaver; for instance, if your employer matches your KiwiSaver contributions up to 7.5 per cent, which sometimes happens in the aviation industry, as an example. Again we must emphasise here that we are simply explaining a range of options; we are *not* offering personal financial advice, which should always be sought from a professional adviser who has all the facts about your unique personal position to hand.

But, with the same cautionary proviso as above, it may be worth considering taking the above-minimum contributions you have been making to KiwiSaver, and instead investing them in a managed fund. This means you will be both investing at the same level as before and also getting access to extra borrowing for your property investing. Put simply, KiwiSaver hurts your servicing; other managed funds don't.

Paying off your student loan early

Another alternative is to pay off your student loan early. You might think 'Why would I ever do that since my loan is interest-free?' That is typically true, and generally many student-loan borrowers will pay down their loans as slowly as possible, since there's typically no interest to pay and inflation will slowly erode the value of the loan.

However, especially for high-income earners, your student loan can stop you from borrowing. That's because, at the time of writing, 12 per cent of any income earned over $20,200 goes towards paying down your student loan. If you are a professional earning $100,000 a year, that's $798 per month going towards student loan debt. That amount doesn't change whether your student loan is $100,000 or $5,000.

When your student loan is small it can be worth paying it off early, so that the money that was going towards your student loan can be used in the banks' test calculations. Let's say your income is $100,000 and your student loan is $5,000. Sure, you could wait to pay it off over seven months, and then reapply for the mortgage. But if you pay it off early, that could mean an additional $236,969 worth of borrowing once you run the numbers through the banks' calculators.

If you're wondering how on earth you can do this when you don't have $5,000 cash conveniently at hand, you can always opt for the Debt Destroyer strategy. (This is explained in Appendix B.) Under the Debt Destroyer, you consolidate all of your extra debts into one loan – usually your home mortgage. So in this case, you increase the size of your mortgage by $5,000 and use it to pay off your student loan. True, there will be some interest costs associated with it, but it means that the bank will assess the repayments over up to 30 years. This means the payments that the bank calculates you pay to your student loan fall from $798 per month to $29.34 per month. This frees up money in the bank's eyes and so frees up cash for more productive borrowing.

You can use the Debt Destroyer strategy for any debts you have with high monthly repayments. Personal loans, car loans, hire purchases (even if interest-free) can all be consolidated to help you borrow more. That $10,000 lounge suite you bought on 48 months interest-free terms? If you consolidated that hire purchase into your home loan that could mean extra borrowing of up to $44,400.

To be clear, we're not suggesting that you take purchases that you're planning to pay interest-free and instead pay them off with interest over the full 30 years of your mortgage. That would mean you end up paying significantly more over the longer term. But you can get the bank to assess the repayments as if it were to be over a 30-year period and then decide to pay it off over four years using the Mortgage Buster strategy. The key is to turn your committed payments into flexible, uncommitted payments, as this paints a different, more positive picture of your situation for the bank.

Am I meant to do all of these?

The purpose of this section isn't to tell you to do every single one of these things, especially if you don't need to do them right now. There is a tendency for people to say: 'That's it, I'm cancelling all my credit cards because Ed and Andrew told me to.' But if you're not trying to borrow more money right now from a bank, that could be unnecessary. You don't need to try to adjust your situation to get your mortgage application through the banks' stress tests yet. Typically, investors start to adapt their situation three months before applying for their next mortgage.

Similarly, if you are a 'slam-dunk borrower' – it's clear your application is going to sail through the bank's assessment team – you might not need any of these strategies. You're going to get approved anyway. But for those investors who are on the borderline, these are the tactics that you can consider (or, better yet, talk to a mortgage adviser about) to see what you need to do to get closer to your goal of purchasing more properties.

Even if you do need to use some of these tactics to get your lending application over the line, you don't have to do all of them. You don't have to extend your personal mortgage term, and cancel your credit cards, and pay off your student loan early, and consolidate your debts, and reduce your voluntary KiwiSaver contributions. But if your ultimate goal is to purchase another investment property and you're stuck, then you do have to do something. That could be employing some of the tactics discussed here, increasing your income, or deciding not to purchase that extra investment property.

If the maths of this all feels a bit overwhelming, remember you're not going to do all this on your own. A quality mortgage adviser should consider each of these scenarios to see whether there is a way to get the lending over the line by adapting your situation in this way. It's not about 'tricking' the bank or doing anything untoward, it's about structuring your debts and financial commitments in such a way that if the worst were to happen you could still afford all of your commitments – and this puts the bank's mind at ease.

When's the best time to invest?

Property investors will often ask us: 'When is the right time to invest in property and grow my portfolio?' Our answer is always the same: when you can. You can't control the banks' or other lenders' policies. Sometimes an email is sent on a Monday morning from a bank notifying mortgage advisers of a change in policy, and all of a sudden money can either be harder or easier to get. That is why we tend to say buy property whenever you have the ability, because your ability to access money can change quickly.

At the time of writing, the Credit Contracts and Consumer Finance Act (CCCFA), a recently updated piece of legislation, is making it harder to get lending approved from the banks. It's not the banks' fault. A new law has been created and financial institutions are responding. This demonstrates that your bank's willingness to lend will change over time. As a result of this law change it has become tougher for some people to access lending. Even when the legislation is loosened, or banks start to interpret the rules differently, it may get tougher again. Take your opportunities as they arise, because you never know when the bank might say no.

CASE STUDY
How a pandemic pushed one couple to pivot their property journey to a whole new level

Many property investors we work with are already active in the market, with a few buy-and-holds in their portfolio before we meet them. But some max-out at a few investments and aren't sure how, or where, to take the next steps to grow their portfolio.

In early 2020, Arana and Anna already owned two properties: the family home and a rental in Papamoa. They were about to settle on a second investment property in Auckland when Covid-19 hit, and the country went into its first lockdown. Not surprisingly, they were worried that buying their third property would end up being a bad decision. Not only were Arana and Anna in the trenches of family life with four young children, at the time the whole economy appeared to be on hold, and daily news articles predicted an impending property crash.

Despite this, lockdown provided an unexpected bonus in the form of time to listen to the *Property Academy Podcast*. After listening to the podcast the pair concluded that while their property strategy was probably on the right track, there was more they could be doing. The trouble was they didn't know what that was.

What did they decide to do differently in the end? They used what they had learned to drill down and identify what was holding them back. Arana and Anna discovered that, as with many investors on 'average' incomes, their first challenge was that while they had good serviceability (income), they did not have enough equity to continue investing.

To rectify this, they started by using the 'sell one, buy two' strategy. They identified that while their Papamoa rental had a lot of equity, it had a very low yield. Selling this property provided enough equity to purchase two new-build properties and pay off their personal mortgage. In addition, they began to look for properties outside of their home city of Auckland, so they could purchase a third investment property at a cheaper price. Anna states they wouldn't have looked at either of these strategies when they started out. Doing so proved to be a success, because they were able to utilise the low LVRs from the new-build properties and the low interest rates that followed. Across 2020–2021 all of their properties appreciated significantly.

Anna admits that expanding their property knowledge and getting advice challenged everything they had thought before about how to approach investment. Even with the challenges of Covid, instead of holding back and waiting to see what happened with the market and their employment, they worked with our team at Opes and continued to invest.

Over the course of a year, this couple went from three properties to five. Selling one ultimately led to buying three. The capital gains achieved on those assets, even over a very short time, has started to provide the basis for them moving closer towards crossing the finish line.

Arana and Anna made two critical changes. The first was being able to clearly see their goals by making the types of projections discussed in Chapter 8, using MyWealth Plan. These goals included:

→ **an early retirement**
→ **creating intergenerational wealth to leave their children.**

The second was getting a second pair of eyes to look at their portfolio and plan with them. This led to their being shown strategies they could use that they'd never thought of, like the 'sell one to buy two'.

Anna admits that taking the leap past one or two investments to buying more properties was a really different way to look at things, and at times hard to wrap their heads around. The much easier option would have been to just 'think about it' and take no action. Like some of our previous case studies, listening to podcasts and reading books can only get you so far: to make change you actually have to act.

RUNNING YOUR RACE

Summary

Your ability to invest in property is often constrained by the banks' willingness to lend. There are steps you can take to continue to expand your portfolio.

→ **Expand your portfolio when you can**. If the bank is willing to lend you money, it's often a good idea to take it. If you're waiting for prices to drop, the bank is likely to turn the lending tap off by the time prices start to tumble.
→ Work with a mortgage adviser to find out what is holding back your ability to borrow – whether that be **equity or serviceability**.
→ Once you know, you can use our **tactics to find a way to increase your ability to borrow**.
→ When you are ready to expand your portfolio, loop back to Chapters 9 and 10 to figure out **what you need in your portfolio and how to find the property**.

With your investment portfolio expanding, your equity will be increasing in line with the market. As that happens you'll be slowly progressing through your own race. At a certain point it will be time to start eyeing up the final stretch, transitioning into the final sprint to set yourself up to cross the finish line.

04

Crossing the finish line

Chapter 18

Strategies to retire on real estate

After putting in the hard yards to build a well-managed portfolio, you're nearly at the finish line. You may be getting close to retirement age (although not necessarily) and want to wind down and work less.

A lot of Kiwis start investing in property because they 'think it's a good thing to do'. They'll build up equity within the properties and at some point think 'What's the exit strategy?' or 'I've got all this equity, now what do I do with it?' That's what this section is about: how your property investing can now serve you. You'll get the game plan for how to take the equity you've built and turn it into cash to live on.

In the crossing the finish line section, you'll take the properties you've already purchased and begin to sell them. You'll then take the money from these sales and use it to either live off or buy properties that enable you to live off the rent. That's what creates your passive income. This stage is about transitioning from investing to grow your assets, to investing to receive an income. Let's dig into it.

The two approaches to crossing the finish line

When it comes to slowing down from work or retiring, there are two ways you can go about it. Earlier in the book we mentioned that Kiwis tend to aim for one of four things when investing in property: a comfortable retirement, passive income, wealth, or to have no money worries. The first two have tended to be the most popular.

What's not well known is that these two approaches – retirement and passive income – are actually different ways to live off your properties.

The Nest Egg strategy

Sell your assets to live a richer retirement

The first strategy – the Nest Egg strategy – is generally the more affordable of the two. You don't need as many assets for this strategy. Here, you build your assets, and then sell them to live a richer retirement. By the time you get to retirement age you've accrued a portfolio of investment properties worth, say, $1 million. Upon retirement you sell those properties, put the money into a bank account (or more likely a low-risk fund), and then gradually spend the money over your lifetime.

We've called this the Nest Egg strategy because you build your assets, then you gradually sell them and spend the proceeds. This means that your assets gradually reduce through your retirement. So when you first retire you're the wealthiest you'll ever be. You then spend that wealth to live, and your assets start to erode from that point. By the time you ascend to heaven's gates your investment assets are gone, but you will still be able to pass on your family home to your loved ones.

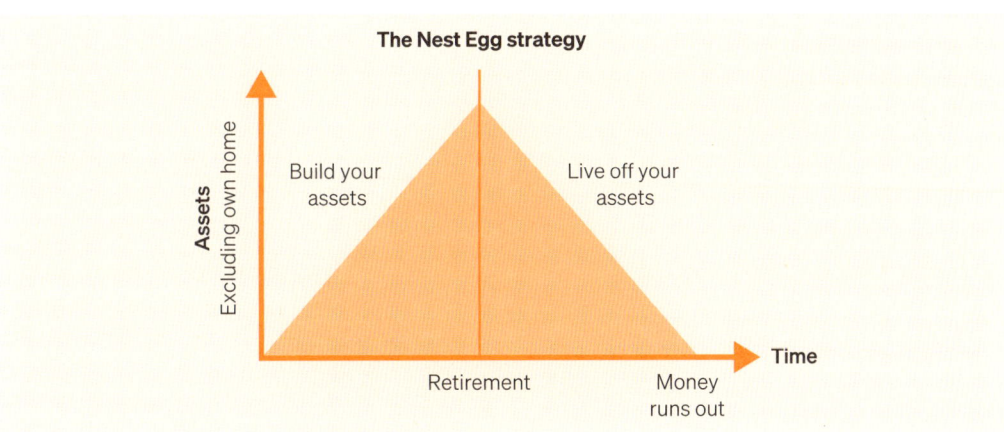

The good news with this strategy is that you don't need as many assets. The downside is that you need a best guess at how long you need your assets to serve you – how long your retirement years might stretch – so you can make sure you have enough money to retire on.

But although your assets reduce over time when using the Nest Egg strategy, you shouldn't automatically think that this is the worse approach of the two. This is actually, by far, the most common approach that the general population of New Zealand uses. In fact, when Massey University reports on how much Kiwis need to retire through their Fin-Ed centre – the gold standard for talking about retirement in New Zealand – they are using this strategy. In 2021, Massey reported that a couple wanting to live a 'choices' lifestyle in one of the main centres would need to retire with $809,000 in the bank to maintain this lifestyle until age 90.[43]

Another example of the Nest Egg strategy in practice is KiwiSaver. At 65, you get access to your funds, and you can spend them over your retirement to supplement your New Zealand Superannuation and your other savings. (Note that while 65 is the current age of eligibility, this may change over time.)

The Golden Goose strategy

Hold your assets to live on a permanent passive income

The second strategy is not as common, but it is arguably much more desirable. That's because under the Golden Goose strategy, even if you live forever you'll be fine. Instead of selling your properties and living off the money, this strategy sees you investing your funds and living off the returns. In other words, you hold on to your assets, which then produce a permanent passive income.

Compare that with the Nest Egg strategy, where your assets reduce over time. If you can build a Golden Goose, you'll not only be able to live off the returns of your assets, but the assets themselves will also stay intact – and then continue to appreciate over time. Of course property prices can go up and down from month to month. But here is the point: regardless of any fluctuations, you are retaining not spending your assets.

In property investment terms that means you build up a portfolio. You then sell your growth properties and buy higher-yield investments. You do this to get rid of your debt so you have no-to-low interest costs. Doing this while buying higher-yield properties increases your cashflow so you can live off the rental income of your properties. With this strategy you don't need to worry about how long you're going to live for; the income keeps on going even after you're gone.

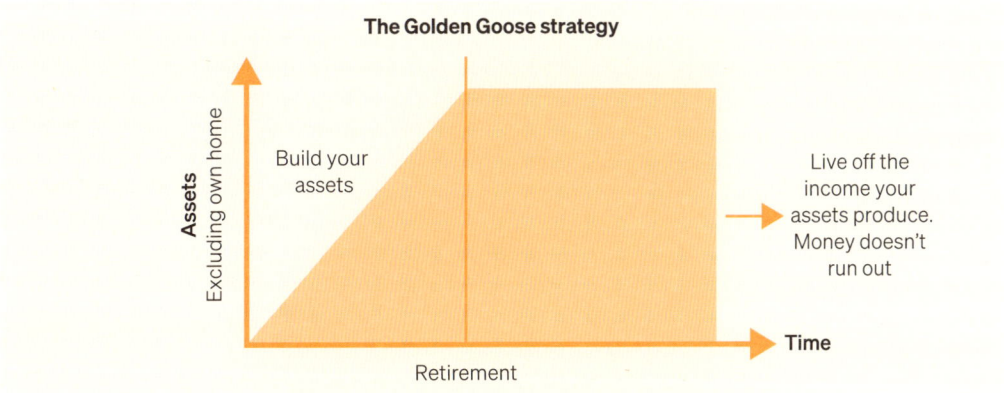

One reason investors like this strategy is that it creates intergenerational wealth, as the generators of wealth (the properties in the portfolio generating income) can be inherited, intact, by children, grandchildren or loved ones. This can make the Golden Goose strategy a good fit for parents and grandparents, because naturally people are driven to look after their families.

That said, some investors prefer SKI-ing – spending the kids' inheritance – and want to sell all their assets and enjoy the fruits of their labours while they can. No judgement here whichever way you go: just pick the strategy that works for you.

How do you calculate the level of assets you need?

First, take the annual passive income you want to live on. Then divide that number by 0.04 (i.e. 4 per cent). That will give you the level of debt-free assets you need.

To give a working example, say that you want an annual income of $100,000 in retirement. Once you divide that by 0.04, you get $2.5 million of debt-free assets. That means that if you own $2.5 million of high-yielding property, and you can pay all the operating costs – rates, insurance, maintenance and more – you can earn $100,000 every year before tax.

This is backed up by both our experience of properties in the market, and the rule of 4 per cent – a widely used rule of thumb in the investment industry, which we first introduced in Chapter 8. This rule says that if you invest in a diversified portfolio you should be able to spend 4 per cent of the value of the portfolio per year without reducing your initial capital. So if you have $1 million of assets, you should be able to spend $40,000 a year and still have $1 million left at the end of the year.

You'll see examples of the sorts of properties that can provide this on page 220.

Which strategy is better?

We've touched on this before, but let's take a closer look, and follow up with a case study. Now it might seem obvious that the Golden Goose strategy is 'better'. Well, yes and no. The *right* strategy is the one that is achievable for you. With the Nest Egg strategy you require fewer assets, and that's not just because you're living off the assets – it also comes down to tax.

Think about it this way. Let's say you want to spend $75,000 a year in retirement. If you opt for Nest Egg, you can sell some shares or property to generate that $75,000. As long as you're outside of the bright line test, you can sip the sauvignon blanc and *not* pay tax. After all, you didn't earn any income, so there's no tax to pay.

But if you take the Golden Goose strategy, you're living off the income your assets produce. This means you're earning income, so there is tax to pay. Right now, to spend $75,000 a year using this strategy, you need to earn just over $100,000 in income from your assets first. (This calculation assumes a one-person household. A couple could reduce this through the use of trusts and clever structuring; see Chapter 14.) You pay the tax and pocket the rest.

Put simply, the first game plan requires no tax be paid. The second one does. So factoring in tax, naturally you need more assets for the Golden Goose strategy than the Nest Egg.

	PROS	CONS
Nest Egg	• Requires fewer assets • Less tax to pay • Still have the family home to leave to the kids	• Need to estimate when you'll pass away • If you live longer than estimated, you'll solely live on NZ Superannuation • Less inheritance to leave behind
Golden Goose	• Don't need to estimate when you'll pass away. The money goes on forever (it's the Golden Goose) • Properties will continue to increase in value, building wealth • Creates generational wealth	• You'll pay tax on the income generated by your properties • Because of the tax implications, this strategy requires more assets

Chapter 18 Strategies to retire on real estate

CASE STUDY
Let's put some numbers around this to bring it to life

You're 45, have two kids and live in Hamilton. Between you and your partner you decide you want to spend that $75,000 a year we've just mentioned in retirement. The plan is to retire at 65 (20 years from now). Pulling up a fresh spreadsheet (or our free MyWealth Plan software, opespartners.co.nz/book), you say to your partner: 'Hey honey, we'll probably live – at a guess – to 82', the New Zealand average.[44]

If you take the Nest Egg strategy, you work out you'll need about $1.7 million (in today's dollars) in debt-free investment assets. That means assets other than your own home, and the money received after you sell your properties, pay the real estate agent and pay back the bank.

That sounds like a lot (and it is), but if you include New Zealand Superannuation in its current form, you only need $1.12 million. That's because, in today's dollars, New Zealand Superannuation will make up about $34k per annum of your $75k – for a couple living together. (Based on April 2021–March 2022 allowances.)

Let's now say you want to take the Golden Goose approach. You apply all the same details, except you don't have to worry about when you might pass on. Based on a 4 per cent net yield on your assets, you reckon you'll need $2.5 million of debt-free investment assets if you don't include New Zealand Superannuation, or $1.5 million if you do.

	NEST EGG	GOLDEN GOOSE
Post-tax income goal	$75,000	$75,000
Debt-free assets needed (excluding NZ Superannuation)	$1,695,000	$2,500,000

The Golden Goose requires 47.5% more net assets than the Nest Egg in this example.

So depending on the numbers you use, you might require 30–50 per cent more assets if you take the Golden Goose approach as opposed to the Nest Egg approach (although this is all dependent on how long you expect to live). If you think you'll live past 90, the number of assets needed starts to become comparable.

199

For the rest of this section, we're primarily going to focus on the Golden Goose strategy. That's because it's not as well known or publicised in New Zealand media, and there's a bit more to it. But, in practice, you can actually use both strategies at the same time, as you'll see in the case study on page 201.

Don't forget about inflation!

If you're a data-nerd, you'll be screaming at this book saying: 'But you haven't talked about inflation yet!' So true. You're savvy enough to have worked out that prices tend to go up over time. In 1974 the price of a litre of petrol was 12.3 cents. By August 2000 it was a $1.21.[45] Today, it is around $3 a litre. Think of it another way: 40 years ago a 50-cent ice-cream was massive. Twenty years later it might be an okay-ish size. Today that 50 cents would barely buy you the cone. The point is that 20 years ago you could buy more stuff for $100 than you can today. And 20 years from now, $100 will buy less than $100 buys today. Why does this matter? Because when you are planning for the future, you can't just think in terms of the dollar-amount income that gets you what you want today.

Take the $75,000 passive income we just talked about as an example. In 15 years, you want to be able to live on the lifestyle $75,000 could buy you today. But in 15 years, $75,000 will only buy you $55,730 worth of stuff in today's money, assuming consistent 2 per cent inflation per year. Which means if you don't factor in inflation, you could find yourself $20,000 short. So, working with the same annual 2 per cent inflation rate, to be living today's $75,000 lifestyle in 15 years, you'll actually need $100,900 income. That means you'll need more assets.

If your head is spinning a bit, and the numbers aren't quite making sense, don't worry – you don't need to build your own spreadsheet. You just need to know that's been taken care of. That's why the companion software to this book, MyWealth Plan, factors in inflation and gives you the exact numbers you need to aim for to hit your goals. You can access this for free at opespartners.co.nz/book.

For ease of reading, all the numbers in this section are adjusted for inflation (i.e. they're all in today's dollars).

When do I cross the finish line?

Most investors we work with tend to transition their portfolios as they approach retirement. At this stage, you might be looking to leave full-time work and have a change in lifestyle. However, age is not the only indicator. The time to start crossing the finish line is when you don't want to rely as much on needing to work for your income, and you have the assets to do so. For instance, you might be 40 years old and have built up sufficient assets to now be in a position where you can earn a passive income from your properties. Even though you decide to continue working, your properties provide the base income that you live on.

One investor we met was in her late thirties when she got in touch for advice around this. She was a listener of the *Property Academy Podcast*, and had built enough equity in one of her properties to comfortably sell and earn a $90,000 passive income per year. She wanted to continue working on her business, which has ups and downs and can be risky. In this case the income from her properties could act as a safety net, ensuring her a good-quality lifestyle and allowing her to weather any storms as she continued building her business.

Alternatively, you might be 65 and want to retire shortly. But if you don't have enough assets to stop working and enjoy a lifestyle you're happy with, then you'll need to continue working to build that asset base. So not everyone crossing the finish line is a retiree. And not every pensioner crosses the finish line at 65.

The maths won't be perfect

One final note. If you're a true data-nerd, you can get a bit obsessed with financial modelling and take it too far. The point of all this isn't to calculate precisely when you'll have $100,000 of passive income with mathematical perfection. That's a fool's errand. Because while the maths can get you in the right ballpark, what really matters is building enough assets to enable you to stop working and live a lifestyle you're happy with.

This is why we (surprisingly) don't advocate for trying to model everything perfectly, and figure out the exact mathematical point to transition. The returns never work out that perfectly. Markets go up and down, and never in a straight line. Instead, use the maths at the start of your journey to create a goal, and then, when it's time to transition, make a judgement call about whether you have enough assets to do it yet, informed by updated numbers. After all, investment returns do fluctuate, and unfortunately the markets don't follow the formulae in our spreadsheets.

CASE STUDY
Thinking big

We were working with an ambitious couple based in Auckland. They wanted to use the Golden Goose strategy to generate an income of $150,000 per year (a big income). If that wasn't ambitious enough, they didn't want to factor the New Zealand Superannuation into their plans. And on top of *that*, they were both 50 and wanted to retire at 60. This is thinking big. They needed just over $4.5 million worth of assets in 10 years to make it happen, adjusting for inflation.

> But although their goals were big, they weren't dreaming. They were already well on their way. By their goal date, they were forecast to have $213,000 in KiwiSaver. They also had four investment properties – one of which was mortgage-free – and they owned a large and valuable family home. So downsizing at some point played a big part in the plan.
>
> Even so, they weren't on track to have a permanent passive income starting in 10 years. They needed more time in the market for their assets to grow to the point where they would provide a passive income. So they decided to use both strategies together. They would start using the Nest Egg strategy, and then transition across once they had enough assets for their Golden Goose. This meant that once they hit 60, they'd sell their mortgage-free investment property. This would allow them to stop working and live off the proceeds until 65, when their KiwiSaver would become available. This would allow them to live for another two years at the income they desired. This all took them through to 67.
>
> The beauty of this strategy is that they then didn't need their Golden Goose to start laying until they were 67. That gave them 17 years to invest and build the assets they needed, as well as an extra seven years in their family home.
>
> Their plan is to invest in another two properties, and, even based on conservative projections, they are on track to massively overshoot their goal. That's not because they want to live off a larger income (although that surely would be welcome), but because if the market doesn't grow as projected they've got a buffer. So they're more likely to achieve their ambitions and win their race.

Although a financial adviser himself, Andrew understands why most people don't use financial advisers. Most of the time, it comes down to trust. While there's little data showing what Kiwis think of financial advisers, across the Tasman only 17 per cent of people surveyed in 2021 said financial planners have high or very high ethics, according to pollsters Roy Morgan.[46] That's down from 25 per cent in 2009.

But while trust in financial planners is on the decline, Andrew believes that a good financial adviser can have their uses. While you can use MyWealth Plan to run your numbers yourself, sometimes you need someone else who can apply a little out-of-the-box thinking and approach things more creatively, as the case study above shows. The trick is to find someone you trust and who knows their stuff.

Summary

How to transition your portfolio at the finish line – a quick summary:

- There are **two types of strategies** to use when crossing the finish line: the Nest Egg and the Golden Goose.
- If you're following the **Nest Egg strategy**, you'll sell your properties, invest the money in a low-risk fund and gradually spend the assets.
- If you follow a **Golden Goose strategy**, you'll sell your property, invest the money in high-yield properties and live off the rental income.
- **The right strategy for you is the one you can actually achieve.**

Chapter 19

Creating a passive income through property

When you're crossing the finish line, the general principle is all about yield, because the simple fact is *you can't live off capital gains*. Let's say your house goes up in value by $100,000 – great. But you can't walk into KFC and feed your family with the equity in your house. We've talked about passive income a lot already, but exactly what is it? Simply put, it's when you continue to get paid once you've set a system up. On top of that, a true passive income takes little effort to maintain, so you're no longer trading time for money. If you step away from your investments, the money still comes in.

To build a serious passive income through property, you need to nix the mortgage and have low levels of debt. That's because when you have a lot of debt, the rent comes in, you pay your rates, insurance and property management fees, and then your mortgage – after which there's often not enough left to live on.

Here's an example of why you need to get rid of debt to earn a passive income. A property with a gross yield of 6 per cent might have 2 per cent operating costs. That leaves a 4 per cent net yield before paying the mortgage. But if you borrow all the money to buy the property and the interest rate on your mortgage is 4 per cent, then that leaves you with no cash.

Let's say this property was worth $1 million and you owned it with no debt against it. The property would earn $40,000 annually before tax. It's the same property, same insurance, same property management, same tenants, but the income is substantially higher because you have less debt and more equity.

	MORTGAGE	NO MORTGAGE
Property value	$1,000,000	$1,000,000
Rent (6%)	$60,000	$60,000
Operating costs (2%)	$20,000	$20,000
Mortgage costs	$40,000	$0
Pre-tax cashflow	**$0**	**$40,000**

The traditional approach to building passive income through property

The traditional thinking in property investment circles used to be:

→ **buy 10 properties with lots of debt**
→ **wait for them all to double in value**
→ **sell half of them**
→ **use the sale proceeds to pay off the debt on your remaining properties.**

You've then got five properties mortgage-free.

These days, it's not that simple. Not just because it's much harder to buy 10 properties, or because the tax rulebook has changed. But because the maths of it doesn't work like this anymore.

Here's the scenario. Fifteen years ago, you bought four properties all at once for $500,000 each. You borrowed all of the money from the bank to do it, and so had $2 million of debt. Over 15 years the properties doubled in value. Your portfolio is now worth $4 million. And since you've stuck with interest-only mortgages, you'll still have $2 million worth of debt. That means you've got $2 million of equity – congrats, you're a property millionaire.

The traditional strategy calls for selling off the first two and paying off the mortgage on the last two. So you sell one of your $1 million properties. You use $500,000 of the money to pay back the mortgage on that property. Then you use the other $500,000, to pay off the mortgage on one of the other properties, ignoring real estate agent fees here. Then you do it all again with the other two properties.

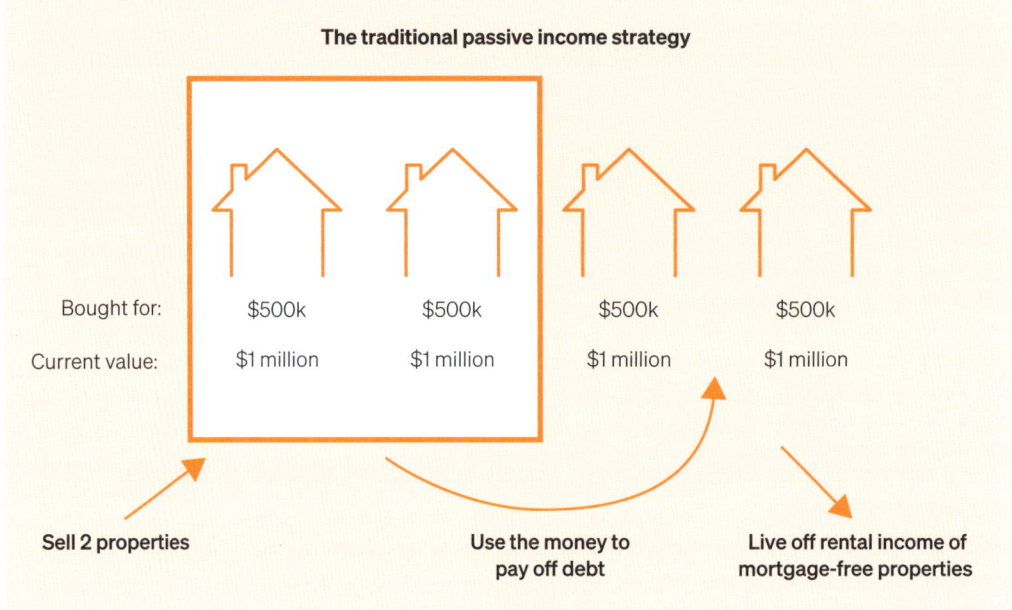

You now have two properties, each worth $1 million with no mortgages. This means you've got total equity of $2 million. The question then becomes: What sort of passive income can we achieve from these properties?

Right now you can get about a 4 per cent gross yield on a standard growth-focused rental property – the sort you needed to buy to use this strategy. That's $40,000 a year in rent per property. Sounds pretty good, right? But you also need to remember that you'll still need to pay for your rates, insurance and maintenance. So you might account for $10,000 of expenses per property. Looking at the portfolio: you've got $80,000 worth of income coming in, and $20,000 worth of expenses. That's $60,000 of passive income for life.

CASHFLOW FOR A GROWTH PROPERTY	
Property value	$1,000,000
Rent	$40,000
Operating costs	$10,000
Mortgage costs	$0
Pre-tax cashflow	**$30,000**

You might be thinking, 'This is great! What's wrong with the traditional approach?' Well, while $60,000 might sound like a pretty good passive income (and it is), you're not living the lifestyle you could be.

This is where yield properties play their part. Rather than selling off two properties to pay down debt, the Wealth Plan way is to sell all four properties – over time – and recycle that equity into high-yield properties. Here's the difference it makes.

Let's say you've sold down your four properties, you've paid off the debt and you have $2 million of equity. You decide to purchase a room-by-room rental in Hamilton and a dual-key apartment in Wellington. The gross yield on these properties is 6 per cent each. This means that together they bring in $120,000 a year in rent, rather than the $80,000 earned in the first scenario.

But of course, running a rental property isn't free. So you need to factor in operating costs. These are often higher for yield properties, because they tend to come with body corporates and higher property management fees. So you allocate $12,500 per property. You're now left with $95,000 in income per year.

CASHFLOW FOR A YIELD PROPERTY	
Property value	$1,000,000
Rent	$60,000
Operating costs	$12,500
Mortgage costs	$0
Pre-tax cashflow	**$47,500**

The only thing that has changed is the properties you have chosen to invest in, yet your passive income has shot up from $60,000 to $95,000. That's a massive $35,000 difference. Just changing property type nets 58 per cent more cash.

While accumulating growth properties sets the foundation to a successful finishing line stage, transitioning later to higher-yield properties makes it happen in practice.

Property vs other investments to create passive income

Of course, property is not the only type of asset you can use to build a passive income. You can use term deposits or funds to produce an income as well. However, there are some key benefits to real estate. First, the income is more stable. Your tenant has agreed to pay a set amount of rent per week. You know what it is, and it rarely changes. Term deposits are stable, too, but the returns of funds and dividends from shares will be variable depending on how the companies and the economy are doing.

Another difference is in how often you get paid. Depending on your term deposit, you might be paid monthly, but any dividends or returns from funds are likely to be paid out only two to four times per year. With property you'll most often get paid out by your property manager twice a month. This frequency of cashflow is often useful for people wanting a regular income.

Finally, there are no fund management fees. If you have $2 million invested in property you'll pay your operating costs and that's it. Put the same amount of money in a fund and you'll pay 0.5 per cent to 1.0 per cent of that $2 million in fees. That's $10,000–$20,000 a year. That means that your fund manager has to produce a high rate of return to justify the same income a property could earn. And as well as the 4 per cent net yield, even high-yield properties tend to grow in value, albeit at a slower rate, e.g. 3.5 per cent.[*]

But that doesn't mean that property is bullet-proof. There are drawbacks that you'll need to keep in mind:

› **Diversification: If you're purchasing a couple of yield properties with little debt, you might only end up buying one or two.** That means your passive income is based off only a few properties. Whereas if you invest in a fund, your money may be used to buy shares in multiple companies and projects, providing greater diversification.

→ **High start-up costs: It won't surprise you that properties cost a lot of money to buy.** If you have $500,000 and a yield property is $1 million, then you might need to invest in an asset

---

[*] The rate we use in internal Opes Partners financial modelling.

that has a lower entry price, like a fund, or take on debt which can diminish the cash the asset produces.

→ **Liquidation:** It takes time to sell a property and costs money to liquidate, as we'll get into in the next chapter. This means that if you need the money quickly, you may run into trouble.

Summary

When you transition over to wanting to build a passive income from property, keep the following in mind:

→ **To build a serious passive income through property you need to nix the mortgages, and get your debt low.**
→ **This is where you transition your portfolio from high-growth properties to high-yield properties.**
→ **Aim for yield properties that have a 5.5–6 per cent gross yield and a 4 per cent net yield – this means that for every $1 million invested, you'll earn $40,000 in passive income.**

In the next chapter, you'll progress to **Step 6: Sell your properties**. You'll learn which properties to look out for and how to structure them to provide a passive income.

Chapter 20

Selling to unlock the equity in your portfolio

To transition into the crossing the finish line stage, you'll need to start selling your growth-focused properties. In this chapter you'll learn when to sell and how to attract a premium price. The principles talked about in this chapter can be used at any point of your property investment journey, and apply when selling your own home, too. So even if you find yourself needing to sell a property while you're in the starting blocks, this chapter is still relevant.

While you're transitioning from running the race to crossing the finish line, you should allocate around five years to sell all your growth properties and replace them with yield properties. That's because you want to sell at the right time and have enough time to spread out your purchases.

How much will I get for my property?

It goes without saying that when you sell your investment properties, you want to get a good price. And the price you get is going to depend on what your property is and the market at the time.

Most property investors forget about, or at least underestimate, the cost of selling property. Immediately, you're probably thinking about real estate agent fees. But it costs more than just paying the agent. There are legal fees, home-staging fees, renovation costs (potentially), advertising costs (definitely), break fees and, if you're not careful, tax too.

All of these costs mean that you don't simply walk away with the difference between your property's price and your mortgage. Instead, you should budget for 5 per cent of your property's value being chewed up by sales costs.

If you sell your property for $1 million and your mortgage is $600,000, you're not going to walk away with $400,000. Instead, you're more likely to walk away with $350,000, with $50,000 going towards sale costs.

Net sale proceeds = Sale price × 95 per cent

When you're thinking about how many assets you'll need to meet your goals, you need to factor in these sales costs to make sure you're not left short. With this factored in, you then need to choose the right time to sell your property.

Choose the right time to sell

More important than finding the right agent is deciding when's the right time to sell. There are two aspects you want to consider: the right time to sell *for your portfolio*, and then the right time to sell *for the market*.

The right time for your portfolio

Although selling your property comes with costs, some of these costs can be avoided. The most obvious one is tax. Let's say you're selling an investment property with a 10-year bright line test, but you've only owned it for nine years. If you sell straight away you'll pay tax on your capital gains, which could be tax of hundreds of thousands of dollars. In that case, it makes sense to wait a few months, get outside of the bright line test, and not pay tax.

The next cost investors need to think about when selling is break fees. This is where you have a contract with the bank to continue borrowing money off them, and break the contract. If two years ago you fixed your mortgage interest rate for five years, you still have to pay the bank for the next three years. If you sell the property and repay the mortgage, there *may be* break fees. The 'may be' depends on whether interest rates have moved up or down.

If interest rates have moved down, you're more likely to have to pay the bank money to break your contract. If rates have moved up since, there may not be a break fee at all. Your mortgage adviser will tell you how much that might be. If it is considerable (e.g. $10,000+), you may decide to hold off selling immediately.

So if you are thinking of selling, it's best to pick up the phone and call your accountant and mortgage adviser. They'll tell you whether you'll need to pay tax, or break fees, or both. Depending on your situation, you may also need to have a conversation with your adviser on moving your mortgages around before selling (read the cautionary tale at the end of this chapter).

After deciding when it's the right time for your portfolio to sell your property, it's time to start thinking about the right time to sell in the market.

The right time in the market

Investors often think they should sell their properties in a hot market when prices are booming. We disagree. You ideally want to sell your properties in a cooler 'buyer's market'. Why's that? Well take a look at this graph of Auckland property prices since the REINZ records began in 1992.

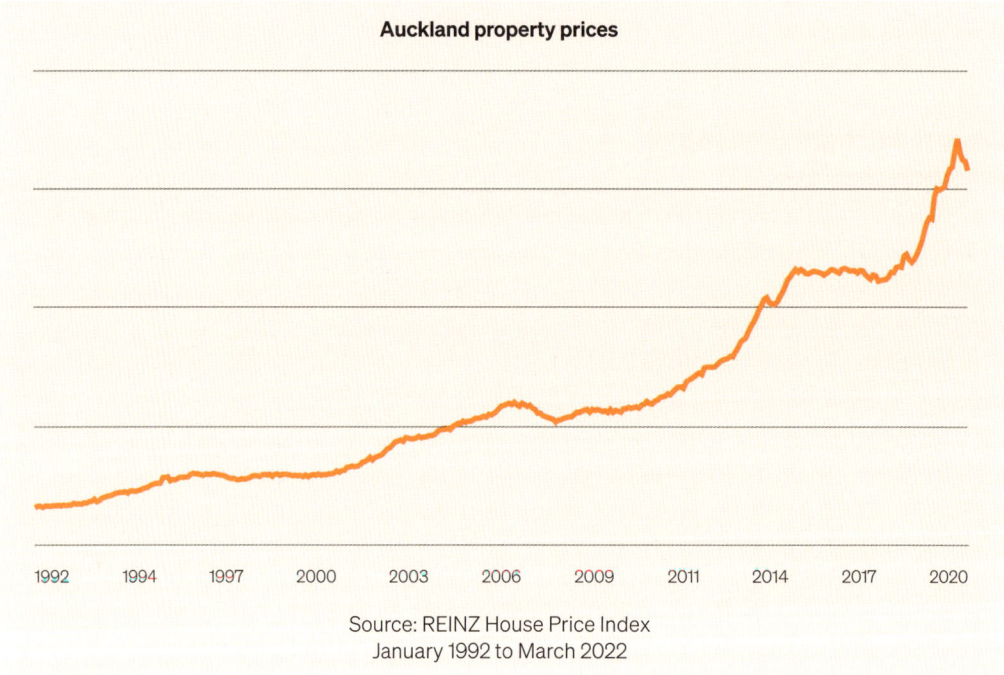

Source: REINZ House Price Index
January 1992 to March 2022

In 2014 house prices were rising rapidly and it was easy to identify that it was a hot market. But it actually wasn't a good time to sell. Had you held on until 2017, where the market had cooled and prices were on the decline, you would have sold for an average of $180,000 more.

The trouble with selling in a hot market is that you don't know whether it's going to peter out or keep going up. That creates the risk that you sell too early and miss out on some of that capital gain. If you sell in a market that has recently cooled, you can be pretty sure that you're not going to miss out on any short-term capital gains. Sure, you might miss the very peak of the market, but you'll often get pretty close.

When property markets cool, prices tend to stay the same or drop only slightly. Selling in a cool market means you can be pretty sure that you've captured all of the growth in property prices and that they're not going up anytime soon.

The drawback of this is that it takes longer to sell a property when buyers are harder to find and properties more available. But you'll often get a better price than if you sold too early.

It takes three to six months to spot the trend. So if you see median house prices in your area staying the same for six months, it could be a sign that the market has cooled and that you've captured all the growth. There are lots of sources for graphs you can use to spot this trend, and we have the latest, constantly updated, on our website (opespartners.co.nz).

One other strategy investors use to time the market is staggering their sales. Instead of selling all your properties at once, you might sell one this year, one next year, and another the year after. This guards against prices changing quickly. Because no one has the ability to perfectly predict property prices, spreading them out spreads your risk of prices lurching up or down. This is why we recommend allowing up to five years to transition across the finish line.

Renovating to sell

Once you decide the time is right to sell, it's time to prepare your property for market. Unsurprisingly, it's generally better to spruce up the place before taking the marketing photos, rather than selling as is.

For instance, when you first bought your properties, you might have purchased them brand-new and off the plans. But by the time it comes to selling them – 10 to 20 years later – they probably need some TLC. If this is the case, it's best to spend a bit of money to tidy them up before you sell. Otherwise, some other investor will come along, buy them off you on the cheap, and then reap the rewards from renovating.

This doesn't necessarily mean pouring tens of thousands in if it's not needed. At this point you can use all of the six Cashflow Hacking steps discussed in Chapter 6, but there are also some more specific tactics you can use to ensure that your property is sale-ready.

Simple renovations

→ **Paint the front step.** When potential buyers come to your property the first thing they will do is bend down to take off their shoes. Their first impression will literally be of your front doorstep,

whether they realise it or not. Painting, staining or scrubbing the entrance will only take you an hour or two and can greatly improve that first impression.
- **Use Bar Keeper's Friend, a cleaning product, to make stainless steel sinks and shower glass look much closer to new.** If you can get the soap scum off the shower glass and basins, the perception of the property will be greatly improved.
- **Replace the rubber strip at the bottom of your shower door, which can discolour and go mouldy over time.** This is the kind of small giveaway that may make your property feel grimy and unloved.
- **Make sure light switches and door knobs are cleaned or replaced.** These small finishings often come in and out of fashion quickly, so can date a property. However, they are cheap to update.
- **Waterblast the front path and/or drive** to get rid of slippery moss and sooty black build-up.
- **Consider hiring a company to complete an external wash of your home, which may cost as little as $350.** Goodbye pollen, road dirt and spiderwebs.

Together, these small actions make a big difference. Plus they are cost-effective, with many requiring just a tin (or two) of elbow grease. A small investment of time, or money if you'd prefer to pay a handyman, can equal a significant pay-off.

After the must-dos, the next best place to spend time and money is on the floors and walls. You might decide to give your property an internal paint job or replace the carpet, that's #5 and #6 from the Cashflow Hacking steps. The reason this has such a big impact on your final sale price is two-fold. First, worn or stained carpet is one of the things that can really turn buyers off. But secondly, buyers often aren't as educated as investors about what home maintenance actually costs. From our experience, a home buyer will generally overestimate what it costs to replace carpet by two- or three-fold (perhaps partly for the inconvenience of doing it). They then factor this in and make a lower offer. A buyer might offer you $10,000 less if the carpet needs replacing. But, in reality, for a three-bedroom home it may cost only $3,500 to $4,000 to recarpet.

So don't skimp on the spruce-up. To put it another way, you wouldn't take your old car with bald tyres and a clapped-out gearbox to the dealers, and expect top dollar as a trade-in. Don't do it with your home either.

Vacant possession

To do all of this, it is best to sell your property with vacant possession. That means selling your property without the tenants. You give them notice, and once they've moved out you can start renovating the property and preparing it for sale.

While some investors might baulk at the prospect of not earning rent while the property is marketed and sold, it can actually cost them $10,000 to $30,000 in the sale price if the property is sold with a tenant. That's because:

- **The majority of tenants don't care as much about the home sale as you do.** So the property is very unlikely to be presented as you would like it during open homes and inspections.
- **Open homes and marketing can be really disruptive to tenants' lives, so you can't expect a tenanted property to be perfectly staged.**
- **If the property is sold with a tenant you will struggle to sell to owner-occupiers.** That's because an owner-occupier will need to settle the property as an investment, and then give the tenants notice, if they are not on a fixed term. That means the soon-to-be owner-occupiers will need to come up with a 40 per cent deposit, rather than the 20 per cent deposit they would need without the tenant. So you limit your market when you sell with a tenant, and often get a lower price than you otherwise could.

To do all of this, you give your tenants notice (90 days if on a periodic tenancy) of your intention to sell the property, and ask them to find a new property to rent. That means you can conduct the renovations without disturbing them. It has the added benefit of not having to trouble them when conducting open homes, or relying on them to keep the place clean.

Home-staging

This leads us to our fifth and final step of selling a property: home-staging. By the time you come to sell your property, your tenants will have moved out, which means there'll be no furniture in the place. You cannot sell an empty house for top dollar.

Great staging can add a return on investment four to five times what it costs, and will help sell the property more quickly. For a three-bedroom home this may only cost around $2,000 (including GST) over a four-week sales period. This means you can often sell the property for $8,000 to $10,000 more than if you didn't stage the property.

Some staging companies will even do partial staging so you can utilise some of your own furniture, if you're selling your own house. You want your property to look like it could be in a magazine. Although prospective purchasers aren't buying the furniture, the first thing they'll look at is the pristine white linen on the bed or the modern, streamlined sofa in the photos. This all helps the buyers imagine themselves living there. Staging helps buyers fall in love with the space . . . and then be willing to pay top dollar for it.

Split-banking

We mentioned earlier that when you go to sell a property you should have a conversation with your mortgage adviser about moving your mortgage around. Here's a cautionary tale of why that's important.

CASE STUDY
Use Split-banking to protect your sales proceeds

I had a couple of Wellington-based investors I was working with who had just retired. They'd invested in property for years and had a portfolio of four investment properties. This couple were in a great position and all of the properties were quietly paying for themselves. They decided they were going to take the Nest Egg strategy, where they sell a property and spend the equity, rather than investing it in a high-yield property. So they sold one, the theory being that with the proceeds of that sale – along with their KiwiSaver – they'd be able to live extremely well for the next decade.

But this was in the days just after the Responsible Lending Code was first introduced. So what did the banks do when the money hit this couple's account? They did a credit assessment to see whether the couple could afford their other investment mortgages. Under the bank's calculations, they couldn't afford their mortgages through their income alone, since they were now pensioners. It didn't matter that the couple had hundreds of thousands of dollars sitting in their bank account that they could use to pay the mortgages for years to come if interest rates rose. And it didn't matter that the properties were cashflow-positive. The bank said no because their pension – their sole source of income – couldn't cover the mortgages under the bank's test conditions.

So without asking, they took the couple's savings, their KiwiSaver and the money from the sale of the house, and paid down debt against the investment properties. For good measure the bank cancelled their credit cards, too. Three days before Christmas. Ho bloody ho.

Now, if the couple was to protect themselves using the Split-banking strategy, what could they have done? Before retiring, the couple could have moved the mortgage on the property – the one they wanted to sell – to another bank. Since they still would have been working, it would have been okay. They could then sell the property once retired, pay off the mortgage to the second bank – and then keep the funds in a separate account. No credit reassessment during retirement. No cancelled credit cards. No crummy Christmas.

What's the moral of the story? Use Split-banking (multiple banks), especially when it comes to planning the transition of your portfolio. Also, keep an eye on new bank regulations

> and codes as they get introduced. And this is *definitely* where you want to work with a good mortgage adviser to talk about how to safely sell properties at this stage of your journey.
>
> You don't want the bank controlling where that money goes (i.e. to other investments or mortgages). Instead, you want to be able to decide *yourself* where and how to use the proceeds to fund your future retirement and investments. There is more on the exact way to use the Split-banking strategy in Appendix B.

Summary

If you follow all the steps listed here when selling your property, you could find yourself selling it for $50,000 to $100,000 more than you would have otherwise. That's why it's important to do the following:

- Factor in 5 per cent of the property's value when calculating the **cost to sell your property**.
- Time the sale of your property to **avoid paying tax or break fees**.
- Time the sale of your property to **sell in a cooler market**, rather than a hot market, to capture as much of the market-made capital growth as possible.
- Conduct **renovations before selling** to increase the property's value.
- Remember that you'll generally achieve a higher price if you **sell with vacant possession** (i.e. no tenants), and with **the property staged**.

Once you've sold your properties, it's time to find crossing the finish line properties. This is the time to go shopping again, looking for high-yielding properties that will help you achieve a passive income.

Chapter 21

How to find 'crossing the finish line' properties

With some of your growth properties sold, it's time to hunt for properties that earn a higher yield. At this point the sorts of properties you look at will be different to those you invested in previously. You're unlikely to be buying a standalone house, a townhouse or even a standard apartment. In this chapter, you're going to learn the five principles of high-yielding properties, along with which types of properties fit these principles and the sorts of yields to aim for.

Five principles of high-yield properties

Just as we have the eight principles of capital growth, there are five principles for finding higher-yield properties. These are indicators that we have uncovered both by investing in property and scrutinising the data. These inform the sorts of properties that you'll invest in to earn your passive income.

Multi-income

Properties that have multiple income streams tend to earn higher yields than equivalent properties that only have one. For instance, a two-bedroom apartment will typically have a lower rental yield than that of a dual-key apartment, which has a studio and a one-bedroom property. Same number of bedrooms, similar purchase price, but a much higher yield with the multi-income. Examples of these include dual-key apartments and room-by-room rentals, which you'll learn more about in a moment.

More-affordable properties

Cheaper properties tend to have higher yields than properties that are more expensive. As part of our internal research at Opes Partners, we scraped data from TradeMe and OneRoof to get an understanding of the yields that property investors are accepting in today's market. We looked at all of the properties available for rent on TradeMe, and then took their valuations on OneRoof to get an indication of the yields real investors find acceptable.

In every city the trend was clear. The cheaper the property, the higher the gross yield. The more expensive the property, the lower the gross yield. The exact reason for this is up for debate. But it seems reasonable to think that if you can afford to rent a really expensive place, you're more likely to buy a home instead. There's not a lot of demand for high-end rentals, so the yield is relatively low. On the other hand, if your income dictates that you can only afford to rent the most affordable properties, then you're probably not going to be able to purchase your own home. Because of that, there's lots of demand for these sorts of properties. So the yields are higher.

Inner-city or close to amenities

Properties that are either inner-city or closer to amenities like hospitals and universities tend to have a higher yield than those that aren't as close. That's because these areas are employment hubs. There are lots of people who want to live closer to work or where they study, and so will rent nearby. For instance, when you look at a heat map of Auckland suburbs by highest yield, you can see that the suburbs right in the middle of town tend to have higher yields than those only five minutes further away.

To be fair, the type of properties that tend to be in the middle of the city are also primarily apartments, and, as you'll see with the next principle, apartments tend to get higher yields.

Apartments

Because apartments are cheaper and tend to be located in higher-density areas in the inner city or around universities and hospitals, this property type also tends to be higher-yielding. Because many apartments can be built on top of a smaller piece of land, the cost of that land is spread over multiple dwellings. This means that a three-bedroom apartment is cheaper to build and purchase than the equivalent three-bedroom house built in the same area.

From our experience, the first things tenants look for is location and the number of bedrooms needed to house their family. A big back yard or renting a standalone house is secondary. That means that apartments can provide what a tenant needs – e.g. three bedrooms in the right area – more cheaply than another type of property. So apartments tend to have higher yields. However, it's important to note that this is not always the case, as we see in the next principle.

Appropriate specs
The final principle of higher-yielding properties is the specification – also known as 'the specs'. That is a fancy industry term for how nice the place is. If you've got marble benchtops, the latest expensive lighting fixtures, and plush, high-end carpet, your property is likely to be more valuable, but it is not necessarily going to achieve the same yield. Sure it might have a higher rent, but not necessarily enough to justify the cost of the high-end fit-out.

For example, you might buy a $1 million property that rents for $40,000 a year ($770 a week) – a 4 per cent gross yield. If you ask the developer to up-spec the property and make it nicer, you might pay an extra $100,000, and for that the tenants are willing to pay an extra $50 a week. You might think 'great, extra money'. But you're spending an extra $100,000 and earning $2,600 a year more in rent. That's a 2.6 per cent gross yield on your extra spend. So you've spent more money, made the place nicer, but for the extra spend you didn't maintain your yield. In fact, your total yield fell to 3.87 per cent.

The point isn't that you should insist that your properties are as grubby as possible. More that you don't need to go overboard in up-speccing everything. Ideally you want to provide a property that has an appropriate level of carpets, curtains and other fittings, that the tenant is actually going to pay for. If you really think these are going to add value to the property when it comes time to sell, add them in just before going to market. That way they'll be brand-new when potential buyers walk through the door.

Properties that meet the five principles of high yield

With these five principles of yield in place, it's time to look at what sort of properties tend to fit with these five principles.

Dual-key apartments
Dual-key apartments are a relatively new style of investment available in New Zealand, but one which is popular in Asia. They have two apartments on the same title, which means they are

legally one property. But they are completely separate, apart from a shared entranceway, and can be rented to separate households and under separate tenancy agreements.

You might have a two-bedroom apartment that has a separate studio or small one-bedroom attached. The key is that both are self-contained. These two units are often rented separately. So you have two sources of income in a relatively compact footprint, which maximises your rental yield. The gross yield you are able to achieve on a dual-key can range between 5 per cent and 8 per cent, depending on where it is in the country and the purchase price. The following case study provides an example of how the numbers can stack up.

> **CASE STUDY**
> ### Ellerslie apartments, Auckland
> At Opes Partners, our property investment company, we found a set of new-build dual-key apartments being built in Ellerslie, Auckland. The most affordable dual-key apartment was $915,000. This comprised a one-bedroom apartment and a studio. At the time of sale, the rent was expected to be $515 for the one-bedroom and $480 for the studio. That's $995 of income per week – a 5.7 per cent gross yield.
>
> To buy a similar one-bedroom apartment and studio separately (i.e. not dual-key) in the same building would cost $1.15 million. So the dual-key apartment was $235,000 cheaper to buy, but would attract similar rent to the two units bought separately. With the rent roughly the same (but the purchase price lower), the gross yield on the dual-key was 5.7 per cent, versus 4.6 per cent if you'd bought the two properties separately.

If this is the first time you're learning about dual-keys, you might think they're an odd type of housing. But there are genuine reasons why they're becoming popular. This is worth knowing because if you're going to buy one, you need to know that there is a resale market, so you can sell the property if you ever need to.

Dual-keys were initially built to avoid the tax man. In Australia or Singapore, buyers pay stamp duty on every property purchase. But since dual-key apartments are legally the same property, purchasers could buy two apartments and only pay one lot of stamp duty. Even though we don't have stamp duty in the Shaky Isles, the same logic applies. It's cheaper to buy dual-keys than to buy two units separately, so the yields are often healthy, which makes them attractive to investors.

They also have a market among home buyers who want a home and an income. A single person might buy a dual-key apartment and choose to live in the studio. They can then rent the adjoining apartment and use the rent from the tenant to pay the mortgage. That means the home buyer can live 'rent-free' in the studio.

These types of apartments also have a place for our aging population. For instance, one elderly lady purchased a dual-key because she needed a full-time carer. She lived in the apartment, and when she needed a nurse to look after her, the nurse could live separately in the studio. And as multi-generational living becomes more popular, it's fair to say that dual-keys will become more accepted and the resale market will continue to grow.

CASE STUDY

Dixon Street Apartments, Central Wellington

A friend of mine signed a contract for an 'off-the-plan' dual-key apartment in Wellington for $525,000 through Opes Partners in March 2017. Unfortunately, there were big delays, and the project took an extra two years to finish. But by the time the development was completed, the value had ballooned. It was now worth around $840,000 – a 60 per cent ($315,000) increase over just four years and two months. While that is an astonishing amount of growth, bear in mind that this was 20 per cent slower than the surrounding Wellington market. After all, this is a yield property, not a growth property.[47]

But the big story here is the rental income and yield. When the apartments were first advertised before construction, the rental income was estimated at around $650 per week, total. By the time they were finished, they were renting for between $1,000 and $1,200 per week. That's a 7.4 per cent gross yield.

In this case, my friend has chosen the strategy where they will live in the studio and use the rental income from the other apartment to pay the mortgage. This is how they will burst out of the starting blocks.

Room-by-room rentals, student accommodation and boarding houses

Another type of high-yield investment worth considering at this stage is a room-by-room rental. This is where you lease one property to multiple tenants. Any property with two bedrooms or more can be rented room by room to gain a higher yield. However, in this situation we're talking about purpose-built room-by-room rentals that are specifically configured for a high yield. For instance, every room within a purpose-built room-by-room rental might have its own ensuite and a kitchenette. The bedroom may be generously-sized, while the common living spaces such as kitchens and lounges are relatively small.

These sorts of properties often appeal to mature students, locum doctors, or similar; people who want a satellite base without the hassles of a whole house or taking on a full tenancy.

One of the investors we worked with purchased a property for $729,000. The property contained four bedrooms, and each room was its own self-contained studio, which could be rented out for $280 per week. That meant the property could earn up to $1,120 per week – an 8 per cent gross yield.

While boarding houses are far less common for your small-sized investor – because they're more expensive – they fit in the yield category so are worth a mention. These are essentially large room-by-room rentals. But, while rented by the room, they often have more of a hostel-type vibe. These tend to provide a very high yield but may suffer from negative sentiment, with many targeted at lower-income tenants or used as student accommodation.

Because boarding houses tend to be larger, they're often treated as commercial investments. That means they'll require larger deposits, and you'll pay higher interest rates and insurance. While all that may sound costly, there is an upside. Because boarding houses are treated as commercial properties, their interest costs are tax-deductible. That means they don't incur the additional taxes that have recently been introduced for other landlords. If you have any mortgage on your boarding house, there are clear tax incentives.

What yield should I be aiming for?

When you are hunting for properties that will earn you a passive income, you must be laser-focused on yield. We aim for a 4 per cent net yield. That means that after you have paid all your operating costs – property management, insurances, rates and more – the property earns you 4 per cent of its asset value. Put simply, if you have $1 million of assets, they should earn you $40,000 after costs and before tax, assuming you have no mortgage. To make this happen you need to be aiming for a property with a gross yield of 5.5–6 per cent, to cover the costs and earn the income.

But a word of warning: you must focus on the money you get *after* paying costs. Not the gross yield overall. Even a small change in net yield will significantly impact your passive income.

Let's say you want a passive income of $80,000 and you have built investable assets of $2 million. You then look at two types of properties.

The first is a $1 million property in an older building. It rents for $60,000 a year, a 6 per cent gross yield. The second property is a new-build apartment in a new hotel complex that also costs $1 million. However, this property only rents for $55,000 a year. That's a 5.5 per cent gross yield.

You might think this is a no-brainer. Go for the older property because the gross yield is higher. That means more passive income, right? Well, that depends on how much the property costs to run. If the older property has a significantly higher body corporate because there is essential maintenance that needs to be undertaken, the older property might have total costs of $25,000 a year. That's a 3.5 per cent net yield. If the newer property has only $15,000 worth of costs, then you as the investor net $40,000 a year in pre-tax profit. That's a 4 per cent net yield.

NEW BUILDS VS EXISTING	EXISTING PROPERTY	NEW BUILD
Value	$1,000,000	$1,000,000
Annual rent	$60,000	$55,000
Operating expenses	$25,000	$15,000
Pre-tax profit	$35,000	$40,000
Net yield	**3.5 per cent**	**4 per cent**

If you invested all your money in the first type of property, you'd end up with $70,000 in passive income. If you invested all of your money in the second type of property, you'd be living on $80,000 worth of passive income.

The point isn't to only invest in new-build apartments. The point is that you need to look very carefully at the expenses when evaluating higher-yield properties. That means triple-checking all of the figures you put into your budget.

This is particularly important around body corporate fees. Don't just take the real estate agent's word for it. Check what the cost is, and whether this is expected to increase over the next 10 years. You will find this information in the body corporate minutes, which you can request when purchasing an older apartment. When looking at these properties, you can use the Return on Investment spreadsheet to ensure you include all the different types of expenses, and to help you easily see the net yield.

Summary

Now that you've sold down your properties, it is time to look for properties that will earn an income:

- Aim for a **4 per cent net yield**. That is: after you have paid all your costs, aim to get a 4 per cent cash return on your assets. That means a $1 million property should earn you $40,000 after expenses and before tax (as long as you have no mortgage).
- The sorts of properties that will earn this return are **multi-income properties**, rather than single family dwellings.
- **Dual-key apartments and room-by-room rentals** are both higher-income properties to consider. If you have enough assets, you might also consider a boarding house.

Once you have your high-income properties, you'll still follow Step 5 (managing your properties) while continuing to live on the income. You will also have reached **Step 8: Live off your income**.

With your properties now earning you a passive income, it's time to kick back and enjoy life. You've done the hard yards. You've chosen risk and investment. You've worked hard for your money. Now it's time for your money to work hard for you.

Chapter 22

What's the future of property?

Investors often message into the *Property Academy Podcast* and ask: 'What's the future of property?' So, let's consult the tea leaves, polish up the crystal ball, and figure out the future of property investment.

To look at what's coming down the line, it helps to see what's happened in the past. Let's start with a recap of the past 20 years in property.

Lessons from 20 years investing in property

Over the past 20 years, the property market has resisted many blows:

→ **Interest rates:** increased (2003–2008), decreased (2008–2021), and increased again (2021–2022).[48]
→ **The leaky homes crisis, which is still ongoing.** Some investors and homeowners have lost hundreds of thousands of dollars. Some have been made bankrupt.
→ **An economic and global financial crisis** (GFC) between 2007 and 2009.

- **The tightening of lending rules** by banks, and the introduction of the Responsible Lending Code, which has made it harder to take on more debt to invest. More recently the Credit Contracts and Consumer Finance Act 2003 (CCCFA) has been tweaked, making it harder for purchasers to borrow.
- **The Christchurch earthquakes**, which damaged half the houses in our second-largest city and unleashed a building boom.
- **Loan-to-value ratios (LVRs)** were introduced in 2014, and have changed at least seven times since then.
- **Property taxes** have changed across governments on both the left and the right. National took off depreciation in 2010 and introduced the bright line test in 2015. Labour then introduced ring-fencing legislation in 2019, lengthened the bright line test to five years, and then to 10 years in 2021. Interest-deductibility legislation has been introduced, tax norms ripped up and new rules written.
- **Foreign buyers were banned** in 2018, since they were 'clearly' the cause of high house prices.
- **Compliance costs have increased**. Healthy Homes legislation has meant that investors have had to spend a lot on heat pumps, insulation and ventilation.
- On top of this, **tenancy laws have become stricter**. It's nigh-on impossible to evict a poor-quality tenant, and it now takes longer to move them on even when you have a legitimate reason.
- As property prices have climbed, **yields have fallen**.
- And of course there was the crisis that was going to cause the property market to fall by 20 per cent – but **pushed up prices by over 41 per cent**.[49] The Covid-19 pandemic and the economic fallout that occurred every time the country got locked down.

You would have expected house prices to crash 36 times with all this going on. But in fact, at the time of writing, house prices are 4.61 times higher today than they were in 2001.[50]

Andrew has been investing in property for almost all of those past 20 years. And you know what the sad thing is? People saw all of these factors happening at different times and decided not to invest.

It's easy to see changing tenancy laws, bank lending restrictions and scary pandemics, and use them as a reason to hold off. Because when you're going through turbulent times, it can feel like it's the end of the world, and the end of property investment as we know it. But then once you come out the other side, bruised but not battered, it all seems so obvious. The history and the facts show that to be true.

What's the future of property investment?

With all of that in mind, what's going to happen to property over the next 20 years? Buckle in for a bumpy ride, because, just like over the past 20 years, things aren't going to be smooth. Following are the seven themes for what could potentially unfold.

Increasing (and decreasing) regulation

This is a bit of a given, and a trend we have seen over and over during the past two decades. Expect more regulation from the Reserve Bank and government, and expect banks to continue their cautious approach to lending money. Tenancy regulation will likely continue to get tougher.

At the same time, some regulations will soften. As the various governments come and go, each will take their turn tweaking the taxes and fiddling with the policy settings. Expect some of the more radical regulations to be eased as the centre parties vie for votes.

The property market will stagnate – property cycles will come and go

At the time of writing, property prices are down around 10 per cent from their peak, and the outlook is that they will continue falling.[51] Even if they lose another 10 per cent, New Zealand house prices will still be over 20 per cent above pre-Covid-19 levels. At some point, prices will flatten out before increasing again. They will continue to follow a predictable and familiar cycle where they increase, decrease and stagnate before moving through the cycle again.

Over the long term, prices will continue to slowly climb through a mix of general inflation and rising household incomes. This will be bolstered by factors such as population growth, immigration, changing tax settings, bank lending policies, and the sentiment of people who buy and sell properties.

The economy will contract

Recessions are inevitable. At some point there will be an economic contraction. Unemployment will increase. Some workers' incomes will decrease, and this will cause widespread alarm.

Property prices will fall. Those property investors who have saved and have taken a conservative approach to budgeting will do well. Those who have been overly gung-ho will face tough times. Some will be forced to sell. Eventually the market will recover and those who have held on will be rewarded.

Chapter 22 What's the future of property?

Younger Kiwis will lose confidence in shares and turn to property

Right now there are thousands of young Kiwis investing in shares through online platforms like Sharesies, Hatch and Stake. They have made enormous gains as stock markets have continued to rally since the GFC. In their minds they are Warren Buffett. They are not.

Many invest heavily in a few big companies and thus far have done extraordinarily well, especially after the Covid-19 pandemic drove markets to new highs. They've made money, and well done to them. But after good times will come the bad, and some of those would-be Buffetts won't have the gumption to stick it out through the tough times when their net worth halves. This will eventually drive some burnt shareholders into property.

In 20 years, news websites will still be writing headlines about a bubble

The newspapers may be gone in 20 years (or at least be well on their way out), but journalists, those on the hard-left and student unionists will still be decrying the state of the housing market and telling us it's all about to permanently crash. These will be the same people who have predicted a permanent crash every week for the past 20 years. They'll be wrong, just as they are today. Just as they were 20 years ago.

First-home buyers will continue to find a way to buy property

You wouldn't think so, but the month before we finished writing this book, first-home buyers were buying the highest proportion of properties since records started in 2005.[52] Even when property prices are at an all-time high, clever young people do what it takes to get into the property market. These are practical youngsters who – in some cases – don't care what they buy, because they see their first home as a stepping stone to their eventual 'forever home'.

Even when the newspapers, and those with a political agenda, tell them it's not possible, young Kiwis will defy the odds and make their home-ownership dreams a reality.

Those who can hang on will and will do well

In 20 years' time, there will have been ups, there will have been downs. It will be a wild ride, and those who have been able to hold on will have seen their wealth increase substantially. They'll be able to retire in comfort and will have generational wealth to pass on to their children and grandchildren. Those who have said 'Stop, I want to get off the property roller coaster' will be less well-off than they would otherwise have been.

And of course in 20 years, you'll all be back here, reading this book to see which parts we were right and wrong about.

Conclusion

This book isn't for everyone. And the tactics we've suggested won't be right for all investors. You may think 'They didn't talk about development' or 'They didn't talk about how I can subdivide properties to increase their value'. All of that has been purposefully left out.

The intention of the book isn't to give you every strategy and tactic that could be used in property investment – that's the point of our podcast. Rather, this book intends to give you a framework and pathway for how to:

- set specific financial goals, using as your baseline the goals other Kiwi investors have set
- outline the level of assets you need to achieve these goals, and then
- find the right properties at the right stage of your life to achieve what you need at the right time.

In essence, this is about how to use property throughout your lifetime to build a passive income and achieve your goals.

The strategies in this book won't be the right fit for everyone. But they can be the right path for regular people who want to take a passive approach to property, rather than being on the other end of a paint brush every weekend for the rest of their lives.

Property investment can seem daunting, but with the right know-how and information it need not be scary. To wrap things up, we'd like to go back to the five principles of the financial fast-track we talked about at the start of the book:

1. **Don't feel down about the state of your financial situation today. You are where you are.** **You need to focus on where you are going and what you'll do to get there**.
2. **Most investors have a wealth gap. There is a difference between the lifestyle they want and what they're currently on track for. To close that gap, you need to build your assets.**
3. **Saving alone is unlikely to be the best way to build wealth and assets, especially if you want a comfortable retirement. Leverageable assets, like property, can produce outsized returns**.
4. **You need to take some risks. That's the only way to get a better return than putting your money under a mattress.**
5. **Growing your wealth through property doesn't mean others have to fall behind. You can help rather than hinder other Kiwis by providing good-quality housing**.

However, the main thing you should take away from this book is that reading this book alone isn't enough. Learning is not enough. Knowledge is not enough. Thinking about it, or listening to podcasts, or attending property investment webinars and conferences . . . None of it is enough. If you actually want to grow your wealth and get the gains from property investment, you actually have to *buy a property*. Only 'doing' will build the life and lifestyle you're after.

Not long ago, Ed spoke at an Auckland Property Investors' Association event about how to choose your property investment strategy. He must have said something good, because at the end of the week he got a phone call. One of the investors wanted to come in for a chat.

This investor was clearly not just a beginner. He seemed to know quite a bit. So why was he sitting in front of Ed? It turns out this investor had spent $25,000 (+ GST) on a property coaching programme (not one of ours), where he had a property mentor for a year to help him with his strategy. The unfortunate thing? He hadn't actually bought a property during that time and was now looking for advice on what to do next.

Now this is not a beat-up on that particular property company. You never know what actually happens between investors and coaches. Sure, it could have been the property coach's fault if they didn't find a way for the investor to take action. But it could have also been the investor's fault, if he messed around and squandered the opportunity. What it *does* go to show is that an investment – whether in time or money – in education *alone* will not make one jot of difference to

CONCLUSION

your retirement or Wealth Plan. *You need to do something with it.* So that's the message. That's the great secret.

You now have the information. You've got the plan. You've got the strategies you can use. And if it feels right, then it's time to put it into action. But to complement that knowledge you might be looking for something else. Perhaps you're also looking for a little motivation. And if you're looking for that ongoing nudge, we're here for you over the long term. You can continue to get your daily dose of get-up-and-go by tuning into the *Property Academy Podcast*. Every single day we release a brand-new episode to keep you in the zone. That includes Christmas, Easter and both our birthdays.

And while the principles of this book will largely stay the same, the data will age. So you can always get the latest data on our website: opespartners.co.nz. We're committed to putting out more information and data about property investment and home ownership than any other company. You will always be able to find it for free; it's just a google away.

One final word. There will always be those who say 'Property is inaccessible' or 'Property is only for people with rich parents'. Hopefully, this book has shown you that this need not be true. And there are also those who will simply state 'It's hard'. And they are right. It is hard.

Getting started is hard. But so is leaving it until later. Achieving financial freedom is hard. And so is relying on the government for your pension. All choices are hard. They come with trade-offs and pros and cons.

But here is the best part of life: you get to choose your hard. You get to choose which path you go down, what you want to pursue, and what you're willing to give up to get what you want.

Now it might sound like we're trying to amp you up to dive head-first into icy waters or walk over hot coals. That's only half true. What we're trying to do is get you pumped to go on this property journey. It's a long journey. One that needs careful planning. One that needs commitment, investment and expertise. One that's going to take time, but through this planning can result the wealth you need to last a lifetime. This is a path to create wealth. This is a way to plan for your future. This is your Wealth Plan.

Appendices

Appendix A: Everything you need to know about getting and paying off a mortgage

When you're setting out on your property path, mortgages seem scary and confusing. Not only are they the most significant financial purchase of your life – leaving you staring down the barrel of decades of debt – but often first-time borrowers are scared to get a 'no' from the bank.

And while it seems like banks have black-and-white rules about who gets a mortgage and who doesn't, in practice there are ways to get around them – exemptions – that you may not have considered.

You'll recognise some of the content in these appendices from the rest of the book. But these appendices pull it all together in one place as a one-stop shop. So, in this first bonus appendix, you're going to learn the basics of home loans, including how to get the bank to say 'yes' more often, and then how to pay off your mortgage even faster. Once you've got these fundamentals down, you can move on to Appendix B, where you will learn our top seven strategies to master your mortgage.

The three types of mortgages

First things first: there are three types of mortgages most commonly used in New Zealand – and each has its own structure, benefits and drawbacks. These are:

→ principal and interest (also known as a 'table mortgage')
→ interest-only, and
→ revolving credit.

There are others. But these are the ones you really need to know about as a long-term 'buy-and-hold' investor or a first-home buyer.

Principal and interest mortgage

The most common type is the principal and interest (P+I) mortgage, also known as a *table mortgage*. This is where you borrow money from the bank and pay it back gradually.

What's unique about this mortgage is that as long as the interest rate stays the same, you'll pay back the same amount each week over the life of the loan. This gives you certainty about what your repayments will be.

However, what happens with your payment each week changes. The amount that goes towards paying the interest on the loan and the amount that goes towards paying back the loan itself (the principal) changes as time goes on. Let's take a look.

> **CASE STUDY**
> ### Same payment, different outcome
>
> Take a $500,000 P+I home loan at a 4 per cent interest rate. Let's say you put it over a 30-year term, with payments being made weekly. Each week you will pay $551 to the bank, and, as long as the interest rate stays at 4 per cent, this payment won't change. But as we've said, what happens with that $551 payment changes week to week.
>
> On your first payment, $385 (70 per cent) would go towards paying interest, and $166 (30 per cent) would be used for paying down what you owe to the bank. Then as you gradually pay off the loan, the bank charges you less interest, since you don't owe as much. That means more of each payment goes towards paying off the loan. So at the start, you pay down the loan very slowly. You're reducing your debt by just $166 initially. As you near the end of your loan period, however, you pay down the loan very quickly.

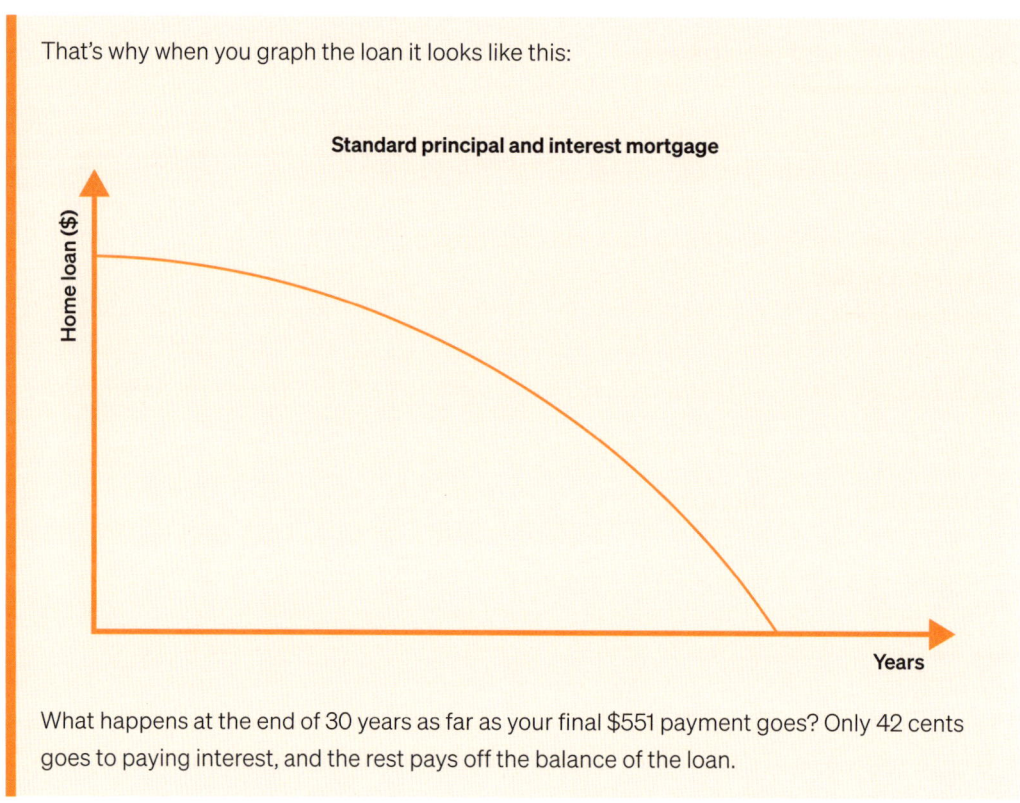

That's why when you graph the loan it looks like this:

What happens at the end of 30 years as far as your final $551 payment goes? Only 42 cents goes to paying interest, and the rest pays off the balance of the loan.

Interest-only mortgage

An interest-only (I/O) mortgage is where you don't pay down any of the debt, and only pay the bank their interest. These types of loans are popular among property investors, but are about half as common among owner-occupiers and first-home buyers. Of new loans to property investors 41 per cent go on interest-only, whereas only 21 per cent of new loans to owner-occupiers are interest-only.

Interest-only mortgages aren't approved forever. You can't get an interest-only home loan for 30 years. For property investors, the banks will let you go on interest-only for up to five years, before you automatically get switched over to a principal and interest mortgage.

Given this, it is better to think about it like an interest-only 'period' rather than another type of loan. For example, if you apply for a 30-year mortgage with a five-year interest-only period, you'll only pay interest in the first five years, and then pay the mortgage off over the remaining 25 years. (But, fear not, that doesn't mean you can't get an interest-only loan for longer. That's where the Extend and Lend strategy comes in, which you'll read about in a minute.)

Appendix A: Everything you need to know about getting and paying off a mortgage

The reason investors gravitate towards interest-only loans is two-fold. First, they improve the cashflow of a property in the near term. An investment property with a $650,000 mortgage and a 4 per cent interest rate will pay an extra $215 a week in mortgage repayments if on a principal and interest loan. So investors who go interest-only do so to lower the outgoings on their properties.

The second reason is that interest associated with some investment property mortgages is tax-deductible. That means the interest costs will help you pay less tax on your investment properties over the long term. So if you have the choice of paying down debt that is non-tax-deductible versus debt that is, you pay less tax if you get rid of debt that is *non*-tax-deductible first. This is often your own home's mortgage, and then some types of investment properties, as discussed in Chapter 14. More on the numbers of this in the Mortgage Buster strategy (see page 247).

Revolving credits

A revolving credit is a flexible loan that's on a floating interest rate. It's a bit like a big overdraft.

If you have $100,000 that you owe through a revolving credit, you might transfer $40,000 into it. You then only pay interest on the remaining $60,000. If you then want to take that $40,000 back out again, you can. Only then do you start paying interest on the full $100,000 again. You can't do any of this with a regular mortgage. If you make an extra payment against a regular mortgage, that's it. If you want to withdraw it again, you need to do a full mortgage application even though it was a voluntary payment.

That's why investors tend to use a revolving credit to make additional, voluntary repayments towards their debt. That way if you get into a tough time, you're able to take the money back out.

Revolving credits are often used as part of a mortgage set-up, as opposed to having the whole amount of a mortgage under a revolving credit. Since these types of loans are on a floating rate, they often attract more interest than if you fixed the mortgage at the one-year rate.

When you set your revolving credit limit, you can either have it as a fixed limit (e.g. $50,000) or a reducing limit. A reducing limit might start at $50,000 but then gets smaller and smaller, just like a P+I mortgage.

If you're using the Lend Before You Leap strategy, which you will learn about as part of the seven strategies to master your mortgage, we prefer to have it as a stable limit that doesn't reduce. That gives you the flexibility to decide what you want to pay off and when.

Where can I get a mortgage?

It might sound a bit weird asking 'Where do you get a home loan to buy a property?' The answer seems obvious: at the bank. But banks aren't your only options. As banks tighten how much they'll lend, and to who, new types of lenders are cropping up. These 'non-bank lenders' are businesses that lend you the money to purchase property, but don't do a whole heap of other bank things like credit cards, term deposits or eftpos cards.

It's important to know about these types of lenders because they are often willing to lend to investors who can't get approved for a mortgage by a main bank. The drawback is that they can charge higher interest rates. That said, sometimes getting a mortgage is better than getting no mortgage at all. If your mortgage adviser hasn't talked to you about non-bank options, it's worth asking about them to see whether an alternative to banks could be a good fit.

Getting a mortgage approved

There are two things you need to get a mortgage approved: you need the deposit, and you need income to be able to afford (service) the mortgage.

Let us ask you this: what's more important, equity or income? If you answered 'income', then you are correct. Obviously, you need both a deposit and income to get your mortgage approved, but income is top of the list. That's because there are ways to get a low-deposit loan, but if you don't have the money to afford the mortgage repayments in good times and bad, you won't get approved.

Let's start with deposits

The amount of deposit you need for a mortgage is primarily set by the Reserve Bank. They set the loan-to-value ratio (LVR) restrictions, which limit how much banks can lend you. Here is a quick summary of the deposit you need:

	BORROWER TYPE	DEPOSIT REQUIRED
Own home	First-home buyer	10 per cent* or 20 per cent
	Second+ home buyer	20 per cent
Investment	Existing property	40 per cent
	New-build property	20 per cent

* Subject to bank approval and buying outside of the LVR restrictions.

While the Reserve Bank says that the majority of borrowers need a 20 per cent deposit to buy their own home, in November 2021, 37 per cent of first-home buyers purchased with a deposit of less than 20 per cent. However, other owner-occupiers usually need at least a 20 per cent deposit. In the same month that over a third of first-home buyers purchased with a low deposit, only 3 per cent of other owner-occupiers accessed a low-deposit loan.

On the other hand, investors buying existing properties require at least a 40 per cent deposit, and those buying new-builds only need 20 per cent.

Is your head spinning yet? Don't worry, that's normal.

It starts to get even more complicated when you start to think about non-bank lenders. Because these lenders will lend money outside of the Reserve Bank's restrictions. At the moment, one non-bank will lend to investors purchasing existing houses with only a 20 per cent deposit. That's half the deposit required at the main banks. Another non-bank lender will lend to first-home buyers with a 5 per cent deposit, as long as they have strong income. First-home buyers who take up this option will pay more interest. But, hey, if you can afford it and this is the only way to get into your first home, it can be a good option.

Now let's turn to income and look at how a bank assesses whether you have enough.

How a bank assesses whether you can afford a mortgage

You might go to a bank's mortgage calculator on their website, plug in the numbers about how much you want to borrow and the current interest rates. You look at the repayments the bank says you'll need to make and say: 'I can afford that, surely I'll get approved.' However, a bank may not agree with you. So how do the banks assess the income side of your mortgage application?

This is where your *uncommitted monthly income* comes in. This is often shortened to just UMI, and is one of the most important concepts when it comes to home loans. In simple terms, this is the amount of money you have left over at the end of the month after paying all of your committed costs like your living expenses, your mortgage and any hire purchases you have. The bank wants to make sure that paying your mortgage won't bankrupt you, so they need to make sure that even after you take on the new mortgage you want, your UMI is above $50. (Although this is different for each bank.)

Even then, the process is not over yet. The banks will then run your application through a series of tests to answer: 'Would your UMI still be above $50 if interest rates went up or you didn't have a tenant for a while?'

SO HOW DO BANKS CALCULATE YOUR UMI?

While your mortgage adviser will run the calculations for you to figure out how much UMI you have, it's useful to understand the process the banks take.

The banks provide spreadsheets to mortgage advisers to get an idea of whether borrowers are in the right ballpark to get a mortgage approved. These spreadsheets aren't made available by banks to the public, and don't exactly mirror the bank's internal software. But they give an indication. A

APPENDICES

good mortgage adviser will run your numbers through multiple banks' spreadsheets to figure out who is more likely to lend you the money.

The bank will first take your monthly salary and remove tax and KiwiSaver contributions. This gives them the money that actually hits your account each month. They then remove your normal living expenses (or if you're particularly frugal they have their own minimum expenses which they'll use). And then come the following tests:

→ **Higher interest rates: They'll see whether you could still afford the mortgage (and any others you have) at a much higher interest rate.** For example, if you'll actually pay a 4 per cent interest rate, your mortgage may be tested at 6.5 per cent. This is called the servicing test rate. Each bank uses a different test rate, which can change a couple of times a year.

→ **Lower rental income: They'll also give your rental income a haircut. If you'll earn $20,000 in rent, they'll scale this back 25–40 per cent.** In some cases after doing that the bank will take off rates, insurance and maintenance before using the rest as part of their calculations.

→ **Maxed-out credit cards: Even if you're not using your credit card, they will test you as if you've already maxed it out and are making the minimum repayments on it.** That's because the day after your mortgage is approved, you could go and max your credit card out. This is the same with any unused revolving credits you have.

→ **Actual expenses: After the introduction of the updated Credit Contracts and Consumer Finance Act 2003 (CCCFA), banks will use what you actually spend each week.** This means they will use your current expenses in their calculations, rather than the minimum amount you could live on if interest rates went higher. This means they effectively want to see you living as if your interest rate was already higher.

→ **Consumer debt: If you're regularly using Afterpay, Laybuy, store cards or any hire purchase, they'll treat it like you'll be making those payments forever, even if those repayments end in a few weeks' time.**

And on top of this, if your income goes up or down because you have bonuses or commissions, you work overtime or are self-employed, they may not include all of that income in their calculations.

With all of this number-crunching, you might wonder how anyone ever gets a mortgage approved. This is one of the reasons why, on average, only 38.1 per cent of mortgage applications per month actually turned into loans in 2021.[53]

It also points to why non-bank lenders are becoming more popular. And while non-bank lenders still follow the above process, they generally are a bit looser on the assumptions. For instance, one non-bank lender might use all of your commission or bonus income in their calculations.

Another might not give your rent the same haircut. Another might use the expenses you say are your minimum ones, rather than looking at your bank statements line by line. The process is the same, but the calculations and assumptions are different. As a result, non-bank lenders tend to be willing to lend you more than a traditional bank.

Now to be fair, we could go down a rabbit hole after information here, and by next month all the details will change. So the key message is that this stuff is complex. And while you can use the Commitment Issues strategy, which you'll learn about in Appendix B, to help improve the income side of your mortgage application, you should still always use a mortgage adviser.

Reasons why your mortgage application might be declined

While some applications might be declined because the would-be borrower doesn't have enough deposit or income, there are two other major reasons why your mortgage might be declined.

Poor account conduct

When a bank lends you money, their number one priority is to make sure that they're going to get it back. So your mortgage may not be approved if you show signs of not being a good payer. In the industry we call this poor account conduct.

When you apply for a mortgage, you'll need to send the bank three months' worth of your bank statements and six months of your credit card statements. As well as looking at what you have spent and where you're spending it, they're also looking for instances where:

→ **you've had payments bounce (e.g. you missed a recurring payment) because you didn't have enough money in your bank account, or**
→ **your account went into unarranged overdraft, or**
→ **your credit card is going over its limit, since even after you hit your credit limit, you'll sometimes find that your credit card will let you keep spending money for a while.**

These indicators make the banks nervous that you may miss mortgage payments in the future, and will make them think twice about lending large sums of money to you.

If this sounds like you, and your application is declined due to poor account conduct, be reassured that it's not a 'no' forever. It usually takes three to six months of 'good behaviour' before the bank will reconsider and approve your mortgage application.

And if you're looking to apply for a mortgage now and you think you'll be hit by this, it's often better *not to apply* for a mortgage just yet. That's because if you get declined, the result of that failed application will stay on your credit record. That can make it harder to get lending, because

APPENDICES

the next bank you apply to will want to know why you got declined. Instead, work with a mortgage adviser to get your finances in order, use the Debt Destroyer strategy, which we'll go over again in Appendix B, and create a record of being a 'good payer'. This will give you a better shot of getting your mortgage approved when you do apply.

Poor credit rating

The second reason your mortgage might be declined is your credit history. When you apply for a loan, the bank will request a credit report from a provider like Equifax, which gets data from debt collection agencies. They're trying to understand if there are any places like Baycorp or Secure Collections chasing you for unpaid bills.

If you have notes on your credit history that could work against you, then it's not an automatic 'no' from a lender. But it is best to front-foot it. You can request the exact same credit report details that a bank or a lender sees for free using My Credit File, which can be found at mycreditfile.co.nz. You can then take your credit report to your mortgage adviser and explain to them anything on there that the bank will pick up on anyway. It's better to explain now rather than defend against questions later.

Interest rates and types of interest charges

Once you've got your mortgage, you need to start thinking about your interest rates. Interest is arguably the most significant factor when taking out a mortgage. If your interest rate is 5.32 per cent or higher for the life of a 30-year P+I loan, you will then pay more in interest than you will in principal payments.

To put that into context, let's say you take out a $500,000 mortgage for 30 years at a 5.32 per cent interest rate and make weekly repayments. *In 30 years, you would have paid $501,093 in interest and $500,000 in principal payments*. This is why there is so much talk about interest rates, and why discussing how you structure yours is essential.

Fixed or floating?

Interest rates can vary over the term of the home loan. You can either choose to 'fix' or 'float' your interest rate. Fixing means your interest rate stays the same for an agreed timeframe. For instance, most banks will allow you to fix your interest rate for six months, 12 months, two years, three years or five years. Some will even let you fix for up to seven years.

Fixing your mortgage rate allows for two things:

- it provides certainty over the size of your mortgage repayments during the period you fix for, and
- it provides more time for you to prepare if interest rates suddenly increase dramatically halfway through your fixed period.

The drawback is that if interest rates fall, you'll either need to:

- wait until your fixed period has ended to take advantage of lower interest rates (and therefore the cheaper repayments that go with them), or
- cancel your current agreement and potentially incur a break fee to get those cheaper borrowing costs.

If you choose not to fix your interest rate, you go on the 'floating' interest rate. The floating interest rate can change day to day based on whatever is happening in the lending market or the broader economy. As the floating interest rate changes, the repayments you make to the lender will also change.

Floating interest rates are usually higher than fixed rates (but not always), so you might wonder why someone would opt for the floating rate. There are three main reasons:

1. **Some types of borrowing, like revolving credits and offset accounts, only come at the floating rate. You can't fix them.** So if you want to access this type of account, this part of your loan will be on floating.
2. **Some opt for the floating rate** if they believe that interest rates will fall, leading to lower borrowing costs.
3. **Others decide to float if they intend to make additional, unarranged payments towards their home loans.** If they tried to do that and had fixed their interest rate, they could have to pay a break fee.

So when choosing your interest rates, it's a good idea to talk to your adviser about your imminent plans around your debts so you can set up the interest arrangements to suit you. If you plan to sell an investment property in three months to pay off your home loan, then clearly don't fix your home loan for five years, because in three months you'll potentially have to pay a massive break fee.

Low equity margins: why did no one tell me this?

One final note on interest rates – and this only really applies to first-home buyers – concerns low equity margins, and *nobody ever tells you about this*. When you purchase with less than a 20 per cent deposit, you don't get access to the main interest rates you see on the billboards, bus shelters

APPENDICES

and TV ads. Those are called 'special rates'. These rates are only for borrowers with an LVR of 80 per cent or lower (i.e. a borrower with a deposit of 20 per cent or more). If you're a first-home buyer purchasing with a 10 per cent deposit, you'll pay a higher interest rate. These higher rates are often known as *low equity margins*.

These are an additional charge added on to the normal interest rate, and typically range from 0.25 per cent up to 1.5 per cent, depending on how small your deposit is. As a general rule of thumb, the lower your deposit, the higher your interest rate will be.

For instance, if your bank is advertising an interest rate of 5 per cent and you wanted to borrow using a 10 per cent deposit, you'd have to pay a margin of 0.75 per cent. That makes your whole interest rate 5.75 per cent.

Appendix B: Seven strategies to master your mortgage

Now that you know the basics of the different types of mortgages, what they do and how the banks assess your mortgage application, here are the strategies for how to either pay down debt more quickly or make it more likely that your mortgage is approved.

We've given these strategies names to make them easy to remember. But not every mortgage adviser will know what the Debt Destroyer or Mortgage Buster is. So you can't just walk in and say: 'I'll have the Mortgage Buster, please.' But you can either work with our mortgage advisers at Opes – Catalyst Financial – or you can hand your mortgage adviser this book and ask them to set things up the way it's described here.

The Debt Destroyer strategy

The Debt Destroyer strategy is most useful for first-home buyers who are struggling to get their first mortgage approved.

First-home buyers often start out with messy accounts and a bit of consumer debt. They might have $2,000 on their credit card, or a $2,500 overdraft that they got when they were a student, some Afterpays, maybe a car loan, their student loan, and perhaps a GEM Visa card with $4,000 on it, too.

The key message is that it is normal for young people to have debt spread across a number of different lenders. But this is also where they can easily veer into 'poor account conduct', where they fall behind on a payment or two because there are so many little payments due at different times, so it's easy to miss them.

This is where the Debt Destroyer comes in. Rather than having multiple payments going out at different times, a borrower will take out a new debt consolidation loan from a bank. They'll use this money to pay off all their other debts. So instead of being surrounded by debt, they've got one larger loan left to focus on. That means one consolidated monthly repayment.

Let's look at an example of the real debts one of the first-home buyers we were working with through Opes First Home had. Here's the debts they had with the interest rates they were paying:

DEBT	AMOUNT	INTEREST RATE
GEM Visa	$1,500	0 per cent
Credit card	$5,000	14.95 per cent
Overdraft	$2,000	10.95 per cent
Car loan	$5,000	12 per cent
Total	**$13,500**	**11.60 per cent average**

So four payments of differing amounts are coming out at different times. But using the Debt Destroyer strategy, this first-home buyer took out a $13,500 debt consolidation loan, paid off all their other debts, and just had one loan to pay back to the bank. The plan was that any extra money they had per week would be put towards paying off that debt more aggressively.

Note, however, that when you use the Debt Destroyer strategy and take out a debt consolidation loan, you will sometimes pay a higher interest rate. The average interest rates in the above example are 11.6 per cent, and the debt consolidation loan our first-home buyer took out had an interest rate of 14 per cent.

However, the point here isn't to save on interest costs, it's to change your behaviour. Instead of having many lenders and many different payments, some of which you might miss, you've got one, so you have the focus to pay down that single debt more quickly.

Debt Destroyer for homeowners

If you already own your own home, the Debt Destroyer strategy works differently. Rather than taking out a debt consolidation loan, which comes with a higher interest rate, you increase the size of your mortgage to pay down the other debt.

Let's say you have the same numbers as the first-home buyer above. You have $13,500 of consumer debt at various interest rates. If you increased the size of your mortgage by $13,500 through a mortgage top-up, you could take the money and pay down this other debt. Rather than paying 11.6 per cent as the average interest rate, you might pay 5 per cent, which helps you save on interest costs.

There is one big thing you need to bear in mind. If you add your personal debts into your mortgage – and use no other strategy – then it could take you significantly longer to pay off your debts. That could mean paying more interest over the long run. That's where you would use the Debt Destroyer to consolidate your debts in your mortgage, and then use the Mortgage Buster – which is coming up next – to pay off your debts in the same period as before.

The Mortgage Buster strategy

The Mortgage Buster is one of the most powerful mortgage strategies. It lets you pay down debt more aggressively, while retaining a lot of flexibility.

Let's say you go into a bank and say you want to pay off your mortgage more quickly. What do you think they will do? Usually they'll say: 'Great, you're currently paying off your mortgage over 30 years, how much extra do you want to pay? Good-oh, we'll shorten that term down to 17 years.'

That's not the best way to do it.

Instead, a better way is to use a revolving credit. The benefit of this is that you can make extra payments against your mortgage. But if the car breaks down or you need access to money, you can also withdraw any money you've got in the account. This means you can challenge yourself to pay down debt faster, knowing that if you go too far and need the money back, you have that option.

If you just shortened the term to increase your repayments, you can't get the extra funds back without making a full mortgage application. Additionally, if you want to decrease your repayments, you again have to submit a full mortgage application to extend your mortgage term again.

So how does the Mortgage Buster work?

First, you have your main mortgage and put it on as long a term as possible. You make minimum repayments against this. Then, you set a portion of your loan up as a revolving credit. This is the one that you try to tackle aggressively over the course of a year.

So if you wanted to pay off an extra $10,000 against your mortgage within a year, you would set up a $10,000 revolving credit and make it your goal to pay that off within 12 months. This gives you a set goal to work towards over a short timeframe.

At the end of the year, you'd take the money you've put into the revolving credit and make one large payment against your main mortgage. This reduces your main loan, but maxes out your revolving credit again. This means you spend the next year paying off the revolving credit to make another lump-sum payment at the end of the year.

What's the point of all this? If you have a small revolving credit (e.g. $10,000), you've got a goal of how much you want to pay off in a year. It's a small, achievable goal and you can see yourself making progress throughout the year, rather than sending any extra repayments into the abyss of an $800,000 mortgage. So the first reason is to challenge yourself.

The second reason is flexibility. Say you take that $10,000 revolving credit goal and start to put in an extra $200 a week. You get halfway through the year and you've paid off $5,000. You're on track.

Then your car breaks down and the motor is fried.

You've got no other savings and you're staring at a $2,000 mechanic's bill. This is where you can access the money in your revolving credit to pay for the bill. Whereas if you'd just increased your fixed mortgage payments by $200 a week, you'd be stuffed. You can't just ask the bank for your voluntary payments back.

The other benefit of setting up your accounts like this is that you can use other money you're saving to help reduce the interest that you pay on your mortgage. For instance, if you have $5,000 saved to go on holiday, you could put this in your revolving credit, so that these savings are used to reduce your mortgage costs in the meantime. You then still have access to spend when you're ready to book your flights.

The Mortgage Buster in practice for an investor

Let's now dig into how an investor might structure their loans to pay down their debts aggressively while using all three different mortgage types at once. This is how you put all of the thinking from the rest of the book into practice.

While an investor may have multiple properties, it's generally better to focus on paying down one mortgage at a time, especially if some of the loans are tax-deductible and others aren't. You'll pay less tax over time if you pay down your non-tax-deductible debt first and then move to paying down the rest. That's why investors with home mortgages frequently put their investment properties on interest-only and focus their efforts on the main home mortgage.

Here's a typical structure of an investor using the Mortgage Buster strategy with three properties: an owner-occupier home and two investment properties.

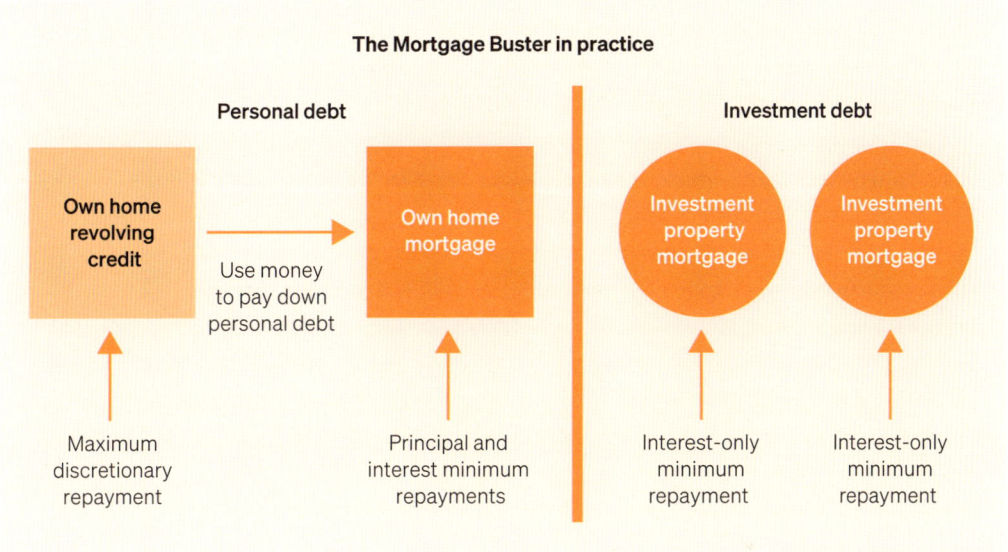

In this case, the investor would put both investment property mortgages on interest-only. The bulk of their own-home loan is on minimum repayments, and then any extra funds they have would be put towards paying down their revolving credit. In other words, instead of spending money paying down the debt on your investment properties, you put that money towards paying off the revolving credit on your personal mortgage.

Why would anyone set up their mortgages this way?

Think back to Chapter 12: remember the story we told you about Tim? He's the investor who had all his properties on principal and interest, but then when interest rates went up he had to sell them early.

The structure outlined above is the sort of structure that Tim probably should have used. That's because when all his properties were on principal and interest, his minimum repayments were very high. When interest rates rose, they went even higher. But the Mortgage Buster strategy reduces your minimum repayments. It's set up so that the payments you have to make are low, and more of your payments are voluntary. That means that if interest rates increased, Tim would have had the flexibility to still pay the same amount, but pay his debt down more slowly so he could hold on to his properties.

This strategy is about setting things up so you still have flexibility as circumstances change.

Should I pay off my own home or an investment property first?

Time and time again investors ask whether they should put their investment properties on principal and interest. Almost always our advice is to pay down your own home first before touching investment debt. The reason for this is three-fold:

1. **If you can get your own home fully paid off, you're less likely to be forced to sell your own home.** It's easy to sell an investment property, but harder to move your own house since you've got to up-end your life. So if things go wrong, it's nice to have low debt on your own place.
2. **Often you can borrow more to buy investment properties if you focus on paying off your owner-occupier home.** This is because most people have lower debt on their own homes than their investments. Let's say your own home is *below* the LVR limit (currently 80 per cent) and your investments are *above* the LVR limit (currently 60 per cent). Every dollar you pay off your own home, you can re-borrow as a deposit for your next investment. But because your investments are above the LVR limit, any money you put in you can't re-borrow as a deposit. This is especially important to keep in mind for investors at the starting blocks and at the beginning of their investment journey.
3. **Currently there is a tax incentive to pay down your own home first. This is because the interest on your investment property mortgages is sometimes tax-deductible, but the interest on your own home isn't.** So if you have the choice between paying off an extra dollar on your own home versus an extra dollar on an investment, you'll often pay less tax if you put it towards your own home first.

But if you have already paid off your own home, and you think the cashflow of your property still works when making principal repayments, then go ahead and start to pay down your investment debt.

The Extend and Lend strategy

The longest that a bank will approve an interest-only loan for is five years. However, that doesn't mean you can't go interest-only on a loan for longer. Here's how it works.

At the end of your five-year interest-only period, you can always apply for another five-year interest-only period. It takes another full mortgage application, but there's no reason you can't keep applying for a new interest-only period every time your last one runs out.

However, remember that your mortgage application is tested on the basis of 'What happens at the end of the interest-only period?' This means that if you have a 30-year mortgage and a five-year interest-only period, they will test whether you can pay the mortgage back over 25 years. If you apply for another five-year interest-only period at the end of that, your mortgage will be assessed to see if you could pay it back over 20 years. Do the same thing again, and then your income is being tested as if you are going to pay off the mortgage over the next 15 years.

Each time you extend the interest-only period, the time you've got left to pay off the loan gets shorter, and so the income the bank needs you to have gets larger. So how do you get around this?

One tactic we use is to extend the mortgage period.

Say you get your 30-year mortgage with five years on interest-only. You get to the end and try to do it again. You've now got 25 years left on your mortgage, so the bank assesses you to see whether you could pay off the mortgage in 20 years (once the new I/O period is over). They think you can't, so they deny you the interest-only period.

No matter: would they approve you if you extended the mortgage term back out to 30 years and applied for a five-year interest-only period on top of that? Then the bank is only assessing you on whether you could pay back the loan over 25 years.

Does that mean you can get an interest-only mortgage forever? No, but you can keep renewing your interest-only period for as long as possible. For example, in the 18 years Andrew has been investing in property, he has never used his own money to pay a dollar of principal payments on his investments. So why doesn't everyone just go interest-only forever? Many investors do for as long as possible. They'll keep their investment mortgages on interest-only and focus their money paying down their personal mortgage. Once that's gone, they might start picking off the other investment mortgages one by one. To be clear, paying down debt is generally a good thing. But some debts (your own home) are more costly than others (investment debt). So you need to pay down the more expensive debts first.

Again, don't worry if you're not following every detail of all these numbers yet. This is all technical and advanced stuff.

That's why we've given this strategy – and the others in this appendix – a snappy name so it's easier to remember.

The Split-banking strategy

So much of property investment is not about the property, but about how you set up the finance. This is where minor changes in how you structure your debts can have a big impact on your ability to grow a portfolio in the future. A good example of this is the Split-banking strategy.

Split-banking is where you will literally split your mortgages across different banks. There are two ways this can be done.

The first approach is if you are purchasing an investment property using a deposit that you have saved (as opposed to borrowing the deposit against your own property). Rather than taking that cash deposit and getting the mortgage from your usual bank, you might decide to get the mortgage from another lender. This is really easy to set up, because you have the savings there already and simply ask your mortgage adviser to recommend a lender to approach, before asking them to submit an application.

The second approach is more common, since many investors borrow the deposit against their own property. This is where you might set up a revolving credit against your own home for the deposit you need. You then take the money from that revolving credit facility and use it as the deposit for the mortgage from another bank. Setting up your mortgages this way takes a few more steps:

1 **Set up a revolving credit with your current bank** for the value of your deposit. For example, you want to buy an $800,000 new-build, so set up a $160,000 revolving credit facility against your own home. In practice, you might apply for a slightly larger revolving credit than you need so that you have flexibility in the purchase price.
2 **Apply for a mortgage from a second bank**, subject to having the deposit. Here you'll disclose that you have a revolving credit facility with your main bank.

Then when it comes time to pay the money to the owner of the property you're buying, you'll transfer the money from your revolving credit to your solicitor (who then pays the current owner of the property). Bank #2 then transfers the rest to your solicitor at the same time.

To be clear, this isn't shady. You're not lying to the banks: it's an open relationship rather than an exclusive partnership. So all of the partners will be in the know. The only challenge with managing the two partners is that you have to meet both their lending criteria.

You're probably wondering why anyone would go to the trouble of using Split-banking. There are three good reasons: you can potentially borrow more, you can retain control over any sale proceeds, and you have more security with your own home.

You can potentially borrow more

There's a bit of an anomaly under the current LVR restrictions. If you buy a new-build you require a 20 per cent deposit. But the day you buy that property and the money changes hands, it becomes an existing property. That means that it now requires a 40 per cent deposit. This impacts your ability to purchase your next investment property if you are borrowing the deposit.

Let's say you have $350,000 of useable equity in your own home that you can use to fund the deposits for investment properties. If we forget servicing for a moment and only focus on the deposit side, this would fund the deposits for $1.75 million worth of new-build properties.

You say: 'Great, I've found a $750,000 new-build that I want to purchase.' This will take $750,000 from the $1.75 million you can purchase with, leaving you with (you think) an extra $1 million left to spend on more new-builds. Not so fast.

If you get the entire $750,000 from your main bank, you have to think about what happens once the property settles. Because the day the property is built and the money is paid, this property requires a 40 per cent deposit. So before you can borrow any additional money for your next investment property, your new purchase will now be taking up $300,000 of useable equity from your main home, because it isn't a new-build anymore. It's an existing property.

BANKING MONOGAMY

What happens if you use one bank when investing in new-builds?

BEFORE YOUR NEW-BUILD SETTLES (IF USING ONE BANK)	
Useable equity in own home	$350,000
Equity required for new-build *before* settlement (20 per cent)	$150,000
Useable equity left	$200,000
What you can buy*	**$1,000,000**

AFTER YOUR NEW-BUILD SETTLES (IF USING ONE BANK)	
Useable equity in own home	$350,000
Equity required for new-build *after* settlement (40 per cent)	$300,000
Useable equity left	$50,000
What you can buy*	**$250,000**

* Assuming purchasing a new-build using a 20 per cent deposit.

That would leave you with only $50,000 left as a deposit. Book a flight to Temuka, because if you're lucky you might be able to buy something there.

What's the alternative? Well, if you'd taken the Split-banking strategy from the start, your main bank won't see your investment property in their equity calculations. That means you'll still have your revolving credit at your main bank. But you'll have kept the additional $200,000 that you can spend as a deposit.

APPENDICES

BANKING POLYGAMY

What happens if you use Split-banking when investing in new-builds?

BEFORE YOUR NEW-BUILD SETTLES (IF USING TWO BANKS)	
Useable equity in own home	$350,000
Equity secured against owner-occupier *before* settlement (20 per cent)	$150,000
Useable equity left	$200,000
What you can buy*	**$1,000,000**

AFTER YOUR NEW-BUILD SETTLES (IF USING TWO BANKS)	
Useable equity in own home	$350,000
Equity secured against owner-occupier *after* settlement (20 per cent)	$150,000
Useable equity left	$200,000
What you can buy*	**$1,000,000**

* Assuming purchasing a new-build using a 20 per cent deposit.

So Split-banking can put you in the position to borrow more than you otherwise could. This is technical: it may take a couple of readings to get your head around this. But the main takeaway is: if you are investing in new-builds, Split-banking is a must. If you don't do it, you start to lose the benefits of purchasing new-builds that the LVR restrictions provide.

You have control over sale proceeds

Next, Split-banking gives you more control over the sale proceeds when you sell. This is because selling a property will trigger a credit assessment. That's where the bank assesses the debt you already have and will make sure that you have the money in order to service the current money you've borrowed.

If you've had a change in circumstances and your income is lower, the bank may think you can't service the debt you have. That means that when you go to sell an investment property, they might take some of the proceeds you got from selling the property and pay down your other mortgages . . . without even asking you. (Remember that case study back in Chapter 20? This is exactly what happened when the bank cancelled Christmas.)

But let's say you used Split-banking and your investment mortgage is at a different bank to your transaction accounts and credit cards. When you sell the property, you won't trigger a credit assessment for your personal lending. This gives you more control over the proceeds of your sale and your own money.

You can keep your own home more secure

Finally, let's say that the worst happens. Your tenant has stopped paying the rent. Your investment property has no income, you're tight on cash and you can't pay your investment property mortgage. This really is the most dire situation you could be in. What happens? Well, if you have both your personal and investment mortgages with the same bank, the lender has the option to force you to sell both properties. It doesn't mean they will. But they can.

What happens if you have them with different banks? The bank can only force you to sell the property that is used as 'security'. So if you can't pay your investment mortgage they can force you to sell your investment property. But they can't force you to sell your own home. This gives you an added layer of protection just in case the worst really does happen.

The Lend Before You Leap strategy

When you invest in property, you'll sometimes need to move quickly in order to secure a deal. That's why one tactic to use is the Lend Before You Leap strategy. This is like Split-banking but with a small twist: you're getting your revolving credit set up in advance so you are able to make a move once you've found the right property. This is more important for existing properties rather than new-builds, since with new-builds you tend to have more time.

To use this strategy, you use the same process described in the Split-banking strategy. You set up a revolving credit ahead of the time you want to invest. You then take it out when you are ready and use it as the deposit at another bank.

If you want to purchase an existing property and your budget is $500,000, you know you'll need a 40 per cent deposit – $200,000 – and that you'll borrow this money against the equity in your own house. Under this strategy you'd set up a $200,000 revolving credit against your own home while you're still looking. Then once you find the property, you've already got your deposit set up. You can then apply straight away to another bank to fund the rest of the purchase if you are using the Split-banking strategy. That's why it's called Lend Before You Leap.

The Commitment Issues strategy

When you first start to invest in property, the main factor holding you back tends to be equity. You don't have enough deposit to purchase your next property. As you start to grow a portfolio of two to four investment properties the issue often becomes income, especially if you earn an average wage. The issue is that in the bank's eyes you don't have enough uncommitted monthly income (UMI) to take on another investment property. And the reason behind this is often that your committed financial payments are too high. In other words, you have commitment issues.

However, there are ways to increase your UMI by decreasing your committed financial payments. These include:

- **Extending the term of your personal mortgage** back out to 30 years. This will decrease your minimum repayments, giving you more UMI so you can borrow more. But you can still maintain the same repayment as you are now using the Mortgage Buster strategy. This also works for any investment property loans you have.
- **Consolidating your hire purchases or car loans** into your personal mortgage using the Debt Destroyer strategy. This extends how many years you have to pay these off, which decreases your minimum repayments. This also increases your UMI, and you can use the Mortgage Buster to pay them off at the same speed you were doing under the previous term.
- **Decreasing your KiwiSaver repayments** to match what your employer contributes (e.g. 3 per cent). If you're currently contributing 10 per cent to KiwiSaver, one option you have is to decrease this so that more money hits your account each pay cycle. This increases your UMI so you can borrow more. This isn't appropriate for everyone, so have a chat with your mortgage or investment adviser before doing this.
- **Cancelling unused credit cards**, especially if you aren't using them. The bank will test you as if you have maxed them out. A credit card limit over $5,000 is often worth cancelling.
- **Paying off your student loan early** can significantly increase your UMI in some situations. That's because 12 per cent of your gross income over $20,200 goes automatically towards paying off your student loan. If you earn $100,000 a year, that's about $800 a month. You can use the Debt Destroyer to use your home loan to consolidate this. Again, this is a strategy that works for some but not others, since it will decrease how much deposit you have. So it won't work for every single person reading this book.

Using some combination of these can turn a mortgage application that would get declined into one that will now get approved.

A good mortgage adviser will work with you to figure out which of these apply to you so you can decrease your committed expenses, which increases your UMI so you can invest in more property.

The Earn, Baby, Earn strategy

The final strategy also increases how much you can borrow from the bank. And it does it by growing the income the bank will use in your mortgage application. That's because the bank treats your various sources of income differently. For instance, the bank might use all of your income from your salary in their calculations. But it might only use 50 per cent of any bonus or commission income you earn. This is what we call 'provable income'. The Earn, Baby, Earn strategy is there to help you increase this.

Yes, that can mean asking for a pay rise if you haven't had one for a while, and you think that you deserve it. But it can also mean:

→ **One partner going back to work** — if they're not currently working (e.g. if they are currently on parental leave).
→ **One partner increasing the hours they work** (e.g. if one partner is currently working part-time).
→ **Renegotiating the way your remuneration package is structured** (e.g. asking your employer to convert commission or bonus income into part of your base salary). This will mean more of your income counts in the bank's eyes.

This is a powerful and important strategy to continually increase the amount you can borrow. The more you earn, the more you can borrow. The more you borrow, the more you can invest. Speaking with a mortgage adviser and applying for a home loan is often a good trigger to have these conversations.

How am I supposed to figure this out on my own?

There are some property investors out there who love the detail of this stuff. They want to understand it and make a good decision. Fair enough, but just remember that the purpose of these resources isn't to turn you into a mortgage master so you can be your own adviser.

Even though we wrote this stuff (and, in fact, the whole book), we both still use mortgage advisers every single time. This appendix isn't a replacement for using a professional. But it *is* meant to prepare you so you can have an informed conversation, ask the right questions, prod your adviser to make sure they've considered all the options, and set you up to get the money you need to invest in property.

Other resources

Opes Partners Want to put what you learned in this book into practice? Your next step is to have a *portfolio planning session* with the team at Opes Partners. In this session you'll work with a property partner to plan out your own property investment portfolio. This includes seeing how close you are to achieving your goals and deciding what to invest in and when. We'll then find the properties that fit with that plan.

opespartners.co.nz

Catalyst Financial Want to get a mortgage to purchase another investment property, or change up your lending? Then Catalyst Financial can help you get the money to invest from the best lender for you. The team can also help you put any of the seven mortgage strategies into practice, so you can either pay down debt more quickly or grow your investment portfolio even faster.

catalystfinancial.co.nz

Momentum Property Want to make sure you're not overpaying your taxes? Momentum Property can help you make sure that you are using the right structures, like trusts and look-through companies, to minimise the tax you pay on your investment properties.

momentumproperty.co.nz

Opes Accelerate If renovations are more your thing, Opes Accelerate may be the right fit for you. This is a renovations-coaching programme, where you'll learn how to renovate properties to increase both their value and their rental potential.

opespartners.co.nz/accelerate

Opes First Home Looking for your first home? Opes First Home can help you get into your first home by project-managing the process for you. You'll work with an adviser who will guide you through the whole process, from figuring out how much you can afford, through to finding the property and negotiating the deal.

opesfirsthome.co.nz

Subscribe to *NZ Property Investor* magazine This publication is the official magazine of the NZ Property Investors' Federation, and every month over 6,000 copies are sent to property investors around the country. It's a great way to keep learning about property investment.

propertyinvestor.co.nz

Subscribe to *Informed Investor* magazine If you want a wider view of investments, *Informed Investor* magazine, which covers shares, funds, cryptocurrency, commercial property, and all types of investments.

informedinvestor.co.nz

Glossary

Asset A resource owned by an investor that can produce a return (e.g. an investment property or a share/equity).

Boarding house A type of yield property where tenants rent a single room or studio within a larger building, usually with shared kitchens and lounges.

Capital growth The increase in the value of a property that happens over time as the market increases in value.

Cashflow The amount of cash produced by an investment property per year (week or month); that is, the money left over once the rent has come in and the expenses have been paid. This can also refer to the amount of cash an investor needs to contribute to a property over a given timeframe (e.g. if the property is negatively-geared).

Central Bank The organisation that regulates and sets rules for the other banks. *See* Reserve Bank of New Zealand.

Code Compliance Certificate Sign-off from a council that a property meets building regulations, and that the property complies with what was stated in its building and resource consent applications. Note: a property may still not be 'finished' even if it has its Code Compliance Certificate.

Commercial bank A business that lends money for purchasing investment property. Also offers traditional money management services like credit cards, debit cards, savings and transaction accounts, revolving credits and term deposits. ANZ, Westpac, ASB and BNZ are all examples of commercial banks.

Debt consolidation loan When a borrower takes out one larger loan to pay off multiple smaller loans. Used to merge many smaller payments into one regular payment. Used in the Debt Destroyer strategy.

Debt-free asset An asset without any debt secured against it. *See* Net assets.

Debt-to-income ratio (DTI) The size of your mortgages compared with the total income you earn from rent and salary/wages. For instance, if your mortgages are worth $500,000 and you earn $100,000, you have a DTI of 5.

Deferred settlement When you agree to purchase a property but don't complete the transaction until more than four weeks later. Often used to renovate a property before you actually own it to minimise mortgage repayments and financing costs.

Depreciation When the value of chattels within your property decreases in value over time. This depreciation is considered an expense and is used to decrease the amount of tax you need to pay.

GLOSSARY

Dual-key apartment A unit where there are two separate apartments contained within one legal title (i.e. two separate apartments within one), usually sharing an entranceway.

Dwelling A legal self-contained residence or unit. Typically lived in by one household.

Equity The value of property minus the value of the mortgage. For example, if a property is worth $1 million with a mortgage of $400,000, the investor has $600,000 worth of equity within the property.

Financial adviser A person who is registered on the Financial Services Providers Register and is legally allowed to offer personalised financial advice.

Fixed rate/Fixed interest rate An agreement with a lender or bank of the interest rate that you will pay for a set amount of time. For example, 4.5 per cent fixed for three years means that the bank will charge you an annual interest rate of 4.5 per cent and that rate will not change for three years.

Floating rate/Floating interest rate An agreement with a lender or bank where the interest rate you pay can change at any time.

Gross yield A measure of how much rental income your investment property generates. Calculated by taking the annual rent and dividing it by the current value of the property. For example, $500 a week for a property currently worth $650,000 means a gross yield of 4 per cent. ($500 × 52) / $650,000.

Growth property A property that will likely increase in value quickly, but will likely not have a high yield.

Healthy Homes Standards The legal standards which every rental property needs to meet in New Zealand before being rented.

Home and income property A type of property where there are multiple dwellings on the same title. The owner will often live in one dwelling and rent the other(s).

Interest deductibility Whether the interest costs associated with your property's mortgage count when calculating how much tax you pay. If your interest costs are deductible, you tend to pay less tax. If they are not deductible, you will tend to pay more tax.

Insurance premium/Premium The regular payment that is made to an insurance company to pay for the insurance policy.

Interest-only loan/Interest-only mortgage Where a borrower pays the bank for the privilege of using the money (the interest), but doesn't pay back any of the original loan.

Landlord Same thing as a property investor.

Leasehold A property where you own the building on the land, but don't own the land itself. You then have a long-term rental agreement with the landowner, which you then pay rent on. Investors should be very, very wary of leasehold properties, because – among other things – ground rents increase faster than rents generally. Leasehold properties can also be much harder to sell.

Leverage The ability to borrow money to purchase a more expensive asset than you could afford. Specifically when that money is lent against the asset being purchased.

Loan-to-value ratio (LVR) The amount of mortgages you have compared with what your property is worth. For instance, if you have a $600,000 mortgage on a house worth $1 million, your LVR is 60 per cent.

Loan-to-value ratio restriction (LVR restriction) A piece of regulation where the Reserve Bank stops banks from lending above a certain threshold for properties. At the time of writing, at least 95 per cent of each bank's lending to investors must be at 60 per cent or less. In effect, that means that the bulk of investors need a 40 per cent deposit or more when purchasing. However, there are exemptions.

Look-through company (LTC) An entity investors use to own their properties. Often used to minimise the amount of tax an investor needs to pay. Not appropriate for every situation and needs to be set up correctly for investors to receive the benefits.

Losses carried forward When an investment property makes a taxable loss, that deficit is used in future years to decrease the amount of tax the investor needs to pay.

Minor dwelling A building that is constructed on a piece of land that already has another house on it. Often used to create a home and income or increase the rent a property achieves.

Mortgage The money a property investor or borrower raises from a bank to purchase a property.

Mortgage adviser A type of financial adviser who deals with a bank on an investor's or borrower's behalf. They usually offer their services with no charge to the purchaser. Instead they earn a commission from the bank/lender when a purchaser successfully borrows money.

Multi-income property A property that has multiple dwellings, tenants or households. *See* Boarding house, Home and income property, Student accommodation, Yield property.

Negative gearing When an investment property runs at a deficit and the investor needs to 'top-up' the property with their personal cash.

Net assets The total value of your properties, minus the total value of your mortgages.

Net yield A measure of how much rental income your investment property generates. Calculated by taking the annual rent, taking away the operating expenses and dividing it by the current value of the property. For example, if a property earns $500 a week in rent and has $10,000 of operating expenses per year and is currently worth $650,000, it has a net yield of 2.5 per cent. ($500 × 52 − $10,000) / $650,000.

Non-bank lender A company that lends money for the purposes of purchasing residential property (and other reasons), but is not a registered bank. Typically, it doesn't offer traditional banking services like transaction accounts, credit cards, debit cards, revolving credits, term deposits or savings accounts.

NZ Property Investors' Federation The national body that represents property investors.

GLOSSARY

It currently has 19 related associations around the country.

Offset facility/Offset loan Similar to a revolving credit except there are two bank accounts – one with a mortgage on a floating rate, one for savings (the offset). The borrower is then charged interest on the mortgage, minus any savings in the offset account. For instance, if the borrower had a $30,000 mortgage on a floating rate and $10,000 in the offset, they would only be charged interest on $20,000.

Owner-occupier A person who owns the home they live in. Also used to refer to the home itself (e.g. 'an owner-occupier home').

Passive income Income that is generated from an asset, rather than generated from working (i.e. exchanging time for money).

Principal and interest loan/Principal and interest mortgage (P+I) When a portion of each mortgage repayment goes towards paying down some of the original loan, and another portion goes towards paying interest to the lender.

Property accountant An accountant who specialises in residential real estate investment. Typically will give advice on how to structure the ownership of properties in order to minimise the amount of tax that must be paid.

Property investor A person who purchases real estate with the intent of holding the property for the long term, and renting the dwelling to tenants. As distinct from a trader (or property trader) who buys and sells properties quickly.

Property Investors' Association A local membership organisation that seeks to educate property investors. There are currently 19 associations in New Zealand that are affiliated with the NZ Property Investors' Federation.

Property manager A person who property investors delegate responsibility to for finding tenants, managing rent collection, conducting quarterly property inspections, organising maintenance, and tenant communication. Usually charges a percentage of the rent collected.

Real Estate Institute of New Zealand (REINZ) A membership body that all real estate agents belong to. It is one of the main property-related data providers in New Zealand.

Refinance When a borrower moves their mortgage from one lender to another. Also commonly used to refer to the process of restructuring loans; for instance, taking out a larger loan on a property after renovations have been completed.

Reserve Bank / Reserve Bank of New Zealand (RBNZ) The central bank of New Zealand, which regulates the main commercial banks. Also has responsibility for setting other policies that impact the housing market, such as LVRs, DTIs and bank capital requirements.

Residential Tenancies Act The main piece of legislation that sets the rules of how landlords and tenants interact. It sets the rules for what both landlords and tenants can and cannot do.

Revolving credit A specific type of mortgage that works like a large overdraft. The revolving credit is secured against a property, and the borrower can withdraw as much money as they like up to an agreed limit. The benefit is that the borrower is only charged interest when they take money out. They stop paying interest when they pay the money back.

Sale and purchase agreement A contract between a buyer and a vendor to purchase a piece of property.

Student accommodation A specific type of high-yield property where students rent by the room. Can also refer to a generic property that is intended to be tenanted by university students, rather than one that is specifically endorsed by a university.

Sunset clause A clause within a sale and purchase agreement that allows the contract to be cancelled if the property isn't completed by a certain date (usually the expected completion date + 12 months).

Table mortgage Same as a principal and interest mortgage. The payments are set out on an amortisation table/schedule.

Tenancy Tribunal The main body that decides and resolves disputes between landlords and their tenants.

Tenant A person who rents a property off a landlord.

Title The legal description of property, including the owner, the owner's legal rights and any restrictions on the property.

Top-up The cash an investor must transfer into their property's bank account if the property is negatively-geared. Also called a cash contribution.

Trust A legal entity used to own and hold property. Often used to protect the assets or lower the amount of tax that an investor has to pay.

Uncommitted monthly income (UMI) The amount of money the bank thinks you have left over at the end of the month – after they've run their financial stress test calculations. This is used to assess how much you can potentially borrow and be able to service.

Useable equity The additional money that an investor could borrow against a property. Used to guarantee the deposit for an investment property.

Vacancy The period where you don't have a tenant in your property so it's not earning any rent. To be conservative, we budget for two weeks a year.

Variable rate/Variable interest rate *See* Floating rate.

Vendor A person selling a property.

Yield A generic term used to describe the rental potential of the property compared with its purchase price or current value. Can refer to gross yield, net yield or cashflow, or the rental potential in general.

Yield property A property that will likely receive a decent amount of cashflow, but may not increase in value as quickly as a growth property.

References

1. CoreLogic, *First Home Buyer Report*, May 2021. Discussed further in episode 631 of the *Property Academy Podcast*. https://www.opespartners.co.nz/podcast
2. https://cffc-assets-prod.s3.ap-southeast-2.amazonaws.com/public/Uploads/Research-2020%2B/Impact-of-financial-stress-on-relationships-RES-Sept-2020.pdf
3. 'Financial stress impacts mental wellbeing', Te Ara Ahunga Ora Retirement Commission, https://retirement.govt.nz/news/latest-news/financial-stress-impacts-mental-wellbeing/
4. *Money and You*, Financial Services Council 2020. Retrieved from: https://www.fsc.org.nz/site/fsc1/Money And You Financial Services Council June 2020 v1.0.pdf
5. Massey University, Fin-Ed Centre, *New Zealand Retirement Expenditure Guidelines*, November 2021.
Assumes that a couple retire at 65 and live to 90. The lump sum has been adjusted for inflation at 2 per cent, and assumes that New Zealand Superannuation will still be available from 65, but adjusted by inflation as opposed to adjusted for wage growth.
6. Statistics New Zealand, New Zealand Census 2018. Retrieved from: https://www.stats.govt.nz/tools/2018-census-place-summaries/new-zealand#housing
7. Statistics New Zealand, New Zealand Census 1936–2018. Retrieved from https://www.stats.govt.nz/news/homeownership-rate-lowest-in-almost-70-years
8. Statistics New Zealand, December 2020. Retrieved from: https://www.stats.govt.nz/topics/population
9. Statistics New Zealand. Retrieved from: https://www.stats.govt.nz/news/new-data-shows-1-in-9-children-under-the-age-of-five-lives-in-a-multi-family-household
10. Kāinga Ora. Retrieved from: https://kaingaora.govt.nz/publications/housing-statistics/ on 05/01/2022.
11. Reserve Bank House Price Index, Key Graph Data, March 1991–March 2021. Retrieved from: https://www.rbnz.govt.nz/statistics/key-graphs/key-graph-house-price-values
12. REINZ House Price Index for Christchurch City November 2003–November 2021.
13. Reserve Bank of New Zealand Data, C31, November 2021.
14. Susan Edmonds, Stuff. Retrieved from: https://www.stuff.co.nz/business/102259396/half-of-all-firsthome-buyers-have-parents-help
15. Real Estate Institute of New Zeland (REINZ), March 2022.
16. Real Estate Institute of New Zealand (REINZ) data, April 2021–March 2022.
17. CoreLogic, *First Home Buyer Report*, November 2021. https://www.corelogic.co.nz/news/record-market-share-nz-first-

References

home-buyers-despite-boom-conditions#.YgjFzO5Bxb9

18 CoreLogic data, Median value by territorial authority, February 2018.

19 CoreLogic data, Average property value by Territorial Authority – Hamilton, March 2021.

20 Core Logic. First Home Buyer report Q3, 2021. Retrieved from: https://www.corelogic.co.nz/news/record-market-share-nz-first-home-buyers-despite-boom-conditions#.YdoZB1hBzLA

21 CoreLogic data, Average property value by Territorial Authority – Hamilton, March 2021.

22 https://www.dulux.co.nz/colour/whites-and-neutrals/popular-whites/okarito

23 Internal Opes Partners modelling. Calculated in today's dollars using a 2 per cent inflation rate, 2 per cent increase in salary per year, 4.5 per cent post-tax, post-fees growth rate on portfolio, 3 per cent employer superannuation contribution, 33 per cent tax and a constant government contribution of $512 per year.

24 REINZ House Price Index, January 2010–January 2015.

25 Opes Partners crunching of REINZ House Price Index data.

26 November 2021, Opes Partners analysis of REINZ House Price Index.

27 CoreLogic. Retrieved from: https://www.corelogic.co.nz/news/property-market-ends-2021-high#.Ydyfp1hBxb8

28 November 2021, Opes Partners crunching of REINZ House Price Index data.

29 REINZ Median Sales Prices 2007–2018.

30 Auckland REINZ House Price Index, January 1992–October 2021, annualised average compounding increase.

31 Wellington REINZ House Price Index, January 1992–October 2021, annualised average compounding increase.

32 Opes Partners analysis of REINZ data. 10-year change in the median price of townhouses and units compared with the 10-year change in the median price of standalone dwellings.

33 Opes Partners analysis of CoreLogic data. Change in average value of properties by city, grouped by numbers of bedrooms, January 2000–July 2020.

34 REINZ House Price Index, Christchurch City, August 2007–January 2009.

35 Ministry of Social Development, Social Housing Register, June 2022.

36 Opes Partners analysis of Ministry of Social Development Data, The Housing Register, September 2021.

37 CoreLogic Data, Torbay, January 2000–December 2021.

38 https://www.facebook.com/groups/nzpropertychat

39 Median Rent in New Zealand (July 2001–July 2021) calculated through Bond Data by Ministry of Business, Innovation and Employment.

40 REINZ House Price Index, New Zealand, November 2020–November 2021.

41 Opes Partners analysis of TradeMe data, August 2021.

42 MBIE Household Income Estimates (based on Stats NZ labour market statistics

REFERENCES

[income] and census data) 1998–2019. Retrieved from: http://webrear.mbie.govt.nz/theme/household-income-median/map/timeseries/2019/new-zealand?right-transform=absolute

43 Massey University, Fin-Ed Centre, New Zealand Retirement Expenditure Guidelines, June 2021.

44 'Life expectancy at birth, total (years)', New Zealand, World Bank, 2019, https://data.worldbank.org/indicator/SP.DYN.LE00.IN?locations=NZ

45 'Petrol prices and taxes', Parliamentary Business Papers, September 2000. https://www.parliament.nz/en/pb/research-papers/document/00PLEcoRP00161/petrol-prices-and-taxes#RelatedAnchor

46 Roy Morgan, Image of Professions Survey, 2021.

47 REINZ House Price Index. Dual-key apartments grew 10.8 per cent growth over this four-year period, while the overall Wellington market lifted 12.2 per cent.

48 1-year fixed mortgage interest rate, Interest.co.nz. https://www.interest.co.nz/charts/interest-rates/fixed-mortgage-rates

49 REINZ House Price Index March 2020–November 2021.

50 REINZ House Price Index July 2002 – July 2022.

51 REINZ House Price Index November 2021–July 2022.

52 CoreLogic, *First Home Buyer report*, Q3, 2021. Retrieved from: https://www.corelogic.co.nz/news/record-market-share-nz-first-home-buyers-despite-boom-conditions#.YdoZB1hBzLA

53 Centrix, Residential Mortgages Conversion Rate (All Providers), January–December 2021

Acknowledgements

A book doesn't get made without a team to make it happen. Thanks first need to go to Steph Zajkowski, who sat with us over many, many Zoom meetings to keep us on task and turn our ramblings and bickering into the book you have in front of you.

Thanks to Christina Wedgwood and Verity Craft from Intelligent Ink who have read and re-read drafts to provide feedback.

Also to Debra Millar from Point Publishing for your help and guidance throughout the project.

Special thanks to Julia Murray, our illustrator who designed the book, the cover and the illustrations. And to Shaun Jury for your attention to the typesetting.

Thanks to all the investors who agreed to be interviewed for the book. Your stories and thoughts bring the book's principles to life.

But most of all, thanks to our business partner and general manager at Opes Partners, Ollie McKenna. If you did not believe in the project, and do what you do, this book would not exist.

Index

access, early 42
accountant, property 132–3, 135, 161, 162, 176, 212, 262
action taking 55–6, 231–2
active buy-and-hold 40, 43
advisers, financial 202, 260
advisers, insurance 170–1
advisers team 122–35: build contracts 128–30; case studies 129, 134; landlord vs investor 130–1; mortgage advisers 125–8, 134; property accountants 132–3, 135; property advisers/coaches/finders 123–4; property lawyers 128–30; property managers 130–2
advisers, mortgage 125–8, 134, 245, 257
advisers/coaches/finders, property 123–4
affordability of mortgages/property 112, 239–41
aims *see* goals
amenities, properties near 219
apartments 109–11, 219–20, 224: apartments vs houses/townhouses and value 109–11
asset 259: asset building 22, 94–6, 231; holding 196–7; net assets 261; requirements 197; selling 48, 195–6

bank accounts 60–2, 137–9, 144, 177: checking regularly 138, 144; offset accounts 61–2; *see also* revolving credit
'Bank of Mum and Dad' 48–9, 80
banking monogamy 253
banking polygamy 254
banks 237–42: break fees 211–12, 217, 243; commercial 259; income tests 78; and mortgage advisers 125; regulations 216–17; rules 234; *see also* mortgages
bathroom 70
bedrooms: extra 68–9; numbers and value 111
boarding houses 223, 259
body corporate fees 224
borrowing ability 190
break fees 211–12, 217, 243
bright line test 163–4
BRRRR (buy, renovate, rent, refinance and repeat) 40, 43, 123, 180–1
bubbles, property 229
budgeting 64–5
buffer account 169, 173
build contracts 128–30
building practitioner, licensed 69
buy and flip/flipping 40–1

capital gains tax (CGT) 163
capital gains/growth 40, 80–1, 179, 259: capital gains vs yield 204; principles 58–9, 100, 104–12
carpet 71
cashflow 117–18, 121, 259: frequency 208; managing 136, 140–3
Cashflow Hacking/renovation framework 67–71, 76, 158, 213, 214
Catalyst Financial 245, 258
Central Bank 259
central suburbs and value 109
chattel depreciation 161, 165
chattel valuation 122, 161
cheaper properties 219
Christchurch earthquakes 89, 169, 227
cleaning 71
Code Compliance Certificate 158, 159, 259
Commitment Issues strategy 241, 255–6
Community Housing Regulatory Authority 159
comparative analysis 115
compliance costs 227
consensus building 168, 173
consumer debt 240
council consent, avoiding 69
Covid-19 54, 74, 188, 189, 227, 228, 229
credit cards 246: cancellation 184, 256; debt 240, 241
Credit Contracts and Consumer Finance Act (CCCFA) 183, 188, 240
credit rating, poor 242
credit report 242
cycles, property 228

debt consolidation loan 246, 259
Debt Destroyer strategy 186, 242, 245–7, 256
debt reduction 179, 186, 204–7, 209
debt-free asset 259
debt-to-income ratio (DTI) 259
deferred settlement 41, 259
deposit 238–9: approval from bank 78; building 38–9; requirements 45–6, 56, 58; saving 14–15; and useable equity 30, 38
deposit finance, obtaining 44–56: action taking 55–6; asset sales 48; 'Bank of Mum and Dad' 48–9; case study 53–5; deposit multiple 45–6, 49, 56; deposit required 45–6, 56; 'Fast Five' ways for deposit 44, 46–50, 55–6; First Home Grant 47, 51–2; First Home Partner 47; government support 47–8, 51–2; income increasing/saving 49; KiwiSaver 46, 47, 52; loan-to-value ratio (LVR) restrictions 45, 58; location of property 52–3, 56; low-deposit borrower 45; misconceptions 50–3; mortgage advisers 45; mortgages 44–6; owner occupier vs rental 52–3; prices for property 50–1, 56
deposit multiple 45–6, 49, 56
depreciation 259
downsizing 94
drawbacks of property 208–9

268

dual-key apartments 221–2, 225, 260
dwelling 260

early access 42
Earn, Baby, Earn strategy 256–7
emotions of property investment 166–73: buffer account 169, 173; case studies 167, 170–1, 172–3; consensus building 168, 173; fears 166; insurance (landlords) 169–71, 173; insurance advisers 170–1; investment focus 171, 173; line of credit 168–9, 172–3; overdraft 168–9; property selection 167, 173; revolving credit 172–3; risk mitigation 166, 171–3; risk tolerance 167, 173
employment: higher income 49, 64; side hustles 49, 64
entities: ownership 132; set-up 132
equity 29–30, 260: building 59–60; equity vs useable equity 29–30; increasing 38, 39, 80–1, 83; realisation 210–17; strategies 178–82, 190; understanding 29–30; useable equity 66, 77–80, 83, 179–80, 263
evaluating properties 113–21: case study 116–20; cashflow 117–18, 121; comparative analysis 115; and goals 120; judgement/subjective factors 115–16, 120; market canvassing 120, 121; numbers 113–14; projections basis 121; return-on-investment method 113–14, 119, 121; return-on-investment numbers 114–16; return-on-investment spreadsheet 114–16; total returns 120, 121
expenses to claim 161
Extend and Lend strategy 236, 250–1

'Fast Five' ways for deposit 44, 46–50, 55–6
fears 166
financial concerns 21–2
financial fast-track 20–7: asset building 22; leverage and property 23–4; need for private landlords 25–7; risk-taking 25; starting and planning 21–2
financial freedom: goal of 90, 91
financial goals, achieving 12
financial modelling 201
finding properties 99–112: affordability 112; apartments vs houses/townhouses and value 109–11; bedroom numbers and value 111; capital growth principles 100, 104–12; central suburbs and value 109; finding growth properties 104–12; growth vs yield properties 99–103, 112; higher-end suburbs and value 109; houses vs townhouses value 110–11; number of properties 104; populations and value 107–9; regions and value 105–7; under valuation properties and growth 111; wealth wheel/balanced portfolio building 103–4
First Home Grant 47, 51–2, 58: house-price caps 51–2, 58; new builds 58
First Home Partner 47
first investment property, calculating readiness for 77–83: calculating useable equity required 78–80, 83; case study 82–3; equity increasing 80–1, 83; formulae 79, 83; goal-setting 81, 83; Lend Before You Leap strategy 78; portfolio planning spreadsheet 81, 83; scoping strategies 77–8; useable equity 77–8

first-home buyers 15, 17, 44–6, 48, 49, 50–6, 58, 59, 229, 236, 238–9, 244, 245–6
fixed rate/fixed interest rate 260: fixed vs floating 242–3
fixtures and fittings 70
flatmates 63, 184
flexibility 248, 250
flipping/buy and flip 40–1: and tax 40
floating rate/floating interest rate 61, 63, 237, 242–3, 260, 262
floor space requirements 68
foreign-buyer ban 227
formulae 79, 83
future of property 226–9: bubbles 229; cycles 228; first-home buyers 229; historical upsets 226–7; recessions 228; regulation 228; shares vs property 229

global financial crisis (GFC) 226
goals: common 90–1; goal gap calculation 96–7; long-term 92; and property evaluation 120; wealth required for 93
goal-setting, investment journey 81, 83, 86–98, 189: asset-building methods 94–6; case study 88–9; common aims/goals 90–1; goal gap calculation 96–7; long-term goal 92; My Wealth Plan 97; passive buy-and-hold strategy 87–8; properties to buy 88; process/schedule 89–97; steps 87, 92–7; Wealth Plan 91–2, 95–6; wealth required for goal 93
Golden Goose strategy 196–7, 200–2, 203
government support 47–8, 51–2
gross yield 260
growth properties 260: finding 104–12; growth vs yield properties 99–103, 112

Healthy Homes: Act 131, 227; Inspection 131; Standards 260
higher-yield properties, finding 218–25: apartments 219–20, 224; boarding houses 223; case studies 221, 222; cheaper properties 219; dual-key apartments 221–2, 225; high-yield property principles 218–20; high-yield properties 220–3; inner-city/near amenities 219; multi-income 219, 225; room-by-room rentals 222–3, 225; specifications 220; student accommodation 222–3; tax 223; yield goals 223–4, 225
historical upsets 226–7
holiday homes 74, 160, 182
home and income property 260
home office expenses 161
homeowners 247
Homes.co.nz 149
home-staging 215, 217
hot vs cooling market 212–13, 217
houses vs townhouses value 110–11

income fluctuations 240
income increasing 49, 184, 256–7
income, provable 257
inflation effects 200

INDEX

Informed Investor magazine 7, 258
inheritance 94–5
inner-city/near amenities 219
inspection reports 177
inspections, Healthy Homes 131, 146
insurance advisers 170–1
insurance premium 260
insurance, landlords/loss of rent 169–71, 173
interest deductibility 140, 155–60, 164, 165, 260
interest rates 226, 242–4: higher 240
interest-only loan/mortgage 236–7, 249, 250–1, 260: vs principal and interest 140–2
intergenerational wealth 197, 229
interior walls 70–1
investment focus 171, 173
investment journey/wealth plan, three stages of 28–35: buying and managing properties (running race) 30–1, 35; case study 33–4; equity 29–30; knowing your stage 31–3; passive income stage (finish line) 31, 35; starting 29–30, 35
Investment Ready programme 63
investment: five core ways 11, 12; lifetime 11; strategies 40

judgement/subjective factors 115–16, 120

Kāinga Ora 26, 159
kitchen 70
KiwiSaver 46, 47, 52, 94, 185–6, 196: reductions 256

Land Information Memorandum (LIM) report 128
landlord 260: being a good landlord 146–8; vs investor 130–1; need for landlords 25–7
lawyers, property 128–30
layout of property 69
leaky homes crisis 226
leasehold 260
lemons 74, 76
Lend Before You Leap strategy 78, 237, 255
lenders 237–8
leverage 23–4, 261: and property 23–4
life stages 13
line of credit 168–9, 172–3
loan to value (LVR) restrictions 45, 58, 79, 179, 180–1, 227, 238, 239, 244, 250, 252–3, 254, 261
locating property 58–9
location of property 52–3, 56
look-through company (LTC) 162, 164, 261
losses carried forward 261
low equity margins 243–4
low-deposit borrower 45
low-maintenance property 57, 65

maintenance 57, 65, 147–8, 153
management, financial 136–44: bank accounts 137–9, 144; case studies 139, 142–3; cashflow management 136, 140–3; checking accounts regularly 138, 144; interest deductibility 140; interest-only vs principal and interest 140–2; mortgage paying down 140–3, 144; mortgage payment types 140–2; revolving credit 138, 144; Split-banking 140
managers, property 130–2, 145, 146, 147, 151, 262
market: canvassing 120, 121; hot vs cooling 212–13, 217; right 212–13
Massey University Fin-Ed centre 196
minor dwelling 261
Momentum Property 258
mortgage 44–6, 234–44: additional repayments 63–4, 65, 243; affordability 239–41; applications declined 241–2; approval 238–41; bank rules 234; break fees 243; case study/example 235–6; Commitment Issues strategy 241; consumer debt 240; credit card debt 240, 241; credit rating (poor) 242; Debt Destroyer strategy 242; definition of 261; deposits 238–9; Extend and Lend strategy 236; extension of term 184–5, 256; fixed vs floating 242–3; higher interest rates 240; income fluctuations 240; increase 247; interest-only 236–7; interest rates/charges 242–4; Lend Before You Leap strategy 237; lenders 237–8; lending rules 228; loan-to-value (LVR) restrictions 238, 239, 244; low equity margins 243–4; lower rental income 240; non-bank lenders 237–8, 240–1; offset accounts 243; pay-down 38, 39, 57, 59–63, 65, 80–1, 83, 140–3, 144; payment types 140–2; poor account conduct 241–2; principal and interest (table) 235–6; revolving credit 237, 243; tax deductibility 237; types 235; uncommitted monthly income (UMI) 239–41; *see also* Mortgage Buster strategy; mortgage strategies
mortgage adviser 45, 56, 125–8, 134, 190, 211–12, 216, 217, 242, 256, 257, 261
'Mortgage Buster' strategy 57, 59–63, 65, 141, 144, 179, 185, 186, 247–50, 256: bank accounts 60–3, 65; extra payments 60
mortgage strategies 245–57: banking monogamy 253; banking polygamy 254; Commitment Issues strategy 255–6; credit card cancellation 256; debt consolidation loan 246; Debt Destroyer strategy 245–7, 256; Earn, Baby, Earn strategy 256–7; existing properties 255; Extend and Lend strategy 250–1; first-home buyers 245–6; flexibility 248, 250; homeowners 247; income increasing 256–7; interest-only 250–1; KiwiSaver reductions 256; Lend Before You Leap strategy 255; mortgage advisers 245, 257; Mortgage Buster strategy 247–50, 256; mortgage increase 247; mortgage term extension 256; new-builds 253–4; own home debt first 250; provable income 257; revolving credit 247–9, 252, 255; security 255; selling 254; Split-banking strategy 251–5; student loan repayment 256; tax 248–9, 250; uncommitted monthly income (UMI) 255–6
multi-income properties 69–70, 101, 219, 225, 261
My Credit File 242
My Wealth Plan software 97, 199, 200, 202

negative gearing 103, 261
Nest Egg strategy 195–6, 203

net assets 261
net yield 261
New Zealand Superannuation *see* Superannuation, NZ
new-builds 57–8, 159, 179, 253–4: advantages 58
non-bank lenders 182–4, 237–8, 240–1, 261
non-rentals 160
number of properties 104
numbers for evaluation 113–14
NZ Property Investor magazine 7, 258
NZ Property Investors' Federation 261–2

offset accounts 243
offset facility/offset loan 262
OneRoof 149, 219
Opes 4, 6–7: Catalyst Financial 245, 258; Investment Ready 63; Opes Accelerate 67, 68, 72, 123, 258; Opes First Home 50, 51, 59, 258; Opes Media 7; Opes Partners 7, 13, 50, 120, 123, 221, 222, 258; Venture Management 139, 147
overcapitalising 66–7
overdraft 168–9
owner-occupier 101, 262: owning vs renting 52–3, 73; vs rental 52–3
ownership structure 161–3

painting 70–1
passive buy-and-hold strategy 40, 43, 57–65, 87–8: additional mortgage repayments 63–4, 65; bank accounts 60–2; budgeting 64–5; capital growth principles 58–9; case study 64–5; deposit requirements 58; equity building 59–60; First Home Grant 58; locating 58–9; low-maintenance property 57, 65; mortgage pay-down/'Mortgage Buster' strategy 57, 59–63, 65; new-builds 57–8; property type 57–8; revolving credit 63, 65; second property prospects 60; tax advantages for rentals 58
passive income: defined 31, 262; goal of 90, 91
passive income creation 204–9, 262: debt reduction 204–7, 209; portfolio transition 208, 209; property drawbacks 208–9; property vs other investments 208–9; traditional approach 205–7; yield properties 204, 207–9
passive income stage (finish line) 31, 35
payments, additional mortgage 243
poor account conduct 241–2, 246
populations and value 107–9
portfolio expansion 178–90: borrowing ability 190; BRRRR 180–1; capital growth 179; case studies 183, 188–9; credit cards cancellation 184; debt pay-down 179, 186; equity strategies 178–82, 190; goal-setting 189; income increasing 184; KiwiSaver 185–6; Mortgage Buster strategy 179; mortgage extension 184–5; new-builds 179; non-bank lenders 182–4; renovating 180–1; sell one to buy two 181–2; servicing strategies 182–7, 190; Split-banking 179–80; student loan repayment 186–7; strategy selection 187; time to invest 187–9, 190
Portfolio Planner 60, 83

portfolio: building steps 12–13; planning spreadsheet 81, 83, 114, 121; right time to sell 211–13, 217; transition 194–203, 208, 209: timing 200–1
price realised 210–11
prices for property 50–1, 56
principal and interest (P+I) (table) mortgage 235–6, 262
process/schedule for investment 89–97
projections basis 121
properties to avoid/lemons 74, 76
properties to buy 88
Property Academy Podcast 7, 73, 82, 89, 104, 164, 188, 226, 232
property coach 231; *see also* advisers
property inspections 131, 146, 177
property investor, definition 262
Property Investors Chat Group NZ (Facebook) 171
Property Investors' Association 262
property managers 130–2, 145, 146, 147, 151, 262
property type 57–8
property vs other investments 208–9

Real Estate Institute of New Zealand (REINZ) 262
recessions 228
refinance 262
regions and value 105–7
regulations, property 131, 228
renovating 38, 39, 40, 66–76, 80–1, 83, 180–1: bathroom and kitchen 70; carpet 71; case studies 72–3, 75; Cashflow Hacking/renovation framework 67–71, 76; cleaning 71; council consent (avoiding) 69; extra bedroom 68–9; fixtures and fittings 70; floor space requirements 68; increasing useable equity 66; interior walls 70–1; layout 69; multi-income 69–70; overcapitalising 66–7; painting 70–1; properties to avoid/lemons 74, 76; renovating to sell 213–14, 217; renovations to avoid 71; renovation framework 67–71, 76, 158, 213, 214; wardrobe 69; windows 69
rent: increases/reviews 131, 177; setting levels 148–52
rental management 145–53: case study 151–2; good landlord 146–8; inspections 146; maintenance 147–8, 153; property managers 145, 146, 147, 151; rent levels 148–52; RightRent system 148–51, 153; tenants' home 146
rentals: cashflow 40; inspections 131, 146, 177; loss of rent insurance 169–70; lower income 240; room-by-room rentals 222–3, 225; tax advantages 58
renter-investor 17
renters: numbers of 25–7; vs house prices 26
Reserve Bank/Reserve Bank of New Zealand (RBNZ) 45, 58, 121, 180, 228, 238, 261, 262; *see also* loan-to-value (LVR) ratio
Residential Tenancies Act 145, 262
Responsible Lending Code 216, 227
retirement: goal of comfortable retirement 90, 91; needs 23; strategies compared 198–9, 203
retiring on real estate 194–203: asset holding 196–7; asset requirements 197; asset selling 195–6; case studies 199, 201–2; financial advisers 202; financial modelling 201; Golden Goose strategy 196–7, 200–2,

271

INDEX

203; inflation effects 200; intergenerational wealth 197; KiwiSaver 196; Nest Egg strategy 195–6, 203; New Zealand Superannuation 196, 199; retirement strategies compared 198–9, 203; rule of 4 per cent 197; tax 198; when to transition portfolio 200–1
return-on-investment method 93, 113–14, 119, 121: numbers 114–16; spreadsheet 114–16, 158, 165, 224
revolving credit 61–3, 65, 138, 144, 172–3, 237, 243, 247–9, 252, 255, 262–3
RightRent system 148–51, 153
risk: mitigation 166, 171–3; risk-taking 25, 231; risks vs returns 12; tolerance 167, 173
room-by-room rentals 222–3, 225
rule of 4 per cent 93, 197

sale and purchase agreement 128, 263
sales, staggering 213
saving 23: insufficient for financial freedom 23; saving schemes 94
scoping strategies 77–8
second property prospects 60
security for borrowing 29
selection, property 167, 173
selling 254: costs 210–11, 217; sell one to buy two 181–2
selling to unlock equity 210–17: break fees 211–12, 217; case study 216–17; home-staging 215, 217; hot vs cooling market 212–13, 217; price realised 210–11; renovating to sell 213–14, 217; right market 212–13; right time to sell portfolio 211–12; right time to sell 211–13, 217; selling costs 210–11, 217; Split-banking strategy 216–17; staggering sales 213; tax 211–12, 217; vacant possession 213–14, 217
servicing strategies 182–7, 190
shares 94: vs property 229
social housing 157, 159, 165
specifications of properties 220
Split-banking strategy 78, 140, 179–80, 216–17, 251–5
starter property 39
starting investment 21–2, 29–30, 35, 38–42: case study 41–2; increasing equity 38, 39; investment strategies 40; mortgage pay-down 38, 39; renovation 38, 39, 40; starter property 39
steps, investment 87, 92–7
strategies, investment 40: active buy-and-hold/BRRRR (buy, renovate, rent, refinance and repeat) 40, 43; buy and flip/flipping 40–1; choosing 43; passive buy-and-hold 40, 43
strategy selection 187
student accommodation 222–3, 263
student loan repayment 186–7, 256
subscriptions 161
suburbs, higher-end and value 109
sunset clause 263
Superannuation, New Zealand 23, 95, 196, 199

table mortgage 263: *see* principal and interest mortgage
tax 154–65, 198, 211–12, 217, 223, 227, 248–9, 250: and accountants 132–3; bright line test 163–4; capital gains tax (CGT) 163; case study 162; exemptions 158–60, 165; expenses to claim 161; interest deductibility 155–60, 164, 165, 237; look-through company 162, 164; management 177; minimisation 160–3, 165; new-builds 159; non-rentals 160; ownership structure 161–3; reducing taxable profit 160–1, 165; reducing tax rate 161–2, 165; return-on-investment spreadsheet 158, 165; social housing 159; tax minimisation 160–3, 165
taxable profit, reducing 160–1, 165
telephone and internet 161
tenancy regulations 227, 228
Tenancy Tribunal 151–2, 169, 263
tenants 132, 215, 263: tenant checks 132; tenants' home 146
The Deal 7
time: and investments 136, 144; time to invest 187–9, 190
timeline for activities 174–7: annually 176; monthly 175; quarterly 175–6; set-up 174–5; twice-monthly 175; weekly 175
title 263
top-up 263
total returns 120, 121
TradeMe 149, 151, 219
travel expenses 161
trust 263
type of property 57–8

uncommitted monthly income (UMI) 239–41, 255–6, 263
under valuation properties and growth 111
useable equity 66, 77–80, 83, 179–80, 263: calculating requirements 78–80, 83; increasing 66; *see also* equity

vacancy 263: allowance for 155
vacant possession 213–14, 217
value increase rate 94
value increase: over time 24
variable rate/variable interest rate 260; *see* floating rate
vendor 263

walls, interior 70–1
wardrobes 69
wealth gap 22, 119, 120, 231
Wealth Plan 91–2, 95–6
wealth wheel/balanced portfolio building 103–4
wealth-building 20–7, 39: goal of 90, 91
websites, property 59, 68
windows 69

yield 227, 263: goals 223–4, 225; net yield 261; yield properties 204, 207–9, 263: *see also* higher yield properties, finding